barcode in back of

Advertising
and the
World Wide Web

ADVERTISING AND
CONSUMER PSYCHOLOGY
A series sponsored by the Society for
Consumer Psychology

Advertising
and the
World Wide Web

Edited by

David W. Schumann
University of Tennessee—Knoxville

Esther Thorson
University of Missouri—Columbia

160101

1999

LAWRENCE ERLBAUM ASSOCIATES, PUBLISHERS
Mahwah, New Jersey   London

Lawrence Erlbaum Associates, Inc., Publishers
10 Industrial Avenue
Mahwah, New Jersey 07430

Cover design by Kathryn Houghtaling Lacey

Library of Congress Cataloging-in-Publication Data

Advertising and the World Wide Web / edited by David W. Schumann,
Esther Thorson.
    p. cm.
    "Edited versions of papers presented at the 1996 Advertising and
Consumer Psychology Conference . . . Bloomfield Hills, Michigan"-
-Introd.
    Includes bibliographical references and index.
    ISBN 0-8058-3148-7 (alk. paper)
    1. Internet advertising--Congresses. I. Schumann, David W.
II. Thorson, Esther. III. Conference on Advertising and Consumer
Psychology (15th : 1996 : Bloomfield Hills, Mich.)
HF6146.I58A38 1999
658.8'00285'4678--dc21
                                   99-17344
                                       CIP

Printed in the United States of America
10   9   8   7   6   5   4   3   2

Contents

Preface

This volume is the result of a series of papers presented at the 15th annual Advertising and Consumer Psychology Conference held at DMB&B, Bloomfield Hills, Michigan, on May 17-18, 1996. The conference was sponsored by DMB&B and the Society for Consumer Psychology, the 23rd Division of the American Psychological Association. The coeditors served as chairpersons for the conference.

We sincerely appreciate the efforts of the authors of these chapters, most of who presented original papers at the conference. We would also like to thank Keith Rinehard, the President and CEO of DDB Needham, whose chapter provided insightful thoughts on the past, present, and future. Professors Sandra Davidson of the University of Missouri, and William Wells of the University of Minnesota, were each asked to contribute original chapters that significantly enhanced the coverage of the topic.

The World Wide Web is a revolutionary environment that holds both excitement and challenge. Advertising has found a whole new medium with which to communicate to customers. With technological advances occurring daily, it will be most curious to see how the growth of this technology-based medium unfolds in the future.

Finally, we would like to dedicate this book to our families. Their patience and encouragement was instrumental in completing this task.

To my wife, Jane, and my sons, Matthew and Jason
DWS

To my two younger children, Kylie and Ian
ET

Introduction

Esther Thorson
University of Missouri – Columbia

David W. Schumann
University of Tennessee – Knoxville

This volume is composed of edited versions of papers presented at the 1996 Advertising and Consumer Psychology Conference, cosponsored by Division 23 of the American Psychological Association (Society for Consumer Psychology) and DMB&B Advertising Agency in Bloomfield Hills, Michigan. Our partner at DMB&B was Charlie Stannard, and we are grateful for his help and hospitality. In addition to the conference papers, several distinguished authors were invited to submit chapters covering topics not included at the conference.

Although many of these papers were initially conceptualized two years ago, they have all been updated - although even two weeks is a long time in terms of changes on the Internet! Nevertheless, these chapters provide a wide-ranging view of issues addressing how advertisers can proceed on the Internet and World Wide Web. Several of the chapters demonstrate the well-known stereotype that when a new medium comes along, the first approach is to treat it like an old medium. For example, much of the early advertising that appeared in online newspapers looked like "print ads." The industry is still struggling with how to measure "reach and frequency" on the Web. And there is certainly an extensive effort to identify consumer segments or targets that somehow relate to systems we already use.

Chapter 1 traces the development of Web advertising from its very beginning as it was represented and discussed in the pages of *Advertising Age*. What can be seen in this history are efforts to define web advertising in a familiar, already known way. Yet, again and again, it is clear that web advertising just will not fit the old mold. Well-known advertising professional Keith Reinhard actually articulates the linkage between old and new as he discusses "old fashioned salesmanship in a new-fangled medium."

On the other hand, much of what the reader will encounter here is a solid conception of how web advertising is different from anything that has come before. Several chapters (see especially chaps. 2, 5, 8, 10, and the practitioner conversation by Bruce Goerlich) focus on the idea of interactivity - where both consumer and advertiser are active in the persuasive communication process. Several chapters focus on how web advertising can be linked with other parts of the complete or integrated campaign (e.g., chaps. 3 and 17). There are chapters on the web's various audience segments, including "browsers and seekers" (chap. 4), children (chap. 6), college students (chap. 7), those with a parasocial response to media (chap. 10), and even those who thrive on hate and bigotry (chap. 11).

Most of the chapters focus on independent commercial sites ("brand sites") on the web, but three chapters consider how web advertising can occur in other formats. Brill considers the role of advertising in online newspapers. Meyer considers web sites serving as catalogs. Nowak and his colleagues examine advertising banners and what factors create their impact.

The book is organized into five sections. Part 1 examines definitions of basic terms like interactivity, icons, banners, hotlinks, hits, advertorials, editorial environment, and shovelware. Part 1 also sets up important theoretical foundations, asking what models of advertising are most appropriate for helping to understand how web advertising works, and what needs to be added to these theories to better account for web advertising. Part 1 also looks to the short, but rapidly changing and controversial, history of web advertising.

Part 2 looks at the structure of web advertising, how it presumably functions to sell products or services, and how well it works. Part 3 looks at four specific applications of web advertising, including a measurement device for ascertaining parasocial responses to sites, an examination of how cyberhate sites look and operate, how advertising fits into online newspapers, and how catalog marketers are moving onto a web format.

Part 4 examines in detail the legal state of Internet advertising, and also looks at the issue of how cybercookies operate and what problems of privacy and consent are involved with cookie-based marketing. Part 5 is the voice of practitioners - those who have pioneered web advertising and promotion, and report back from the front lines on what works and what fails.

Although there remain a few naysayers concerning the future of web advertising, the reader of this volume will be able to see, we think, just how incredibly high-impact this new medium has become and will continue to become. The researcher will see how many fascinating and important questions there are to ask. The historian will see lots of stumbles, but a new form of advertising that is getting longer legs and picking up some serious speed.

The editors thank the authors for their contributions and patience. And now, if you'll excuse us, we need to log on and go cybershopping.

Part 1

Definitions, History, and Theoretical Foundations

1

Web Advertising's Birth and Early Childhood as Viewed in the Pages of *Advertising Age*

Esther Thorson
University of Missouri – Columbia

William D. Wells
University of Minnesota

Shelley Rogers
University of Missouri – Columbia

On October 4, 1993, *Advertising Age* (*Ad Age*) inaugurated "INTERACTIVE Media & Marketing" (a section henceforth referred to as INTERACTIVE), a new department in the popular and influential trade journal. World Wide Web advertising actually began just about the same time, early in 1994 (Briggs & Hollis, 1997). In the subsequent five years, advertising on the web has grown exponentially. Because appearance and disappearance of web advertising sites is common, and because ideas about what the Web will mean to advertising, both as a process and as an industry, come and go almost as quickly as the various sites themselves, *Ad Age's* INTERACTIVE section provides a fascinating chronicle of the beginnings of *Web* advertising that is perhaps unlikely to be available anywhere else. For that reason, this chapter examines nearly five years of INTERACTIVE, discussing trends in the major issues that any new advertising medium must deal with: effectiveness with its audience, pricing, evaluating cost effectiveness, defining basic measurement units so a common language of web advertising can be developed, linkage with other media, either online or traditional, and so on. We also look at what this material means for academic and industrial researchers who must decide which aspects to invest in first, and what questions must be articulated.

Some Precipitating Stories

Reasons for the creation of INTERACTIVE can be seen in headlines from the weeks that preceded its appearance: "Video goes 3DO. Games to benefit from newest technology" (*AA*, 1/11/93, 1). "Time Warner hits road running. Ad presentations set for 'superhighway'" (*AA*, 5/24/93, 1). "NBC dials interactive. New service lets viewers call 800-number for more advertiser info" (*AA*, 8/12/93, 1). "Most technology is 'bullshit' says Rosenshine. BBDO's chairman takes a hard look at 'nonsense' about agency of future" (*AA*, 9/20/93, 4). "It's a battle for new media. In the fight to purchase Paramount, contenders weigh interactive impact" (*AA*, 9/27/93, 1). The issues covered in these stories all pointed to the importance of "interactivity" for advertising, as well as for a variety of other marketing activities.

THE BIRTH

Consistent with the focus on interactivity in general in the precipitating stories, the first few months of INTERACTIVE focused on a variety of different media. The first words from the new department were, "The interactive digital age has set off a gold rush. . . " (*AA*, 10/4/93, 27). That metaphor led to an interview with Vincent Gross, "AT&T's project director for interactive TV and multimedia." He said:

> This is a very big sandbox, and I think there's going to be a lot of winners. It's nothing less than a revolution in the way television is going to work. . . . (*AA*, 10/4/93, 27)

The next week featured more predictions. In a speech to a *Business Week* symposium, Keith Reinhard, CEO of DDB Needham Worldwide, said:

> Now we tell the customers what we want them to know. In the age of multimedia, we must tell customers what they want to know.

He followed that with

> We must remember. . . that advertising messages will be chosen by the customer. This will spell doom for ads that insult intelligence or offend sensibilities. The ads must be not only inviting but irresistible. (*AA*, 10/11/93, 40)

It is important to note that Reinhard is apparently conceptualizing Internet advertising as appearing in independent sites created by advertisers, rather than as appearing in content web sites such as newspapers and magazines. He is also focusing on the idea that this will be "pull" advertising, that is, that the consumer will have to go looking for it, rather than having it delivered.

By the end of its first month, INTERACTIVE had printed additional enthusiastic predictions. The most dazzling of the dazzlers came from Gerald Levin, Chairman - CEO of Time Warner. In describing the "Full Service Network," he was about to launch in Orlando, he predicted,

> It's our belief that this technology will alter the way Americans inform, entertain, and educate themselves. This is not some dreamy future. By April 1994, we will hook up our first 4,000 customers. (*AA*, 10/18/93, 24, 27)

So, the first words were entirely enthusiastic: "This is going to be a very big sandbox"; "This will spell doom for ads that insult intelligence." "This will alter the way Americans inform, entertain and educate themselves." As we shall see when we get to 1998, these predictions, although not true yet of the masses, were clearly true for the large and ever-growing segment of web users.

The Early Naysayers

Not every early voice joined the enthusiastic chorus. An article entitled, "A new kind of sticker shock?" envisioned an era in which "our cable bill, which used to average about $26.00 a month, is now a whopping $135.00." It wondered how many viewers would write checks for that much in-home entertainment. An article headed, "But skeptics warn marketers to watch out for rough road ahead" described an "almost endless lists of pitfalls" facing advertisers. The list included,

> If the arithmetic doesn't work for advertising on cable in a 30-channel universe, why should it work in a more segmented universe at higher cost?

and "We're going to have another consumer revolt, and this one will be about privacy" (*AA*, 10/25/93, 24).

Another reported called, "Cerritos test shows there's more to learn about interactive television" said,

> GTE has only 3,000 Main Street subscribers, hardly an enthusiastic response to what is billed as the wave of the future by many media prophets.

It quoted Michael Noll, dean of the Annenberg School of Communication at the University of Southern California, as saying, "People don't need it. You pay bills sitting at your table, not on a living room couch," and it quoted a

Cerritos respondent as saying, "Right now I can't say it's changing my lifestyle. I don't think I'd miss it if we didn't have it" (*AA,* 10/25/93, 20).

Other Interactive Media

Meanwhile, *Ad Age* was reporting other digital events that would affect interactive marketing and advertising. In the first issue of INTERACTIVE, it described a test by Sega of an all-videogame cable channel (*AA*, 10/4/93, 28). In the next issue, it described a 16-market tour of "Planet Bubble Yum," a virtual reality game (*AA*, 10/4/93, 30). Later, it mentioned "Hollywood Online," where subscribers to online home computer services could "access 15-second video clips, film star biographies, production information" and play dates of upcoming movies (*AA*, 10/11/93, 41). It described QB1, an "interactive football game" where patrons in "more than 1,300 establishments" could "play along" with the NFL by guessing what quarterbacks would call next (*AA*, 10/11/93, 41).

In "France says 'oui' to interactive kiosk," *Ad Age* described an in-store workstation where customers could get odor-profiled by answering lifestyle questions (*AA*, 1/8/93, 25). Earlier, it had described CD-ROMs where customers could view and buy from Spiegel, Lands' End, Patagonia, and Neiman-Marcus catalogs (*AA*, 10/18/93, 26); and, from the beginning, it had noted that home shopping channels with 800-numbers are important players on the interactive stage. All of these interactive marketing innovations would eventually become strategies available within the world of web advertising.

The first half of 1994 continued to see *Ad Age* focus on a variety of interactive new media, but not the Internet or the World Wide Web. For example, INTERACTIVE reported progress in videogames (*AA*, 1/10/94, 19); *AA*, 3/7/94, 18), kiosks (*AA*, 1/17/94, 13; *AA*, 2/21/94, 17), CD-ROMs (*AA*, 1/19/94, 18; *AA*, 1/17/94, 14; *AA*, 3/14/94, 21), and home shopping (*AA*, 1/17/94, 17; *AA*, 2/28/94, 19), and it reported impressive forays into interactive media by all the major print and electronic media (*AA*, 1/10/94, 16; AA, 1/17/94, 16; *AA*, 2/21/94, 16; *AA*, 3/7/94, 22; *AA*, 3/21/94, IM-6). Then, suddenly in May, *Ad Age* recognized the Internet. In reporting interviews with "readers and online industry experts," *Ad Age* (5/2/94) said,

> Surprisingly, there seemed to be no doubts about the commercialization of the Internet, a global network of computers that has long serviced as a haven for academics, researchers and government workers. The Internet's estimated 10 million to 20 million, mostly well-heeled users are simply too desirable an audience to be passed up by marketers. (p. 23)

Aside from two major errors, this statement turned out to be more than mildly prescient. First, it called academics, researchers, and government workers "mostly well-heeled," and second, it failed to perceive that probably more important than reaching an upscale audience was what could be done within the Internet medium itself - the incredible creativity and variety in types of information and interaction that would rapidly begin making its appearance!

A second major occurrence, during the spring of 1994, was a speech by Edwin L. Artzt, then Chairman-CEO of Procter & Gamble, to the annual conference of the American Association of Advertising Agencies. Mr. Artzt said,

> Our most important advertising medium – television – is about to change big time . . . . We can't be sure that ad-supported TV programming will have a future. (*AA*, 5/23/94, 24)

That speech, later called "the shot heard 'round the advertising world," reverberated for two reasons. First, it startled the advertising industry. When the chairman of a three billion dollar advertiser suggests that ad-supported television - and by extension, the ads and the ad revenues and the ad careers that go with it - "might not have a future," people listen.

Second, it identified the essence of interactive marketing communication. Speaking of contemporary television, where semicaptive audiences watch most of the advertisements most of the time, Mr. Artzt said,

> Procter & Gamble, in a given year, has to sell 400 million boxes of Tide - and to do that, we have to reach our consumers over and over throughout the year . . . . The only way you can achieve that kind of impact is with broad-reach television . . . . (*AA*, 5/23/94, 24)

But, in the interactive future,

> It's going to be harder than ever before just to reach consumers with our advertising, much less reach them with the frequency and regularity we need to build loyalty to our brands. (*AA*, 5/23/94, 42)

He added,

> This is a real threat. These new media suppliers will give consumers what they want and potentially at a price they're willing to pay. (*AA*, 5/23/94, 42)

As it turned out, Proctor & Gamble was already climbing aboard the new media engine, and would attempt to use its marketing clout to determine the direction of that engine, but at this time, Mr. Artzt was worried about a potential shift in power from marketer to customer. As we will see in 1998, however, marketers may have figured out a way to harness the Web, but to use it to continue to deliver advertising messages to customers, just as it does via television.

FAST FORWARDING NINE MONTHS - 1995

In March, 1995, about 18 months after the birth of INTERACTIVE and about nine months after the "shot heard 'round the advertising world," we find that *Advertising Age* was taking stock. In a twelve-page special section called "The New Business of New Media," the trade magazine reported more surprises. The lead article was "Building a new industry." It began,

> Interactive media.   Skeptics call it the great zero-billion-dollar industry, full of pipe dreams and fancy schemes, overwhelming type and underwhelming results. But that description . . . misses the mark completely. There are already billions of dollars being made . . . .

To get to "billions of dollars" - 11.1 billion, to be exact - *Ad Age* totaled revenues from eight activities:

Videogames	$ 3.8 billion
Home shopping/infomercials	$ 2.8 billion
CD-ROMs	$ 2.5 billion
Commercial online services	$ .8 billion
Interactive 800-numbers	$ .4 billion
Internet	$ .4 billion
Kiosks	$ .3 billion
Virtual reality	$ .1 billion
Total:	$11.1 billion

Note the order of magnitude: Videogames on top, interactive TV - the innovation that was to "alter the way Americans inform, entertain and educate themselves" - in the cellar. For perspective, remember that in 1994, revenues from old-fashioned linear television were about $29 billion (*AA*, 8/7/95, 13).

THE WEB BECOMES THE DOMINANT
INTERACTIVE MEDIUM

In its discussion of this reordered industry, INTERACTIVE featured the World Wide Web. It said,

> For marketers, the Web has swiftly emerged as a key new-media platform. By the end of last month, there were more than 2,500 commercial sites on the Web, many of them home to such mainstream brand names as MCI, Reebok, Volvo, and Club Med. In the first two months of this year, *Advertising Age* ran more stories about the Web than it did in all of 1994. (*AA*, 3/13/95, S4)

As we are about to see, the movement toward the Web as the dominant medium of interactive advertising was not to slow, but to speed.

"The New Business of New Media," also carried full-page advertisements. Silicon Graphics ran a message that highlighted its Netscape home page. It said,

> Introducing WebFORCE from Silicon Graphics. Not all Web sites are created equal. The most popular spots artfully combine graphics and text with audio and video. But authoring those kinds of media-rich Web pages has been extremely difficult. And most servers lack the horsepower to handle hundreds of visitors simultaneously.
>
> WebFORCETM systems change all that - easily giving you power to author and to swerve the most compelling content on the World Wide Web. See exactly what we mean, once and for all. Stop in at <http://www.sgi.com> or call 1-800-800-7441. (*AA*, 3/13/95, S11)

In another full-page message, Poppe Tyson - a small company that before the Internet, had specialized in direct response marketing - said "So Not Every Ad Agency in the World is Trying to Look Electronic." It continued,

> Online. Interactive. Multimedia. Whatever you call it, ad agencies are falling all over themselves to get into it . . .. But for Poppe Tyson, it's already a proven part of our clients' communications portfolios . . .. Please visit our web site at <www.poppe.com> or contact Nicholas Buck the traditional way at 415.969.6800. (*AA*, 3/13/95, S13)

Here, we have a new systems manufacturer and a former direct marketing supplier staking claims to multimedia via traditional linear print. Ads like these would rapidly proliferate, and, as INTERACTIVE came to fill more and more space, its presence was clearly supported by this proliferation.

In the months that followed "The New Business of New Media," INTERACTIVE paid even more attention to the Internet. It had already begun "CyberCritique," a "monthly review of the latest online marketing efforts" (*AA*, 3/6/95, 18). In July, it featured a "Web Builders Showcase" that presented web sites from Convergent Media Systems, Organic Online, Renaissance, Executive Arts and Proxima - among others. The Proxima site said,

> Proxima, Inc., an Internet Services Studio, specializes in the design and development of creative Web sites for corporations and organizations. Proxima has designed and implemented over 50 Web sites in 1995.

> From online catalogs that sell your products in a secured environment
> to creative informational sites, Proxima provides a full lifecycle of
> Web development services that will make your site an Internet
> success. So let's talk! (*AA*, 9/11/95, 41)

This was thus the beginning of what would become the central focus of INTERACTIVE - advertising on the Web. Even at this point, however, there were skeptics. In May, 1995, *Ad Age* ran an opinion piece by John Emmerling, chairman-chief creative officer of Emmerling Post. Emmerling declared,

> In this country today there are just two mass "image" media. Only
> TV and magazines given national advertisers the tools they need to
> quickly extend a pervasive image-building message - in color - to
> tens of millions of average Americans. . .

and he concluded,

> . . . in the year 2000, new media will remain a nice little boutique
> reaching a selective group of upscale, educated types. (*AA*, 5/15/95,
> 19)

Moreover, as *Ad Age* itself had often noted, fewer than one third of U.S. households have computers and fewer than half of those machines have decent Internet connections. As we look at the rest of 1995 and INTERACTIVE through early 1998, we find that Mr. Emmerling was apparently listening to the wrong muse.

Skepticism for web advertising probably reached an all-time high later in 1995. Yet, that did not stop advertisers and marketers from speeding onto the information superhighway. Indeed, 64 new web companies made it into *Ad Age* headlines. The questions being asked became more practical and focused not on whether, but how, will this new medium prove to be a viable and profitable advertising vehicle? Articles in 1995 promised more inventiveness, as marketers and advertisers experimented with ad gimmicks: coupons, scavenger hunts, giveaways, games and recipes. The idea was to create independent company or brand sites and somehow lure consumers to those sites. What we learned by year's end was that only a few gimmicks worked, and those that did work sometimes attracted the wrong kind of customer (*AA*, 06/12/95, 16).

Meanwhile, web advertising could be said to be going through a defining phase. Tracking of users' visits to the sites, and pricing for advertising located on content sites were two of the most hotly debated issues of the year. Marketers and advertisers argued in *Ad Age* about how best to measure clicks and create ads at a price that was appropriate to the amount of traffic and/or the selling impact of the site visits.

Many small advertisers took a "wait and see" approach. Others, including big names - like Fox, Chrysler, *Sports Illustrated*, and ESPN - jumped onto the Net to prove that online advertising could be profitable (*AA*, Spring 1995, 54). Companies that already had a web presence, like Time Inc.'s Pathfinder site, were going commercial to "keep down consumer costs" (*AA*, 04/10/95, 19). Most of the companies reporting they were on the Web in one way or another indicated they did not expect to be operating in the black for another two to three years (*AA*, 10/23/95, 24).

As noted, skepticism about web advertising was high during 1995. *Ad Age* headlines conveyed the unpredictable nature of the new medium. Some of the headlines read: "Uncertainty Rules at Interactive Ad Meet," "Riding the Run-Away New Media Cow," "Pricing on the 'Net Confounds Some Marketers," ". . . Fear of Unknown Slows Advertisers," and "Interactive Payoff Still Far Away." A dominant reason for this skepticism was that so many of the big name web advertising pioneers, including major corporations and media such as Toyota and *Rolling Stone*, leaped into cyberspace without sufficient preparation - and of course without any maps for the unexplored commercial territory of the Web. Many learned the hard way of the dangers of web advertising: "Those who think they know the technology are walking before they're crawling," warned Christine MacKenzie, manager of corporate advertising at Chrysler Corporation. (*AA*, 02/20/95, 12). "The safest thing to do always is to say no, and then you're covered," noted Les Brown, a consultant and critic who covered TV's formative years for *Variety* and *The New York Times*, and who wrote the *Encyclopedia of Television*. "If the answer is yes and it doesn't work, the client will say 'What did you get me into?'" (*AA*, special edition, Spring 1995, 54).

Marketers, however, at this point in the development of web advertising, were afraid that they would lose too many potential profits, not to mention being seen by customers as failing to be on the leading edge. New media proponents were quoted as saying the potential growth of Internet users validated using interactivity. Indeed, online revenue services were estimated to rack up $3.3 billion in revenues by 1997, which would be up 22% from 1995, according to a report from Dataquest, San Jose, CA. (*AA*, 08/21/95, 19).

Thus, 1995 saw many stories of failure or at least disappointed expectation, but the up- side was that the explorations led to clearer articulation of important problems. How does a company get a customer to its site? What information should that site contain? How does the company get return visits?

Pricing was perceived as one of the most important issues for marketers. How much should an interactive ad cost? Ad rates in late 1995 varied from a few thousand dollars up to $1 million. HotWired, for instance, charged advertisers $30,000 for an eight-week sponsorship, and ESPN charged $1 million for a one-year sponsorship of ESPNET (*AA*, 2/20/95, 13). In fact, rates like those of ESPN caused some advertisers to decide not to join in the great online experiment (*AA*, Spring 1995, 54). "Making ads affordable is the key to making this online odyssey work," said Richard Segal, Jr., managing director of Cincinnati, Ohio-based agency Hensley, Segal, Rentschler. "In order for us to move this boulder of Internet marketing, we're going to have to make it affordable so everyone from entrepreneurs to major corporations is willing to try it" (*AA*, 02/20/95, 13).

Interestingly, *Playboy* publisher Richard Kinsler was content to leave his ad rates right where they are - as some of the priciest on the Web. Sponsoring a *Playboy* article online was priced at a whopping $50,000 per quarter, and a hypertext link from *Playboy* to another home page was priced at $30,000 per quarter. Playboy allowed marketers to test the site for one month for $10,000 plus a small premium (*AA*, 06/19/95, 15). The claim at the time was that because the site was getting some 800,000 hits a day, marketers should be willing to foot the bill.

Another heated debate begun during 1995 concerned whether advertisers should pay for the number of users that were exposed to a banner advertisement on a web page, or for the number of users who clicked on the ad's hotlink for more information (*AA*, 10/09/95, 21). Large, established sites with lots of traffic argued for exposure, but those on the opposing side argued that pricing based on exposure alone was not appropriate for the Web because it did not take into account who the user was and the extent to which that user interacted with the advertising (*AA*, 07/10/95, 16).

Of course, as attention turned to how to count exposures, the issue of who should be doing the counting also arose. Nielsen Media announced it would independently monitor HotWired's traffic from its own remote servers and launch an Internet measurement service for agencies and advertisers (*AA*, 06/19/95, 18). Just four months after Nielsen announced its tracking intents, the advertising industry's Coalition for Advertising Supported Information & Entertainment, and the Advertising Research Foundation released a set of guiding principles for interactive media measurement (*AA*, 10/09/95, 22). In fact, in that document, the call for third-party audience measurement was high on the list.

An important additional audience measurement problem is that, although competing computer programs track user activity at a site, they fail to tell the advertiser who is accessing the site. Without this information, targeting is not possible (*AA*, 09/04/95, 14). In talking about the issue of audience measurement, Jayne Spittler, senior VP-director of media research, Leo Burnett USA, commented, "Part of the confusion is that people think there will be a one-size-fits-all solution that will solve everybody's problems," said (*AA*, 10/09/95, 22). And Adam Shoenfeld, an analyst at Jupiter Communications, similarly noted, "I would expect that we're going to get piecemeal solutions to all these small problems first and then some shakeout before a standard is in place" (*AA*, 09/04/95, 15).

Also during this time, low budgets forced many fledgling web site owners to resort to the egg-on-the-wall" pricing tactic "of throwing ad rates up to see if they stick" (*AA*, 10/02/95, 34). One such company, *Utne Reader* magazine, was forced to downsize after being online for just three months. Before making its online debut, Utne had lined up six major sponsors - including Saturn - each of whom paid $24,000 for an eight-week sponsorship. Nevertheless, the online magazine was forced to lay off employees and reduce ad rates by nearly 40% (*AA*, 07/10/95, 16; *AA*, 10/23/95, 24). Was the downsizing of Utne caused by poor pricing? John Hegeman, VP-marketing administration at MGM/UA argued that a more plausible explanation for pricing difficulties stemmed from a lack of understanding of the selling value of web advertising. "The one thing we don't have is an understanding of what the value is of links from site to site or what the value is of sites in general" (*AA*, 04/24/95, 14).

Matthew Cutler, director of business development with Boston-based net.Genesis suggested that, "You shouldn't speak of buying advertising on the Internet in the traditional sense. What you are doing is buying association with a content provider" (*AA*, 02/20/95, 13). This was one of the first articulations of the idea that advertisers should prefer locating themselves in a content area (e.g., a newspaper, a magazine, or even with another advertiser) rather than having their own site. This approach came to be known as "piggybacking."

The argument for piggybacking was that advertisers should work in partnership with online publications. The more publications understand how a particular product is sold, the more they can come up with creative ways of linking, or piggybacking, that site with others.

"They call it new media for a reason," pointed out Scott Heiferman, president of Interactive Traffic. "Just like a great print ad won't do anything if it isn't well placed, a great online site won't do anything if it isn't strategically linked. And many traditional agencies need help in getting up to speed in interactive" (*AA*, 07/24/95, S16).

Finally, the focus of INTERACTIVE in 1995 was on predicting size features of web advertising. For example, early in 1995, it was reported that 37% of 1,000 people polled said they did not know what the "information superhighway" was (*AA*, 02/27/95, 3). Later in the year, it was reported that "online consumers are expected to grow from 10 million in 1995 to 29 million in 2000 (*AA*, 07/10/95, 17).

It should be noted that by mid-1995, advertisers were most commonly simply putting up a banner ad in a content area or mounting their own web page and hoping for some traffic (*AA*, 10/09/95, 21). For those using their own web sites, coupons, recipes, scavenger hunts, sweepstakes, games, and prizes were given trial runs to determine what consumers valued. Pillsbury, for example, began a recipe site and received a 12% click rate after inviting 90,000 of Prodigy subscribers to drop by. This click rate was said to be more than "twice the average number of looks such solicitations usually receive" (*AA*, 6/05/95, 19).

Perhaps the mostly widely publicized value-incentive approach was CompuServe's $1,000,000 Internet scavenger hunt. CompuServe hoped the hunt would attract new Web-comers and drive up connect time revenue of old Web-timers by providing a "highly addictive game" (*AA*, 06/12/95, 16).

The problem with incentive-type techniques, however, was that they could become gimmicky, explained Rick Spence, an analyst with Dataquest. "There's a potential danger that consumers walk away with a bad feeling that you won't want associated with your product," he pointed out (*AA*, 06/12/95, 16).   In addition, the use of a scavenger hunt or sweepstakes to attract may not necessarily be the target a web marketer wants to reach. "Probably the most attractive people with a lot of money don't have time to be playing games," Spence said (Ibid.).

Critiques of the gimmick approach led some advertisers to develop their own "content" sites. For example, Toyota was one of the first companies to offer an "ad-free" site that emphasized lifestyle features. Visitors could learn how to plant a garden or plan a trip by linking to other sites. Although the intent was noble: To build "a sense of community," the outcome was troublesome because the links led visitors to other sites, often never to return (*AA*, 10/16/95, 22).

Thus, at the end of 1995, we find that two of the critical issues have been formulated and some initial experiments are being carried out. Web content areas were trying out different ways to price advertising located in their site. Both advertisers and content providers were innovating what material was located at the sites. Research suppliers were trying to find a measurement and evaluation approach that would provide web marketers with the information they needed about customers.   INTERACTIVE has now passed its second birthday, and we pass into 1996.

1996 — THE COOPERATIVE PHASE

Up to this point, much of what has challenged online advertisers has been technical - issues of measuring and tracking audiences, or of determining most effective creative elements in web sites. Although these issues continue unabated in *Ad Age* into 1996, this year sees new challenges that can be said to be mostly educational in scope. For example, if the Web is to grow, it will need promotion and marketing of its own (*AA*, 09/09/96, 26). It will need to develop a far better understanding of which ads reach out to consumers. As a result of these needs, some of the changes that 1996 brought included smaller web sites, smarter banner ads, the birth of advertorials, and the fact that many advertising competitors became one another's best friends.

Intermedia Promotion

Advertisers in 1995 were so fixated on attracting clickers via the Web itself, that they overlooked traditional, more reliable media like TV and magazines as ways to attract consumers to the Web (*AA*, 10/14/96, 51). According to a 1996 survey conducted by Market Facts, half of 500 respondents said they visited a web site because they saw the web address mentioned in a magazine or newspaper ad. Consistent with this apparent impact of linking traditional media with web advertising, Pepsi-Cola launched an outdoor ad campaign for its Pepsi World (*AA*, 04/01/96, 36). Although it is too soon to know if intermedia efforts such as Pepsi's will pay off, such efforts may be responsible for increasing the awareness of the virtual highway. Indeed, last year, the Internet was a term recognized by 82% of Americans, but is now nearly ubiquitous at 94% awareness (*AA*, 10/14/96, 46).

On the other hand, critics say that it will take a lot more than advertising on a billboard to send consumers running to web sites - especially given that 44% of current web users sampled said they never look at banner ads (*AA*, 10/14/96, 51). In addition, advertising a web site in a traditional medium may work well for larger companies, but what about the little guys?

As noted previously, piggybacking was an innovative approach developed by online advertisers in 1995, but it gained widespread popularity in 1996 (*AA*, 4/22/96, 26). Sports sites, such as ESPN, were among the first to use business-to-business links in order to increase traffic to other sites, with the expectation that the link would be reciprocated (*AA*, 01/29/96, 26).

Newspaper giants, such as *The New York Times* were finding that they, too, must seek partners in building web sites. Low profits (less than an average of $50,000 each for 395 newspapers) sent newspapers in quest of appropriate links. Proponents argue that this could be the 'make-it or break-it' "factor for how the publications fare on the Web" (*AA*, 4/29/96, S6).

Smaller advertisers also were taking note of this coordinated strategy. Freemark, an ad-supported e-mail provider, is hanging on the coattails of big brands like Radio Shack and PC Week. "We're a small company and we don't have brand-name recognition," notes Doug McFarland, Freemark's exec VP-general manager. "We could hire a big agency and spend millions of dollars, but we've chosen to associate our name with a number of companies to receive value from them" (*AA*, 4/22/96, 26). Proponents argue that online companies that do not form alliances with big corporations (and vice versa) will be left standing alone in cyberspace (*AA*, 10/21/96, 28).

On the other hand, name association does not guarantee ad profits or even visits to a linking site. Time magazine is repositioning itself on the World Wide Web by focusing more on the Time name and less on Pathfinder, the corporate site for all Time Warner brands (*AA*, 10/07/96, 46). Apparently, Time Warner wants to increase the 50% traffic flow it receives from Pathfinder by creating a separate site. This switch is amiable to Pathfinder because it will continue to bring traffic to its site (Ibid.).

Growth

Web ad spending reached an all-time high at $66.7 million in the first half of 1996 (*AA*, 10/02/96, 1). That number was estimated to grow to $3.8 billion by 2000 (*AA*, 10/28/96, 40). A less sanguine finding is that the growth rate of online users has slowed to 50% in 1996 (*AA*, 09/09/96, 47). The number of hours spent online in a month fell from 16 to 12 hours between May 1995 and May 1996 (Ibid.). And, 82% of 500 people who had been online in the past six months reported going there primarily to gather news and information (*AA*, 10/14/96, 46).

Advertorials

In an effort to establish a profitable model for the Web, advertisers took note of the growth information, and many switched from entertainment-oriented ads of 1995 to an information-oriented approach, or advertorials - ads that combine editorial content (*AA*, 11/08/96, S3). Advertorials were argued to be the next "lucrative deal" for virtual advertising (*AA*, 11/08/96, S3). Media companies claimed that if a sponsored site was carefully designed, users would not be confused about where content begins and an advertisement ends (*AA*, 04/01/96, 29).

Critics disagreed, saying advertorials add to the blurred lines that already exist in cyberspace (*AA*, 11/08/96, S3). For example, Kraft Foods opened an area in *The New York Times*, inviting users to take a Maxwell House coffee break. Users are then linked to a "co-branded content area" that offers *Times* book reviews and crossword puzzles (*AA*, 04/01/96, 29).

Microsites

Building mini- (or micro-) sites, like Kraft Foods did, became a popular ad strategy in 1996. Sites like Levi Strauss, Pepsi-Cola and Toyota reported downsizing and dispersing their sites to better target their audience (*AA*, 10/21/96, 40). Larger sites like these "were launched at a time when Web advertising was all about getting consumers to spend a lot of time with a brand on the Web" (Ibid.). That notion did not pan out. This trend did not mean, however, that web advertising sites would disappear altogether because they were still valuable for things like conducting transactions, generating sales leads, and providing general information (*AA*, 10/21/96, 49). What marketers were learning was that to engage a consumer in a particular brand, an advertisement must (in many cases) appear outside of their web site (Ibid.).

Local Appeal

Online marketers were also learning that a mass market appeal on a worldwide medium is equivalent to the shotgun approach of advertising preelectronic days. The shift now is to target microgroups of consumers, even on a local basis (*AA*, 11/08/96, S8). One such company, Cox Interactive, reported concentrating its energy "on developing local 'city sites' and specialty niches." One of its sites, for example, targeted outdoor enthusiasts in the Western United States. Cox Interactive believes that people want information that is personally relevant to them, and that local content sites will be the key to accomplishing this (Ibid.).

Virtual and Interactive Sites

Not only were web sites going local in 1996, they are going virtual and interactive. It was argued that advertising material would no longer exist at a fixed Uniform Resource Locator (URL) (i.e., a web address). Instead, "it will be dynamically generated, demographically targeted and capable of existing in multiple places in multiple formats" (*AA*, 10/21/96, 48).

The interactive capabilities of the Web were used more for building relationships in 1996. Online businesses began reporting that they were sending customized e-mails to consumers who solicit questions about products. This interactive tactic was predicted to build respect and brand loyalty (*AA*, 09/09 96, 42).

Targeting Younger Audiences. There are more than 7 million North American children under the age of 18 with Internet accounts (a.k.a. the "Net-Generation"). If this market is to be tapped, marketers must learn to "attract the attention of young people who are reaching higher levels of income." Online ad spending is expected to grow as marketers look beyond the banner ad for what else they can do on the Net. The cost-per-impression model will be traded for a direct marketing model that pays according to performance. Subscriber fees continue to generate low revenues, and web measurement persists in its infuriating spiral.

1997 — THE TARGETING PHASE

Online Ad Spending

1997 was the first year that marketers articulated a commitment to online advertising. Online ad sales showed a healthy growth, as first quarter sales in 1996 ($29.9 million) rose to $168 million during the second quarter of 1997. In other growth developments, the Computer Network reported second-quarter revenues of $8.3 million, an increase of 46% from first quarter. Rival site ZDNet formalized a rate card for sponsoring site content, e-mail messages, banners, microsites, and advertorials. Switching to a rate card pricing approach almost doubled second quarter revenues for ZDNet (*AA,* 8/4/97, 26).

Search engines scrambled to find new revenue streams by rounding up cobranding sponsorships. Yahoo reported $13.5 million in revenue, up 42% from first quarter. Excite's revenue grew to $9.5 million - a rise of 26% over first quarter, and Infoseek's revenue jumped to $7.7 million - an increase of 25%. In fact, some online businesses - such as Wired Digital - are expecting to earn a profit in 1998.

An important discussion point during 1997 concerned what factors were fueling this kind of growth. First, many businesses had finished with the first phase of creating their web sites and therefore were implementing their advertising plans. Most consumer-oriented companies concentrated their efforts in 1996 on building their web sites and determining their business model. In the first half of 1997, we were beginning to see the implementation of those plans in terms of ad placement (*AA,* 8/4/97, 24).

A second reason for a rise in ad spending was that advertisers were learning what drives traffic to a site - namely, making a site fun, easy to navigate, useful, and interactive. Simply putting up a web page or throwing up a banner was not perceived as being enough to attract users. The concept of linking to key sites to drive traffic was also being left behind in 1997. One of the biggest problems with links was, as noted before, that they take web users from the screen they are originally viewing. In essence, links drive users away from sites instead of driving them to sites, as was originally thought in 1996 (*AA,* 2/24/97, 74).

Instead of links, advertisers became more concerned with concepts of proximity and immediacy. Internet users are argued to want product information now, but they do not want to download multiple sites to get that information (*AA,* 3/10/97, S16).

Smart Banners

What we find in 1997 is that the rash of improved technologies "allow advertisers to deliver customized information and even perform a transaction without ever leaving the confines of a banner, icon or frame" (Ibid.).

First Virtual Technologies, for example, launched a new technology called "Virtual Tag" that allowed advertisers to embed a number of forms within a banner that streams additional information into the ad. Users could then receive information and purchase products by clicking in a "smart" ad banner. There was only one problem with Virtual Tags: Users needed to have an account with First Virtual in order to conduct business (*AA,* 2/4/97, 74).

IN2, an agency specializing in interactive banners, aimed "to bring qualified users to advertisers' sites through interactive polling, searching, and other direct response activities within banner ads" (*AA*, 8/25/97, 20). IN2 polling banners were claimed to garner a 10% to 30% click-through rate for its client iVillage - a community-based web site. IN2 developed a drop-down banner for iVillage that asked users to rank their preferences for various Parent Soup (an area of iVillage) discussion groups, including teens, pregnancy, and toddlers. In this way, iVillage was able to gain insights concerning editorial content. In a campaign for Barnes & Noble, IN2 developed an interactive ad that allowed users to search for book titles. *Ad Age* reported that click-through rates jumped to 26% during the first four days the ad ran.

Thus, online ad spending appeared to be up, partly because advertisers were beginning to use "smart" ad banners that delivered product information fast and within the same screen.

Direct Marketing Model

A third reason for the increase in online revenues was argued to be the fact that advertisers began to be more creative with pricing models by offering more options to sponsors. CNET, for example, developed a creative sponsorship of "The Intel Screamer of the Week," a branded area of CNET, where visitors vote on their favorite Web sites. Rival site ZDNet came up with a new rate card that allows advertisers to sponsor site content, e-mail messages, banners, microsites, and advertorials. According to VP-General Manager Jim Savage, the company doubled its revenue shortly after implementing the rate card (*AA*, 8/4/97, 26).

In-House Orientation

A study conducted by Mediamark Research Inc., *Ad Age*, and Bruskin/Goldring Research indicated that advertising agencies may be losing out when it comes to interactive work (*AA*, 3/10/97, S4). Just 30% of 301 telephone respondents named their ad agency as the lead resource for interactive marketing projects. Many marketers (54%) said they preferred interactive specialists (e.g., CKS Group, Poppe Tyson, or TN Technologies) for their online needs. Others (26.9%) indicated that they would turn in-house for online projects before using an ad agency. The primary reason that marketing executives gave for not using their ad agency more was agency lack of interactive experience. Peter Levitan, president of New Jersey Online, said the advertising community is "behind the curve when it comes to the Internet" because they do not understand the value of Internet marketing (*AA*, 5/12/97, 72).

Others predicted that as marketers invest more money in online media, agencies will begin to see the value of having a staff to buy and plan the advertising (*AA*, 3/10/97, S19).

How should an agency handle its interactive business? Should an agency separate or integrate the interactive component? Anderson and Lembke, a San

Francisco agency, formed separate online media divisions, hiring 30 new media staffers. Interactive specialist Modem Median boosted its interactive department and reported expecting to invest $40 million in online advertising in 1997 (*AA*, 3/10/97, S19).

On the other hand, BlairLake Chairman David Epstein pointed out that "most ad agencies have found that adding an interactive function in-house is like adding a television studio - it just doesn't make sense." In fact, even if ad agencies do decide to integrate online advertising, only 27% of marketers polled indicated that they would use their ad agency for Web projects (*AA*, 3/10/97, S4). Naming an interactive agency of record seems to be a rage of the past. The new trend is to divvy up work that utilizes "people with the right skills to get the job done" (*AA*, 3/10/97, S10).

Targeting Locally

Targeting became easier and more feasible in 1997. Until this time, targeting in cyberspace had been a difficult task; primarily it was not known who was using the Web, at which sites and when. With all the new technology shaping up, marketers may soon be able to "hatch the fabled golden egg of 'one-to-one marketing' on the Net" (*AA*, 8/4/97, 28). PC Meter expanded its measurement reach by splitting into two divisions: One to provide comparative research on web sites and one to track consumer and business usage trends (*AA*, 2/24/97, 78).

Another company, RelevantKnowledge, said it planned to pick up where PC Meter left off - providing data about business usage (*AA*, 4/21/97, 52). Web publishers claim their sites are under-reported by PC Meter because about 85% of their traffic occurred during business hours. RelevantKnowledge will provide data of 30 demographic breakdowns, ranking top sites in a variety of categories. This kind of data was argued not to allow clients to compare sites to each other, but to compare pages within a site.

With data like these, advertisers were predicted to "look more favorably on the Web," as they were given "tools" to target microgroups, such as teens, African Americans, and women. (*AA*, 5/26/97, 36; *AA*, 7/28/97, 32; *AA*, 8/11/97, 18).

One of the main shortcomings of the Web was acknowledged to be geographic limitations. During 1997, marketers came closer to having the ability to target a particular geographic group by asking users to register their zip codes (*AA*, 6/2/97, S18). This method of determining who is using the Web was presented as being more accurate than previous methods of observing domain names. Advertisers who use geographic targeting reported good advertiser response (*AA*, 3/24/97, 30). The Weather Channel, for example, reported planing to target specific regions with allergy updates.

Yahoo! targets users through a combination of localized content, such as its nine city-specific information services. Wells Fargo, Honda, and American Airlines are among those who have taken advantage of the site's localized ad targeting (*AA*, 3/24/97, 30).

Traditional Media Go Online

Newspapers, radio, and TV stations had been trying to figure out how to get their piece of the superinformation highway in the sky since its earliest days. In 1997, the effort by media to online became even more intense.

The Wall Street Journal launched a career site, a job listing site for the executive marketplace, that was aimed at generating revenues from client listings and advertisers (*AA*, 8/4/97, 26). NBC-IN hoped to attract traffic to its site by selling national advertising sites, and television stations sold local spots (*AA*, 5/12/97, 72). NBC projected that the average viewer would access NBC-IN once a week, see eight pages per visit and stay an average of 40 seconds per page.

Katz Radio Group teamed up with World Wide Radio to make media buying on radio web sites easier and more common. Senior VP-director Gerry Boehme stated that the Internet would help radio stations extend their current business model by providing a forum to do visuals and offer coupons (*AA*, 6/2/97, S12). Radio station WNNX, Atlanta, claimed to make nearly $1 million annually from its three-year-old web site (*AA*, 6/2/97, S12). They suggested their success came from "going beyond the ad banner." The station marketed Internet access software for companies like Internet Atlanta, and it sold sponsorships of web events to advertisers such as Anheuser-Busch and America Online (AOL).

WFTC-TV, Minneapolis, targeted children. Although concerns of pornography and kids' privacy issues have created parental wariness, WFTC offered a link from the Fox 29 Kids Club to the Federal Communication Commission's Children's Programming Guidelines (*AA*, 6/2/97, S16). Once kids enter the Kids Club area, they can play games, enter contests, or submit "Fridge Art" - freeform drawings that are either, snail-mailed to the station and then scanned onto the site, or e-mailed by the kids themselves.

Policing the Web

Almost every week in 1997, another crisis in Internet advertising was reported (*AA*, 6/16/97, 46). For example, Time sued CompuServe, alleging the online service wanted to cut short a two-year, $7 million deal (*AA*, 3/24/97, 28). Ticketmaster Corporation sued Microsoft Corporation, alleging the company was deriving ad revenue from its link to the Ticketmaster site (*AA*, 5/19/97, 68). Three adult web sites were secretly switching users to an international phone line, charging $2 per minute for the rest of the computer session before they were closed down by the Federal Trade Commission (*AA*, 2/24/97, 78). Web sites that targeted children were asking for demographic information without the parents' consent before the FTC's Children's Advertising Review Unit (CARU) proposed guidelines that would require getting parental consent in writing and putting such requests in language kids can understand (*AA*, 6/23/97, 16).

Although the FTC began pressuring Washington to step in to regulate the Web, President Clinton made it clear that his approach was (mostly) "hands-off" (*AA*, 5/12/97, 66). The hands-off recommendation apparently extends to obscenity on the Internet. Rather than set limits, Ira Magaziner, leader of the Internet task force, said the U.S. government should focus on "assuring that competition remains free." Even though privacy and protecting children do remain the two areas that will need special Internet regulation, the task force was not, at least late in 1997, expected to propose solutions.

To summarize the online situation late in 1997, banner advertising accounted for 54% of total web revenues, but the banners were themselves "getting smarter." Media issues continued to be a problem (*AA*, 1/26/98, 38). There was generally no consistency on web sites in terms of how the owners of the site processed, reported on, and placed ads. This meant that managing only advertising campaigns remained unwieldy and labor-intensive. Because it remained unclear just what had to happen for an online ad to be effective, there were fierce arguments about "cost per thousand" of online as compared to other media. One could calculate CPM in one way and show it costing either much more, the same, or much less per "exposure" (*AA*, Spring 1998, Special Report, 18A).

MOVING INTO 1998

Innovations continued to appear early in 1998. Interstitial ads, which appear while users are waiting for screens to download, became much more common. Newspapers continued to experiment with charging either for their whole site, or for at least part of it (*AA*, 1/26/98, 40). Newspapers also began banding together to create sites like <Cars.com>, which would provide all automotive information from the *Chicago Tribune*, the *Los Angeles Times*, and *The Washington Post*. Several companies, including Microsoft with its new "Sidewalk," attempted to break into the hold newspapers have over local information by providing detailed city information (*AA*, 11/24/97, 25).

Legal and issues continued and increased in type and number. For example, spamming (sending an e-mail that pretends to be from someone else) became a problem as users of Juno (free e-mail system) and AOL received faked messages (*AA*, 12/1/97, 68). The FTC began a program of examining the Web for invasion of privacy problems (*AA*, 1/16/98, 45). Microsoft continued to be investigated by the U.S. Department of Justice for allegedly forcing computer makers to include Internet Explorer browser on Windows 95 (*AA*, 11/17/97, 3). There were continuing security problems with online commerce transactions (*AA*, 11/17/97, 56). Also, there were increased trademark problems when advertisers found someone was using their name on the Web (*AA*, 11/17/97, 56).

One of the most controversial new developments was the "push" ads, where ads were delivered to users via e-mail or through their server. An *Ad Age* survey of web users showed there was a favorable response to received news uninvited, but 71% of the sample said they would not sign up for incentives where they could get cash or prizes for accepting push advertising (*AA*, 11/10/97, S1).

SOME CONCLUDING REMARKS

Although this chapter must end sometime, *Ad Age*'s INTERACTIVE goes on every week; its size and the amount of advertising it carries continues to grow. Forrester Research most recently predicted that web advertising, at around $2.4 billion at the end of 1997, would grow to $17.4 billion by 2001 (*AA*, 11/14/97, 24). From its inception in the fall of 1993, then, INTERACTIVE has provided a delightful window on interactive marketing, and now most particularly on web advertising. The claims, the ideas, the arguments are laid out for anyone who wants to know what is going on in this infant field of marketing, and who wants to hear prognostications about the future.

REFERENCES

Briggs, R. & Hollis, N. (1997). Advertising on the Web: Is the response before click-through? *Journal of Advertising Research, 37*(2), 33-45.

2

Understanding Interactivity Of Cyberspace Advertising

Harper A. Roehm
Curtis P. Haugtvedt
The Ohio State University

> We'll interact with advertising where once we only watched; we'll seek out advertising where once we avoided it. Advertising will not go away; it will be rejuvenated.
>
> *Michael Schrage (1994)*
> *MIT Media Lab Fellow*
> *Ad Age Columnist*

Marketing communications on the Web provide benefits to both consumers and marketers. Many of these benefits stem from the form of the interaction between the web site and the consumer. Consider Zeke, an individual in the market for binoculars. Although he had little expertise, he did have some beliefs about binoculars. For example, he believed that well-performing binoculars would be very expensive because of the exacting nature of the optics. Similar logic led him to believe that it was important to match the type of binoculars to the intended use, such as hunting, bird watching, or watching sports. His search for information about binoculars began with locating and reading a *Consumer Reports'* study on binoculars published in 1988. Although the report contained a great deal of information, he was somewhat skeptical about the usefulness of this information primarily because (1) the information was relatively old, and (2) there was little information about the use of binoculars for bird watching. This motivated him to "surf" the World Wide Web. In less than five minutes, he located a web page devoted to providing information, updated monthly, on binoculars for bird watching. Not only was there a great deal of important and current information, it was in a medium where Zeke could customize the input to his own needs. With the click of the mouse, he was able to go directly to the information of interest to him, avoiding extraneous information about monoculars or photography. He was able to go directly to guidelines on how to evaluate and select binoculars. In addition, the site contained an analysis of different brands. The site also allowed him to reorganize brand information consistent with his specific needs. After analyzing information on the site, he purchased a pair of binoculars with which he has been very satisfied.

Only weeks after the purchase did he realize a number of things. He realized that for basic information about binoculars, the *Consumer Reports* study was nearly as informative as the web page. One significant limitation, however, was that the study did not have any specific information on binoculars for bird watching. This initially created doubts as to the usefulness of the information. Because the web page provided information about the product related to how he was planning to use it, he realized that he had given more weight to the web page information in his purchase decision.

Based on additional web browsing, Zeke concluded that many web sites allowed him to communicate with other people who have similar interests. Web sites allowed him to e-mail others, post or review questions and answers on usenets, listservers, or bulletin boards, and even get involved in the dialogue of chat-lines. This provided him with entertainment, social outlets, and new information sources. He noticed that web pages containing graphics, colors, photos, movies, and sound created more vivid, interesting, and more informative sites. He also noticed that many web sites provided objective information (similar to the birding web site) so he and other "surfers" could learn about products from an objective source, not just the company selling the product. Overall, he realized that the web provided a means to learn about and purchase products - sometimes much more informatively and conveniently than actually visiting a store or calling a mail-order catalog operator. In sum, the example of Zeke is real (with names changed to protect the innocent) and serves to illustrate some of the important characteristics of the Web and its potential impact on consumers.

The World Wide Web is a new, interactive means of communication. This computer-mediated communication (CMC) is the union of hardware, software, and computer know-how that allows millions of people to "surf" the Net in search of entertainment, information, sense of community, and/or commercial exchange (Schrage, 1994). It is estimated that in 1998 the Internet reached approximately 50 million consumers worldwide (Wang, Lee and Wang, 1998). The Web provides the capability of developing interactive advertising or computer-mediated advertising (CMA), in which the salesperson is a computer program (Schrage, 1994). Businesses have been quick to recognize this new medium. $336 million was spent in web advertising in 1997 (O'Brien, 1998). The Web is becoming so popular that businesses are rushing to have a presence on the Web - perhaps without diligent consideration of important differences between web advertising and the use of traditional media. Some companies are perhaps not giving enough attention to these differences. Clearly, although the Web represents a tremendous opportunity for marketers now and in the future, much needs to be learned to be successful. Similarities and differences between traditional and computer-mediated communications need to be addressed in detail.

One of the most important differences is that the Web is (or has the potential to be) highly interactive. That is, people can control what information they see, for how long, how many times, and in what order. Additionally, they can post questions and even respond to questions. Negroponte, *WIRED* senior columnist and MIT Media Lab Director, believes that advertising will see a " . . . total inversion: Instead of advertisers soliciting response, they'll respond to solicitations by potential customers." Others agree. Don Peppers and Martha Rogers predict that there will be a new tone to advertising - marketers will have to better satisfy consumers in their product search, entertainment, and buying experiences. In fact, they predict that "In the one-to-one future, the consumer will be the one in the driver's seat and the advertiser will be thumbing a ride" (Schrage, 1994, p. 3).

In this chapter, we develop the idea that advertisers can also be in especially good positions to achieve their goals, once they understand how to effectively use this new medium. We suggest some ways that we can begin to understand how consumers process information in this new interactive medium and how marketers can affect that process in order to better satisfy the customer. The end result of such understanding should be improved profitability and greater customer loyalty.

Our approach to answering these questions is to utilize current theories from various social science disciplines such as social psychology, consumer psychology, and communication disciplines. In addition to addressing practical issues, we believe this new medium offers unique opportunities to explore existing theories in new and exciting experimental designs and data collection methodologies. Such research may provide more insight as to the boundary conditions of current theoretical perspectives and existing empirical studies and may stimulate the development of more comprehensive views. Speed of data collection and development of knowledge may also be accelerated by the new technologies - issues of importance to both basic researchers and practitioners.

Before describing some of the research opportunities, we briefly explore some of the benefits and costs of the web-based communications to consumers and marketers. To do this, we begin with a conceptualization of the web interactivity. This framework will then be used to describe a program of research on the development of effective interactive marketing communications.

BENEFITS OF INTERACTIVITY

In moving to the Web, many researchers and practitioners argue that the consumer garners more benefits and control than does the marketer. That is, the balance of control and power shifts in favor of the consumer. Cross and Smith (1995) suggested that balance between the interactive marketer and the customer will look something like Table 2.1:

TABLE 2.1
The New Interactive Marketing Balance

Interactive Marketer	Interactive Customer
New selling channels	Convenience
Targeted messages	Fewer irrelevant messages
Measurability	Availability
Ever-present messages	Access to peers' dialogue
Customer dialogue	Informed decisions
Loyalty	Speedy response
	Ads on demand
	New sources of information
	Product satisfaction

Modified from Cross and Smith (1995).

Benefits to Consumers

Using the Web, customers can easily seek out information about a number of products and services from their homes, can ignore advertising or parts of advertising they perceive as irrelevant, can pick specific ads in which they are interested, and, most importantly, can potentially control the content of the information presented to them. Additionally, in a competitive environment, such as when a customer uses an Internet search engine, the consumer has the additional option of looking at a competitor's offering and information at relatively low cost in terms of time and effort.

Many web sites are available that provide objective information on an industry and its products, like an online *Consumer Reports*. For example, if someone was interested in purchasing a Gateway 2000 computer, he or she might visit Gateway's web site to find out about their product offerings. In addition, he or she may also go to C/net's web site, one that serves as one of the *Consumer Reports* for computer software and hardware. The consumer can go to this site and validate any claims made by Gateway and determine how C/net's experts compare Gateway's products to others. The potential consumer can even initiate or join in dialogue with other interested parties. What makes this medium even more beneficial is that these services are available 24 hours a day, seven days a week. All of this results in a situation where consumers may be able to make more informed decisions.

As the previous example illustrates, there are a number of advantages for consumers. In the realm of advertising, many experts suggest that marketers have lost much control to the consumer. Peppers and Rogers (1995) noted that advertising has worked in the traditional mass-media paradigm has been simple: Figure out the likely prospects and aim standardized messages at that target market using mass media for delivery. A primary goal in such approach has been media efficiency - enhancing the chances that the specified audience is likely to see the media vehicle chosen. This will change in the interactive age. Peppers and Rogers suggested that advertising will be invited by consumers because of inducements on the part of business (e.g., free phone time or computer time) as part of an exchange relationship. In other contexts, consumers may actually solicit businesses to bid to provide their services or products.

Interactive Marketers' Benefits

Marketers have a new advertising and selling medium to target/reach their established customers as well as reaching new customers (see Table 2.1). Marketers can target messages by customizing the message based on the interaction with the customer. They can track these new customers' activities by getting them involved in marketing research such as surveys. This new medium can help generate loyalty. A web site is an ever-present source of company and product/service information, where information specific to particular needs and interests can be obtained quickly and easily, with visual aids, organized guides to walk through particular problems, and even dialogue with other product users, and so on. Executed appropriately, this can result in greater customer satisfaction and loyalty.

Defining Interactivity

Interactivity of the web provides a number of benefits to both consumers and marketers. Characterizing the issue of interactivity in terms of communication processes, Heeter (1989) used six elements to define interactivity: complexity of choice available; the amount of effort users must exert; the extent of responsiveness to the consumer; the capacity of monitoring information use; the ease of adding information; and the potential to facilitate interpersonal communication. Steuer (1992) defined interactivity as "the extent to which users can participate in modifying the form and content of a mediated environment in real time" (p. 84). Thus, for working purposes, interactivity refers to some level of real-time dialogue in which the involved entities (human or otherwise) play both the role of sender and receiver of information at some point in the dialogue. In the case of interactive marketing and the Web, the two entities are the marketers and the consumers who have "hit" or entered the web page. Interactivity in this context, when carefully executed, *might* resemble conversations between salespersons and customers.

In addition to allowing customers control of the information accessed, including the order and extent of the information, web pages can be developed to allow such a great level of interaction that it is conceivable that the customer thinks he is actually having a conversation with the web page. The web page can be programmed to ask questions and to respond to consumers' answers or other input such as requests or questions. Online advertising affords consumers the opportunity to perform in-depth analyses of the product or service and/or company's claims relative to their products or services. Consumers may post questions about the product or claims made about it and they can instantly respond with praise or criticism after product or service experience. Additionally, we suggest that interactivity should also refer to the ability of marketers to customize their communications to the personality style or needs of particular consumers.

In its current state, the web context lacks some of the dimensions of the most interactive medium, the personal selling environment. Web programming cannot "read" and interpret nonverbal cues, such as amusement or curiosity. A salesperson can "read" a customer's puzzled look and act accordingly. Future developments, however, may enhance the personalized nature of the interactions.

As mentioned previously, some commentators believe that interactive web advertising is shifting the power and control to the consumer relative to more traditional media forms (e.g., Schrage, 1994). We suggest, however, that both marketers and consumers will gain some type of control. In the following section, we examine how interactivity can empower both the customer and the marketer. We recognize, however, that this distinction is somewhat artifactual and that the notion of customization is very much an iterative process.

One of the key dimensions of interactivity is the ability of consumers to participate in the formation of the content of the communication and its presentation. Steuer's (1992) definition of interactivity focused primarily on this perspective. Another perspective is that interactivity can include the marketer's ability to customize the advertising message presented to the consumer. Heeter's definition implied such customization when she referred to the extent of "responsiveness" to the consumer and the potential to "facilitate" interpersonal communication. Based on this interpretation, we suggest that interactivity has two dimensions: (a) control and (b) message (see Table 2.2).

The source of control dimension refers to who controls the nature of the interactivity, that is, whether it is consumer-controlled or marketer-controlled.

For instance, the consumer's ability to influence the information presented on screen from a web site would be characterized as consumer-controlled interactivity. The consumer interacts with the web page in order to view particular information. A marketer can set up a web page to ask consumers questions about their interests, and then provide information corresponding to the consumer's interests. In this case, interactivity can be used to manipulate the content and/or the form of the communication to adapt to a particular receiver with the goal that it is clearer or more effective.

TABLE 2.2
The Two Dimensions of Interactivity

Dimension 2 – Control	Dimension 1 – Message	
	Form-oriented	Content-oriented
Customer-controlled:	Selection of advertising layout or communication style (e.g., cosmetic features, video vs. print)	Selection of the product attributes to be assessed (arguments in favor of the product)
Marketer-controlled:	Changing wording, Highlight certain attributes and/or use different layouts or message sources	Changing the attributes presented each time the person comes back to the site (message arguments)

The message dimension of interactivity is broken down into (a) form-oriented interactivity, referring to the use of interactivity to manipulate the message form (or how it is said) and (b) content-oriented interactivity, which refers to the use of interactivity to manipulate the content of the communication (i.e., message copy). This is similar to the distinction between cosmetic and substantive variation (Schumann, Petty, & Clemons, 1990). For instance, a message argument (i.e., ad copy) with the same content in terms of information can be presented in different forms or different wordings (cosmetic features). Similarly, different product attributes or message arguments can be presented (substantive features). In the following sections, we explore how these two dimensions, cosmetic and substantive variation, when combined, provide a more detailed conceptualization of interactivity.

Customer-Controlled, Content-Oriented Interactivity. Zeke's satisfaction with the birding web site was caused not only by its trove of important and current information, but also because the medium's interactivity allowed Zeke to customize the information for his own needs. He was able, with the click of the mouse, to go directly to the information of interest to him, avoiding the extraneous information. He also had control of the order and the length of time the information was presented.

This form of customization of the persuasive message is a type of interactivity that is driven by the consumer and focuses on the content of the message. We call this customer-controlled, content-oriented interactivity.

Customer-Controlled, Form-Oriented Interactivity. Zeke might also be able to control the nature of the spokespersons or endorsements appearing on the web page (e.g., see what the experts or people just like himself have to say) or to see a video rather than read the information. Of course, the same basic product information could be presented in different ways. Some consumers may be more influenced by the visual presentation of information, whereas others may prefer print or audio versions of the information.

Marketer-Controlled, Content-Oriented Interactivity. To this point, we have discussed only the role of consumer-controlled interactivity. We believe types of interactivity or customization controlled by the marketer could improve the persuasiveness of the communication (as assessed by attitudes toward the brand, requests for additional information or salesperson callback, purchase intention, or online purchase). For example, suppose Nikon has a web page that included information about the company, its product line, warranties, service, locations of nearest dealers, and so on. In addition, Nikon provides general objective information about binoculars, such as the information found in *Consumer Reports*. At this point, this information is consumer-controlled because Nikon has simply provided a web site that allows consumers to use interactivity to control the type of information presented, as well as its order and the length of presentation.[1] What if Nikon also attempts to customize the message to the customer? This is accomplished by collecting information about the consumer while he or she is interacting with the web page.[2] The web page programming would initiate a dialogue in which the web program asks questions and the consumer responds. These responses could be utilized real-time to customize the form of the message.

---

[1] Of course, Nikon's content decisions should be driven by their customers and may change as Nikon learns more about what customers are looking for, reflecting an iterative process between consumer- and marketer-control.

[2] Database marketing concepts could also be used so that a repository of information on a particular consumer is kept, with the consumer's consent, and used to customize the web experience each time the consumer comes to the web site. This could be accomplished by assigning a customer identification number that is required to gain access to the web site. This would allow marketers to gather information about all the transactions a customer has in the web site.

This customization might involve simply personalizing the message by inserting the customer's name in various appropriate points in the web page presentation. A more persuasive type of customization would be to ascertain the customers' goals or interests and customize the persuasive message by highlighting particular aspects of the product that would be of interest to the customer given his or her goals or interests. This type of interactivity is marketer-controlled, content-oriented interactivity.

Binoculars, like many products, contain a long list of features. To enhance the effectiveness of its web-based advertisement, the Nikon web page could have ascertained Zeke's intended uses of the binoculars by providing a number of options such as, bird watching, boating, hunting, watching sports, and so on. Zeke could then have responded by checking, "bird watching." The Nikon web page in turn could present the most relevant and important information (i.e., a subset of the binocular features relevant to bird watching) in a prominent fashion while still allowing access to the full list of attributes.

The same model of binocular can be advertised differently based on the customer's intended use. For instance, in the case of a boater, the "floating strap" feature of these binoculars is one of the first pieces of information provided in the boater's case and/or a picture of a person using the binoculars on a boat in a rain storm, highlighting that they are waterproof. In the case of the birding, the clarity of vision attribute might be highlighted by the picture of the magnification capabilities (i.e., instead of a boater using the binoculars in the rain as in the case of the boater message), and/or highlighting the product's quick focus feature that would be particularly important when spotting a moving bird. Two different ads with different information would have been provided.

Marketer-Controlled, Form-Oriented Interactivity. With marketer-controlled, form-oriented interactivity, the actual information or arguments presented do not change. Customization can involve rewording or even highlighting certain attributes or arguments and/or endorsers or the use of video - without changing the content. The different forms would be available in anticipation that some forms would be more effective than others in persuading certain consumers.

CUSTOMIZED ADVERTISEMENTS AND INFORMATION PROCESSING

The foregoing discussion has outlined some of the ways in which web-based advertisements might be customized. Very important theoretical and practical questions are raised with the use of such techniques. Under what circumstances will a customized advertisement lead to more positive attitudes toward a product or service when compared to a noncustomized advertisement? How does customizing influence the manner in which persons cognitively process material from web-based advertising? Will consumer knowledge of the customized nature of the advertisements influence their effectiveness (cf. Friestad & Wright, 1994)? To what extent will the attitudes formed or changed from experience with interactive advertisements predict behavior and/or enhance loyalty?

Although such research is very much in the early stages, we believe that theories and methods from social and consumer psychology will prove extremely valuable in attempts to answer such questions. To conclude our chapter, we consider how customization might influence the extent of consumer elaboration. We also discuss research methods that might lend insights into such processes.

A fundamental goal of advertising is the creation of positive attitudes toward some person, issue, or object. A great deal of accumulated research now supports the idea that persons sometimes form their attitudes through extensive elaboration (central route to persuasion) or by giving greater weight to simple inferences or peripheral cues (peripheral route to persuasion; Petty & Cacioppo, 1986). Theory and recent empirical work guided by the Elaboration Likelihood Model supports the idea that even though individuals might develop equally positive attitudes through the central route or peripheral route, attitudes formed via the central route will last longer over time, be more resistant to change in the face of attack, and more predictive of behavior (see Haugtvedt & Wegener, 1994; Haugtvedt, Schumann, Schneier, & Warren, 1994; Petty, Haugtvedt, & Smith, 1995; Haugtvedt & Priester, 1997).

The extent of elaboration is one basis for strong attitudes. Persuasion researchers use at least two tools in order to understand the extent to which persons engage in active elaboration of advertising content versus using simple heuristics in the attitude change process. One approach is to ask persons to report the kinds of thoughts that were going through their minds when they engaged in the task, and content analyses of the thoughts can be used to make inferences about the extent of elaboration (Petty & Cacioppo, 1986). Another approach is to vary the content of the persuasive message such that one version contains strong arguments and the other version contains relatively weak arguments. If persons are not thinking extensively about the content, then individuals exposed to the different versions will report similar attitudes; but, if they are thinking extensively, individuals exposed to the strong arguments will have more positive attitudes than individuals exposed to the weak arguments (Petty & Cacioppo, 1986). Of course, such a manipulation of argument quality would likely be used only in laboratory-based studies to assess the extent of elaboration - one would not want to use weak arguments in real advertisements!

There are, of course, many ways to customize advertisements. One approach we are interested in pursuing involves using our understanding of a consumer's personality style as a basis for changing the nature of the advertisement presented to the individual. For example, an individual who sees him or herself as "versatile, wise, and conceptual" might be presented an advertisement in which those characteristics are used to describe users of a particular product. Existing research suggests that such matching will enhance behavior but the processes by which this occurs is unclear (Brock, Brannon, & Bridgewater, 1990). One possibility is that matching the ad with the consumer's self-perception will enhance the extent to which a person is motivated to think carefully about the product. Alternatively, encountering an advertisement for a product that "fits" one so well might lead one to find the product to be very appealing without much additional reflection. The use of argument quality manipulations, in addition to the customization, will help us in understanding the circumstances in which one process is more likely than the other.

Theoretical perspectives from the influence of personality on persuasion (e.g., DeBono & Snyder, 1989; Haugtvedt, Petty, & Cacioppo, 1992; Haugtvedt & Petty, 1992) might be contrasted with work on social perception by Gilbert and colleagues using the interactive web page as a experimental paradigm to better understand the processes of persuasion (e.g., Gilbert, Jones, & Pelham, 1987) and consumer decision making (Bettman, Johnson, & Payne, 1991). Sophisticated computer programming of web sites will also allow researchers and marketers to obtain some insight as to the order of consumer activities, as well as the amount of time they spend on various aspects of a site. Such data might be helpful in learning how consumers develop and later use knowledge about products in the purchase and use decisions (e.g., Huffman & Houston, 1993). To the extent that purchases take place via the web page (or can be linked to web page activities), extremely valuable insights may be provided.

In sum, our goal in this chapter was not to present all of the possibilities for customizing advertisements but rather to highlight some possibilities and to illustrate the linkage of current theory and research methods to understanding web-based advertising effectiveness. Developing, implementing, and main-taining web sites that "interact" in an effective way with the consumer will require time, effort, and money. Useful future research, therefore, will involve investigating message forms that vary in the level of customization in an attempt to answer the critical question, does it pay to implement interactive advertising?

REFERENCES

Bettman, J. R., Johnson, E. J., & Payne J. W., (1991). Consumer decision making. In H.Kassarjain & C. Robertson (Eds.), *Handbook of consumer behavior.* Englewood Cliffs, NJ: Prentice-Hall, 50-84.

Brock, T., Brannon L., & Bridgewater C. (1990). Message effectiveness can be increased by matching appeals to recipients' self-schemas: Laboratory demonstrations and national field experiment. In S. Agres, J. Edell, & T. Dubitsky (Eds.), *Emotion in advertising*. New York: Quorum Books, 285-314.

Cross, R., & Smith, J. (1995). Customer-focused strategies and tactics. In E. Forrest & R. Mizerski (Eds.), *Interactive marketing*. Lincolnwood, IL,: American Marketing Association, NTC Business Books, 5-28.

DeBono, K. G., & Snyder, M. (1989). Underlying consumer decision-making: The role of form and function in product evaluation. *Journal of Applied Social Psychology, 19*(5), 416-424.

Friestad, M., & Wright, P. (1994). The persuasion knowledge model: How people cope with persuasion attempts. *Journal of Consumer Research, 21*, 1-26.

Gilbert, D. T., Jones, E. E., & Pelham, B. W. (1987). Influence and inference: What the active perceiver overlooks. *Journal of Personality and Social Psychology, 52*(2), 861-870.

Haugtvedt, C.P., Petty, R.E., & Cacioppo, J.T. (1992), Need for Cognition and advertising: Understanding the role of personality variables in consumer behavior. *Journal of Consumer Psychology, 1*, 239-260.

Haugtvedt, C.P., & Petty, R.E. (1992). Personality and persuasion: Need for cognition moderates the persistence and resistance of attitude changes. *Journal of Personality and Social Psychology, 63*, 308-319.

Haugtvedt, C.P., Schumann, D.W., Schneier, W., & Warren, W. (1994). Advertising repetition and variation strategies: Implications for understanding attitude strength. *Journal of Consumer Research. 21*, 176-189.

Haugtvedt, C.P., & Wegener, D.T. (1994). Message order effects in persuasion: An attitude strength perspective. *Journal of Consumer Research. 21*, 205-218.

Haugtvedt, C.P., & Priester, J.R. (1997). Conceptual and methodological issues in advertising effectiveness: An attitude strength perspective. In W. Wells (Ed.) *Measuring Advertising Effectiveness*. Mahwah, NJ: Lawrence Erlbaum Associates, 79-93.

Heeter, C. (1989). Implication of new interactive technologies for conceptualizing communication media use. In J. Savaggio & J. Bryant (Eds.), *The information age: Emerging patterns of adoption and consumer use*. Hillsdale, NJ: Lawrence Erlbaum Associates, 53-75.

Huffman, C., & Houston, M. J. (1993, September). Goal-oriented experiences and the development of knowledge. *Journal of Consumer Research, 20*, 190-207.

Obrien, J. (1998, September). Web advertising and the branding mission. *Upside, Foster City, 10* (9), 90-94.

Peppers, D., & Rogers, M. (1995). Customer-focused strategies and tactics. In E. Forrest, & R. Mizerski (Eds.), *Interactive marketing*. Lincolnwood, IL: American Marketing Association, NTC Business Books, 113-134.

Petty, R.E., & Cacioppo, J. T. (1986). *Communication and persuasion: Central and peripheral routes to attitude change*. New York: Springer/Verlag.

Petty, R. E., Haugtvedt, C. P., & Smith, S. (1995). Elaboration as a determinant of attitude strength: Creating attitudes that are persistent, resistant and predictive of behavior. In R. E. Petty & J. Krosnick (Eds.), *Attitude strength: Antecedents and consequences*, Ohio State University series on Attitude and Persuasion. Mahwah, NJ: Lawrence Erlbaum Associates, 93-130.

Schrage, M. (1994). Is advertising finally dead? <http://www.wired.com/ wired/2.02/ features/advertising.html>.
Schumann, D. W., Petty, R. E, & S. Clemons, (1990). Predicting the effectiveness of different strategies of advertising variation: A test of the repetition-variation strategies hypotheses. *Journal of Consumer Research, 17*(2), 192-202.
Steuer, J. (1992). Defining virtual reality: Dimensions determining telepresence. *Journal of Communication, 42*(4), 73-93.
Wang, H, Lee, K.O., and Wang, C (1998), Consumer privacy concerns about Internet marketing. *Association for Computing Machinery. Communica-tions of the ACM*, New York, Mar 1998, *41*(3), 63-70.

3

Current Advertising on the Internet: The Benefits and Usage of Mixed-Media Advertising Strategies

Ann E. Schlosser
Alaina Kanfer
University of Illinois

Definition of Advertising:

> Paid, nonpersonal communication through various media by business firms, nonprofit organizations, and individuals who are in some way identified in the advertising message and who hope to inform or persuade members of a particular audience. (Krugman, Reid, Dunn, & Barban, 1994)

In the past five years, we have seen the Internet increase 25-fold. According to January 1998 estimates, the commercial domain is the largest domain on the Internet with 28% of all Internet hosts (Network Wizards, 1998). Moreover, the commercial domain is by far the largest and fastest growing on the World Wide Web with an estimated 63% of all sites on the Web (Gray, 1997). It appears that businesses are increasingly taking part in the new marketing forum available in cyberspace. Yet, many companies are growing disillusioned with the commercial possibilities of online advertising, and some have suggested that the Internet is better suited for interpersonal communication and personal sites rather than commercial sites (Bayers, 1996). Executives are questioning whether the potential of the Internet is real or just hype, and some companies are considering decreasing or removing their investment in online advertising. Questions remain, however, whether these online businesses are currently taking advantage of the Internet's capabilities and hence its potential benefits. Moreover, are these businesses integrating their online marketing strategy effectively with other traditional advertising media? Or, are their online advertising strategies actually precluding them from attaining the potential benefits of online advertising? Our research attempts to address these questions.

Potential Benefits of Advertising Online

For businesses, advertising on the Internet offers potential benefits that are not available through traditional advertising media. This new medium has caught the attention of advertising and marketing experts in several fields, and a range of research has just begun to highlight the differences between online and traditional advertising.

Information Richness. The broadcast nature of television, radio, billboard, and print constrain a traditional advertisement to one short, memorable message (Cronin, 1994). With the Internet, the advertising message is no longer so constrained. The Internet allows for communicating to consumers substantially more content-rich product information (Coalition for Networked Information, 1994; Cronin, 1994; Hoffman, Novak, & Chatterjee, 1995; Serafin & Ralston, 1995).

Ease of Updating. Maintaining an online ad is less costly than maintaining traditional ads and lacks the delays of other media (Hoffman, Novak, & Chatterjee, 1995; Sussman & Pollack, 1995). Furthermore, online information can be quickly and easily changed and updated (Cronin, 1994; Jennings, 1996; Solomon, 1995).

Brand Information. Whereas certain brand-relevant information is often considered too frivolous, given the space limitations of a traditional ad, the online ad can contain more brand-relevant information important for building brand image (Badgett, 1995). For instance, the site can contain trivia about the company, provide detailed information about the organizations it sponsors, and link to interesting image-related sites (Sadikin, 1995).

Data Collection. In exchange for this information and/or other product incentives, the company can easily and inexpensively collect detailed data about their Internet market (Cronin, 1994; Hoffman, Novak, & Chatterjee, 1995; Williamson, 1995a), as well as obtain precise measures of which pages in their sites were visited, for how long, how the individuals came to the site, and where the visitors originated (Williamson, 1995a, 1995b). The Internet also has the capabilities to gather consumer reactions to current products and ads as well as product and ad concepts through such means as online focus groups (Thorell, 1994).

Global Exposure. The Internet also reaches a worldwide audience. Clearly, the Internet expands the company's market to include global markets, allowing those from around the world to visit the web site (Hodges, 1996; Unger, 1996). Companies can respond to this global accessibility easily by having pages available in languages other than English. Gaining brand recognition from a global market could give a company the competitive advantage it needs in a marketplace that is increasingly expanding its borders (Krugman, Reid, Dunn, & Barban, 1994; Wilkie, 1994).

Customization. The Internet's interactive nature allows for greater flexibility than traditional media in type of information transmitted and the method of transmission. For instance, decisions regarding whether the information should be technically advanced or simple (Raman & Leckenby, 1995), whether the information should be textual, graphic, video or auditory (Anderson, 1995; Brueckner, 1994), and whether a product demonstration or detailed product description is used, can all be made by the consumer rather than the advertiser (Badgett, 1995; Coalition for Networked Information, 1994; Cronin, 1994).

Enhance Customer-Company Relations. Internet advertisements can also be used as a customer service vehicle. For instance, relationships can be enhanced through being available upon demand all day, every day (Hoffman, Novak, & Chatterjee, 1995), reducing purchase uncertainty through online product trials or demonstrations (Hoffman, Novak, & Chatterjee, 1995), and providing online, up-to-date, accurate technical support (Cronin, 1994).

Role-Playing. Another important feature of the Internet is its capabilities in creating a more persuasive and engaging ad. Through the use of interactive games and contests, the online site can encourage role-playing (Raman & Leckenby, 1995). Through role-playing, the consumer generates arguments in favor of the product (Petty & Cacioppo, 1981), which is often more persuasive to the individual than other-generated arguments (Pratkanis & Aronson, 1991).

Purchase Facilitation. Finally, the Internet can facilitate purchase decisions not only by providing detailed product and purchase details (e.g., by finding the nearest dealer and quoting prices), but also by giving consumers the option of buying at that moment from their own homes. This removes the gap between ad exposure and purchase response (Anderson, 1995; Hoffman, Novak, & Chatterjee, 1995), creating the opportunity for the ultimate in impulse buying (Jennings, 1996).

In this chapter, we examine whether current commercial sites are incorporating features that allow the companies to achieve the nine potential benefits outlined previously: providing detailed product information; supplying accurate, up-to-date information; building and fostering brand image; collecting information about their on-line customers; reaching and enhancing relationships with a global market; allowing customers to tailor the advertising experience to meet their own needs; enhancing customer-company relations by providing accurate, personalized customer service; engaging customers in role-playing; and facilitating purchase decisions.

The Incorporation of Online Advertisements with Print Advertising

In the midst of all of these potential benefits of online advertising, there is the challenge of attracting visitors to one's site (Sadikin, 1995; Sussman & Pollack, 1995). One solution is to advertise the site online by renting space on a site or purchasing keyword-search space (Hodges, 1996). However, relying on this approach alone, poses several problems, one of which is that the audience is limited to those already on the Internet. In addition, it is unlikely that the online ad will reach all potentially interested Internet users; hence, there will be those who remain unaware of the site.

Another, more compelling solution to attracting consumers to the site is to promote a site through the use of traditional media (Sadikin, 1995; Unger, 1996). Print media is particularly useful because the interested consumer can directly refer to the print advertisement when typing the Uniform Resource Locator (URL). This reduces the likelihood of errors due to hastily copying on paper or memorizing the URL from a television, radio, or billboard advertisement. Recent evidence suggests that the use of one mixed-media strategy (promoting a web site in magazine ads) has increased at a nearly exponential rate (Huffenbeger, Kanfer, Scholsser & Ryan, 1998; Kanfer, Schlosser, & Ryan, 1996). Table 3.1 compares four magazines from the date when the first ad containing a URL appeared and the percentage of ads having URLs at the present time of the study. The results indicate that among these magazines, the first URL for a commercial web site appeared in *PC Computing* in November, 1994, and that just over one year later, 50% of all the ads in *PC Computing* contained a URL, with similar growth rates in the other publications. In addition, preliminary research suggests that using magazines to locate sites on the Internet is far from uncommon; 65% of respondents reported finding out about web sites through magazines (Gupta, 1995).

The way in which advertisers incorporate the online site and the print ad varies, however. For instance, many advertised URLs take the consumer to the homepage, which may or may not directly link to the product advertised in the print ad. The prominence and context of the URL in the print ad, the degree to which the print ad attempts to persuade consumers to visit the web site, and the amount of information describing the web site also varies considerably.

TABLE 3.1
Comparison of the Presence of URLs

Magazine	Date of First URL	Percentage of Print Ads With URLs in Jan., 1996
PC Computing	November 1994	50%
Newsweek	April 1995	32%
Money	May 1995	28%
Glamour	September 1995	10%

RESEARCH QUESTIONS

In this research, we focus on the mixed-media strategy of advertising online and publicizing the online exhibit in a magazine ad. Our two primary objectives are to (1) assess the degree to which online advertisers are currently taking advantage of the potential benefits of advertising on the Internet as outlined previously, and (2) assess the degree to which web sites and print ads are integrated.

METHODOLOGY

Selection of Ads

From a list of magazine categories used in prior market research studies (Magazine Readership, 1979), categories were selected to provide a broad range of the magazine markets which varied in technical knowledge, sex, and age. Among those selected are business, news, beauty/fashion, entertainment, youth, and food/home magazines. Within these categories, the magazines with the highest circulation statistics according to the most recent *World Almanac* (1995) were chosen as the source of print advertisements included in the study sample. The magazines selected were *Business Week, Newsweek, Glamour, Rolling Stone, Seventeen,* and *Better Homes and Gardens.* Only the most recent issue at the time of coding was evaluated (the issue available the week of April 8, 1996). Those advertisements less than one sixth of a page or in the classifieds section were excluded. Of the remaining print ads, those listing a URL referring to a site on the World Wide Web were analyzed along with their web sites.

Measurement

Features Capturing the Nine Benefits of Advertising Online. To benefit from a web site, the advertiser must include features that would allow the site to yield that benefit. For instance, one cannot expect a company to benefit from the global accessibility of the Internet if the site does not contain such content as currency information, international shipping fees, and product availability for countries outside the manufacturer's. Thus, to measure the degree to which a commercial web site is utilizing the Internet in ways to attain the potential benefits, four features per benefit were identified that would help in attaining that benefit. These features were specific to an identified benefit, many of which were provided in the literature as examples of the potential benefit. Care was taken to ensure that each feature was independent from the other features within and across benefits. Each feature was coded dichotomously as either present (1) or absent (0) in the web site. For each advertised web site, a score between 0 and 4 was obtained for each potential benefit by aggregating across the four features for the benefit.

The following are the nine benefits, each with an example feature: (1) provides content rich information (e.g., do they elaborate upon product/service features or provide detailed performance data?); (2) updates information and informs their visitors of updates (e.g., do they have a "what's new" or "what's coming" section?); (3) builds brand image (e.g., do they have links to other interesting sites or have trivia about the company and its product?); (4) employs data collection methods (e.g., do they request feedback about the web site or existing products?); (5) responds to the potentially global market (e.g., do they have pages about their product or their company translated into other languages?; (6) gives consumers the option of customizing the information (e.g., do they have the information at various levels of technicality, available in graphical, textual, auditory, and/or video form?); (7) attempts to enhance customer-company relations (e.g., do they provide an e-mail address for consumer questions/comments or have an online discussion page?); (8) encourages role-playing (e.g., do they have interactive games or product simulations?); and (9) facilitates purchase intentions (e.g., do they offer multiple purchasing methods including online methods?).

Additional questions were asked to learn more details about current online advertising practices. For example, the judges coding the sites indicated the ease of finding certain items (e.g., whether such features as a "what's new" section were listed on the initial page or homepage), how frequently time-sensitive items (e.g., press releases, prices, product availability) were updated, which data collection methods and incentives were most commonly used, how technically advanced the sites were, and whether the sites were using recommended methods for tying offline sales to the web site (e.g, by providing "computer coupons").

Including all features for each benefit would result in an overwhelming amount of information for the consumer to sift through without good navigational tools. Many web style guides mention the importance of including navigational tools such as a search engine (Levine, 1995; Richmond, 1995; Snyder, 1996). To investigate the advertised sites' use of navigational tools, we identified four tools and coded the site as either having each navigational tool (1) or not (0). The ease of finding these tools (e.g., whether they are located on every page) was also assessed. To receive information regarding the coding items for the nine benefits and the navigational tools, please contact the authors.

In addition to these objective measures of the site, there was one subjective measure: whether the judge liked the site. This measure was added after all of the coding was completed to capture the judge's overall impression of the web site. This was coded dichotomously: The judge either liked the site (1) or did not (0).

Because the inclusion of a feature might vary by product type, the judges recorded the product advertised in the print ad. When more than one product was advertised, the product featured prominently in the ad was selected. If all of the products were similarly displayed, one of the products was randomly selected. The products advertised in the print ads were later categorized as technically advanced (i.e., requiring more technical information such as cars, computer equipment, financial products; these are often products that require a large monetary investment, thereby motivating consumers to seek detailed information) or technically simple (requiring less technical information such as food, beverages, and clothing; these are often products that require a relatively small monetary investment).

Integration of Web Site and Print Advertisement. To examine the integration of the web site and the print ad, we noted the size and placement of the URL in the print ad, whether the ad made specific reference to the URL, and whether the advertised product could be easily located on the web site. We also compared the web site's and print ad's number of product visuals and the amount of product information.

Sample

As reflected in Table 3.2, there were 5 to 24 print advertisements with URLs in each magazine (excluding those less than one sixth of a page or in the classifieds section), with the most appearing in *Business Week* (*n* = 24; 50% of total ads in that magazine) and the fewest in Seventeen (*n* = 5; 6% of the ads in that magazine). There were a total of 65 distinct ads listing URLs, with 95% of the ads covering a full page or more.

TABLE 3.2
URLs Present in Magazines Sampled

Magazine	Number of Ads with URLs	Percentage of Ads with URLs
Business Week	24	50%
Newsweek	12	35%
Rolling Stone	22	30%
Better Homes and Gardens	13	10%
Glamour	9	6%
Seventeen	5	6%
TOTAL	85 total ads, 65 distinct ads	17%

Of the 65 print ads 10 displayed multiple products. All of the advertised products within a print ad were from the same product category (e.g., computer software, cosmetics), and therefore random selection of one of the products did not influence the type of product examined (i.e., whether it was technically advanced or simple).

The features capturing the nine potential benefits of a web site, additional details of the web site, navigational ease, the subjective measure, product type, and the integration of the web site with the print ad were examined for each of the 65 ads. The judges coding the sites were three trained undergraduate and graduate students working with the authors.

RESULTS

Making Use of the Benefits of a Commercial Web Site

To assess the degree to which the 65 advertised web sites incorporated features that would help them attain the nine benefits, the number of features present were summed for each benefit such that the highest score possible was 4 (incorporates four features for that benefit) and the lowest score possible was 0 (incorporates no features for that benefit). The scores averaged across all 65 sites indicate that, overall, the sites included approximately half or fewer of the features for each benefit ($M = 1.65$ across all sites and benefits; only two of the nine benefits had average scores above 2, indicating that on average, sites included more than half of the features for that benefit).

On average, the web sites included more of the features to take advantage of the content richness of the medium and the ability to build brand image (see Table 3.3). Most sites used the content richness of the medium to elaborate on product features (75% of all sites). Fewer displayed their products with more than one visual (46%). In terms of building brand image, most sites had details about sponsored events (62%) and linked to interesting sites outside their web site (59%). Fewer sites, however, attempted to build brand image through the use of customer testimonials (31%). Furthermore, most sites virtually ignored those features addressing the global accessibility of the medium and its role-playing capabilities.

One might argue that having multiple features for each benefit is unnecessary and that having at least one feature is sufficient for the company to attain that benefit. Although most of the sites included at least one feature from six or more of the nine benefits (see Table 3.4 below), only 12% of the sites incorporated into their web site at least one feature from each of the nine benefits.

TABLE 3.3
Mean Benefit Scores

Benefits	Mean (SD)
1. Content-Rich Information	2.32 (1.39)
2. Ease of Updating	1.18 (0.98)
3. Build Brand Image	2.51 (1.00)
4. Collect Detailed Data	2.11 (1.20)
5. Global Accessibility	0.74 (1.11)
6. Customized Advertisement	1.91 (0.98)
7. Enhance Company-Customer Relations	1.66 (1.11)
8. Role-Playing	0.69 (0.80)
9. Facilitate Purchase Intention	1.72 (1.24)
10. Navigational Tools	2.26 (1.16)

Furthermore, although all of the sites incorporated at least one feature to build brand image (see Table 3.5), the majority of sites failed to include at least one feature to attain the benefits of the global nature and the role-playing capabilities of the medium. In addition, nearly one quarter of the sites failed to have at least one feature taking advantage of the ease of updating the information and facilitating purchase intentions. This included such features as notifying visitors of upcoming changes to the site and locating the nearest store or dealer, neither of which are difficult features to incorporate into a site, although they do require an ongoing commitment to keeping the site current.

Although for most of the nine benefits, 75% or more of the sites included at least one of the four identified features, it is questionable whether a single feature alone can attain the benefit. For instance, looking more specifically at the features incorporated into the site for the ease of updating, we find that nearly half of the sites mentioned when the site was last updated (44%) and what was new at the site (48%), but few mentioned whether they regularly update the site or announced upcoming features of the site (less than 15%). In addition, although the Internet allows for the gathering of detailed customer information, most sites collected demographic and customer contact information (51% or more), with fewer gathering reactions to web sites or to products (less than 35%). Most sites enhanced communication with the company (thereby enhancing company-customer relations) through the availability of the company's e-mail address (68%). Few enhanced relations, however, through more novel methods such as adding the customer to a newsgroup or listserv (35%) or having a discussion page (20%). These novel features would allow the company to share more information with the consumer and build brand image as their ongoing relations with customers are displayed. This technique would also provide more information about their online consumers.

TABLE 3.4
Cumulative Benefits

Number of Benefits with at Least One Feature	Percentage of 65	Cumulative
0	0%	0%
1	2%	2%
2	0%	2%
3	0%	2%
4	3%	5%
5	5%	10%
6	26%	36%
7	20%	56%
8	32%	88%
9	12%	100%

Perhaps most surprising is that the sites made little use of the interactive nature of the medium. For instance, most products were presented textually (94%) and/or graphically (77%) with few being presented auditorially or as video (less than 20%). In addition, only a few sites offered information at various levels of technicality (44% or less), and had such technically advanced features as words running across the bottom of the screen (14%) or frames (6%).

These advanced features can be useful in guiding the consumer to particular pages within the site. For instance, words running across the bottom of the screen can be used to attract attention to a particular feature of the web site. In addition, frames can be used as a navigational device by having them serve as a table of contents alongside the main text.

Furthermore, only a few sites encouraged impulse buying on the Internet by taking online orders (18%). This finding is especially important in light of how many businesses express disappointment with online sales. Only 43% of these sites located the nearest store or dealer, and few mentioned such details as their return policy (14%) and their product availability (11%). What is more, few made attempts to tie offline purchases to the web site through an order form that could be faxed/mailed (20%). Only 2% provided coupons via the Internet that could be redeemed online or offline.

The currency of the time-dependent information appears to depend greatly upon the type of information being updated. For instance, of the sites listing prices, only 18% had updated the prices within the last month. The "press release" pages, however, were kept much more current. The vast majority (73%) of those having such a page updated it within the last month. This result may be due to prices not changing as often as new press releases are generated. Furthermore, once press releases are created, they can easily and inexpensively be put on a web site along with a date.

TABLE 3.5
Features Incorporated by Benefit

Benefits	Number of Features Incorporated				
	0	1	2	3	4
1. Content Rich Information	11%	25%	14%	23%	28%
2. Ease of Updating	25%	45%	22%	6%	3%
3. Build Brand Image	0%	20%	26%	37%	17%
4. Collect Detailed Data	11%	20%	31%	25%	14%
5. Global Accessibility	59%	25%	5%	9%	3%
6. Customized Advertisement	5%	31%	42%	15%	8%
7. Enhance Company-Customer Relations	14%	35%	28%	17%	6%
8. Role-Playing	51%	31%	17%	2%	0%
9. Facilitate Purchase Intention	23%	19%	28%	25%	6%
10. Navigational Tools	8%	19%	29%	29%	15%

By including the features of many of these benefits, the online site can become quite complex, thereby requiring the accessibility of navigational tools.

Overall, the sites made use of approximately half of the navigational features under investigation ($M = 2.26$, see Table 3.3). Most sites had home and section icons on each page (69%), but few had an overview of the site (31%). Moreover, although web style guides agree on the primary importance of a search engine (Levine, 1995; Richmond, 1995; Snyder, 1996), less than half of the sites had one to assist consumers in navigating through a site (34%). Of those with a search engine or an outline of the site, only approximately half (59% and 55%, respectively) of the sites had the feature located on every page. If these features are not accessible from every page in the site, then the consumer must learn how the site is organized in order to recall where such navigational tools are and are not available.

It appears that many commercial sites lack the features that would allow the company to benefit from having an exhibit on the Internet. Most of the included features increase the volume of information, but few made use of the interactive, global features of the medium. Moreover, although the sites were complex and content-rich, most commercial sites failed to include many of the navigational tools necessary to assist visitors in finding their way around the site.

Navigational tools, however, appear to be an especially important feature of a site. The only feature significantly related to liking the site was the availability of navigational tools ($r = .42$, $p < .001$). This suggests that regardless of how much information is available from a site, how many interesting bits of trivia are included, how many visuals, contests, games, or online discussions are present, visitors will have a favorable impression only if multiple navigational tools are available.

To examine the relationship among the benefits, we applied a principal factor analysis to the ad by benefit (65 x 9) matrix. The first three factors have eigenvalues greater than 1 and together explain 53% of the variance. Additional factors each explain less than 10% of the variance. After applying a Varimax rotation, the following factor pattern was indicated (only those items with values greater than .40 are included within a factor, see Table 3.6 below).

The first factor appears to capture the interactive nature of the medium, thereby allowing the consumer to be an active participant. This first factor, which accounts for more of the variance than the other two factors, includes the benefits of letting the consumer customize the advertisement, encouraging role-playing, and having multiple navigational tools available so the consumer can navigate easily around the site. The second factor appears to capture the company's commitment to having an ongoing, online communication with consumers. That is, they offer up-to-date information, they collect detailed information about the consumer, and they include features to enhance company-customer relations - all of which require significant human labor. The third factor appears to capture attempts to enhance sales by providing both sales and brand-image information. This factor includes providing detailed product and brand information, providing such information for other countries, and providing purchase-related information. Hence, there appear to be three components to current Internet advertising strategies: site interactivity, communication with the company, and traditional sales-based content. Although the first component, interactivity, is the most discriminating among the online ads, the benefits characteristic of the third component, traditional sales approaches, is most common among online advertisers.

Finally, the examination of product types reveals that sites with technically advanced products incorporated more features of each benefit than those sites with technically simple products (see Table 3.7).

This is especially the case for the inclusion of rich product information, updates, brand information, and navigational tools. In terms of information richness, more sites marketing technically advanced than technically simple products elaborated on product features (84% vs. 67%, $x^2(1, 65) = 2.75$, $p = .098$), provided detailed performance data (66% vs. 39%, $x^2(1, 65) = 4.48$, $p < .05$), described multiple products (75% vs. 42%, $x^2(1, 65) = 7.10$, $p < .01$), and had multiple visuals of the same product (59% vs. 33%, $x^2(1, 65) = 4.43$, $p < .05$).

TABLE 3.6
Benefit Factor Structure

Benefits	Factor 1	Factor 2	Factor 3
1. Content Rich Information			.73
2. Ease of Updating		.79	
3. Build Brand Image			.69
4. Collect Detailed Data		.57	
5. Global Accessibility			.55
6. Customized Advertisement	.84		
7. Enhance Company-Customer Relations		.67	
8. Role-Playing	.54		
9. Facilitate Purchase Intention			.50
10. Navigational Tools	.72		

In terms of keeping the information updated, more sites marketing technically advanced than technically simple products had a "what's new" section (66% vs. 33% respectively, $x^2(1, 65) = 5.54$, $p < .05$), a "what's coming" section (22% vs. 6%, $x^2(1, 65) = 3.41$, $p = .065$), a "press release" section (72% vs. 39%, $x^2(1, 65) = 7.47$, $p < .05$), and mentioned how often the site was updated (22% vs. 3%, $x^2(1, 65) = 5.35$, $p < .05$).

Regarding the inclusion of brand information, the only feature included more by sites promoting technically advanced rather than technically simple products was the inclusion of details about sponsored events or other supported causes (81% vs. 42%, $x^2(1, 65) = 10.35, p < .001$).

In examining the inclusion of navigational tools, those sites with technically advanced products were more likely to have a search engine than were those sites with technically simple products (50% vs. 27% respectively, $x^2(1, 65) = 7.35, p < .01$), and were somewhat more likely to have an outline of the site (41% vs. 21%, $x^2(1, 65) = 2.87, p = .09$).

Although the average number of features allowing customers to customize sites was no higher for sites with technically advanced products as opposed to technically simple products, the sites with technically advanced products were more likely to have information available at various levels of technicality (53% vs 15%, $x^2(1, 65) = 10.46, p < .001$). In addition, more sites with technically advanced products provided price information than did sites with technically simple products (63% vs. 36%, $x^2(1, 65) = 4.44, p < .05$). This last finding may be due to the larger monetary investment (and, hence, consumers' greater concern with pricing) for products that are technically advanced versus simple.

TABLE 3.7
Benefits by Product Types

Benefits	Technically Advanced	Technically Simple	$t(63)$
1. Content Rich Information	2.84	1.82	3.17*
2. Ease of Updating	1.59	.79	3.60*
3. Build Brand Image	2.81	2.21	2.51*
4. Collect Detailed Data	2.28	1.94	1.15
5. Global Accessibility	.97	.51	1.66
6. Customized Advertisement	2.00	1.82	.75
7. Enhance Company-Customer Relations	1.69	1.64	.19
8. Role-Playing	.75	.64	.56
9. Facilitate Purchase Intention	1.88	1.58	.97
10. Navigational Tools	2.63	1.91	2.59*

*$p < .05$

Incorporation of Mixed-Media Advertising Strategies

In addition to examining whether online commercial sites are incorporating features that would allow them to benefit from being on the Internet, we also examined the use of print media in guiding a consumer toward a site and toward a specific product or service.

We found that although a growing number of magazine ads included URLs, it appears that the URL still played a minor part in the print ad. For instance, the URL was often listed in small print, near the copyright information (40%). Only a few advertised the web site (5%) rather than the company or a product. Furthermore, few advertisements guided the consumer directly to the online product information. For 59% of the sites, it was difficult to find the advertised product on the web site. That is, there was no immediate reference to the product advertised in print on the first page to which the advertised URL linked. In fact, for 9% of the sites, the product advertised in the print ad could not be found anywhere on the web site. In contrast, within its print ad, Kodak guided the consumer directly to online information of the advertised product. Although their URL, <www.kodak.com>, was in small print near the copyright information, it instructed the consumer to click on "What's Hot" and then "Serious Fun," which led the consumer directly to information on the advertised camera and additional product-related information.

Overall, the web sites contained more information about the advertised product than the print ad did ($M = 1.53$). Not surprisingly, this was especially true for the technically advanced products ($M = 1.72$) than for the technically simple products ($M = 1.33$, $t(63) = 2.19$, $p < .05$). That is, due to the complexity of the technically advanced versus the technically simple products, it is more likely that such products as computers would have significantly more information in the web exhibit than the print ad, whereas such products as tweezers and shoes would have only slightly more information in the web exhibit than in the print ad.

Advertising one's web site in other media may be a viable solution for attracting people to a site. However few advertisements directed the consumer's attention to the URL, much less listed the benefits of visiting the site. Moreover, even fewer advertisements guided the consumer directly to the web page where the product was described, often leaving the consumer to hunt for the product. This can often be quite an endeavor without the presence of such navigational tools as a search engine or outline. Hence, although more information is included in online ads than in print ads, there does not yet appear to be effective integration of print and online advertising.

CONCLUSIONS AND DISCUSSION

Benefits of Online Advertising

The results suggest that on average, commercial web sites incorporate approximately half or fewer of the identified beneficial features of advertising on the Web. Most web sites are taking advantage of the content richness of the medium and the ability to build brand image while ignoring the benefits attainable through its global accessibility and role-playing capabilities.   It appears that commercial web sites include many of the features that traditional media are capable of handling (e.g., listing product descriptions and specifications textually and graphically, listing information about the company and upcoming sponsored events). However, most sites do not include many of the features unique to the Internet (e.g., online discussions, the choice of textual, graphical, auditory, and video product descriptions, interactive games, product simulations, online purchase orders). Indeed, the factor analysis results suggest that current online advertising can be described in terms of a three-pronged approach involving interactivity, customer-company communication, and traditional content. Commercial web sites appear to concentrate on this third factor. Taken together, these findings suggest that online businesses may be transplanting their marketing strategies from other media to the Internet, thereby missing many of the beneficial possibilities offered by the interactive, time- and space-independent features of the Internet.

Although most of the sites did include at least one feature from six or more of the nine benefits, many of the commonly included features were static broadcast messages (e.g., product specifications) rather than interactive (e.g., interactive contests). In addition, many of these features increased the volume of information, thereby increasing the complexity of the web site. The potential benefits attainable from these features may not be realized if the resulting volume of information overwhelms the consumer.

One way to avoid overloading the consumer with information is to provide navigational tools. Indeed, the results of this study indicate that navigational tools are an especially important feature of a site: The more tools available at the commercial web site, the better it was liked. The results also suggest that commercial web sites include navigational tools that allow the consumer to move easily between pages (e.g., by having home and section icons on every page), but lack those tools that would assist consumers in information acquisition (e.g., by having a search engine or some outline or overview of the site). These latter tools are those argued to be necessary features of a site, especially a complex one (Levine, 1995; Richmond, 1995; Snyder, 1995).

It is possible, however, that some of the beneficial features identified might be more applicable to certain types of products than others. We explored this possibility in terms of how technically complex the advertised product was. We found that in comparison with those sites promoting technically simple products, sites promoting technically advanced products incorporated more features using the content richness of the medium, the ease of updating, and the ability to build brand image. Furthermore, the sites marketing technically advanced products included more navigational tools than did those marketing technically simple products. It is possible that sites exhibiting such technically advanced products as computers and cars have more product information, have information that changes more frequently, and are more likely to have such image-related information as trade shows and sponsored events, than sites exhibiting such technically simple products as lip gloss and beverages. As a result of having more information overall, the importance of navigational tools might be especially salient to the design of web sites promoting technically advanced products. Even though sites marketing technically advanced products currently include more of the beneficial features than the sites marketing technically simple products, a future empirical question is whether sites with technically advanced products benefit more by including these features in their sites than those with technically simple products would.

Although our study does not directly assess whether incorporating the beneficial features into a site leads to a successful site (indeed, this would be difficult to assess given the lack of agreement in the field over the appropriate benchmark to use in identifying web site success), one can imagine the likely consequences of ignoring many of the unique features of the Internet. For instance, because all sites on the Internet are globally accessible, a site that ignores its global audience might turn away potential customers who identify the site as applicable only to certain regions. Such an identification might be difficult to later counteract. Moreover, ignoring such interactive features of the Internet as its role-playing capabilities and its ability to enhance company-customer communication may lose the majority of the Internet audience who are less interested in sites infected with "brochureware" or "brochuritis" (Sadikin, 1995; Sussman & Pollack, 1995). Such sites are unlikely to encourage repeat visits. Experimentally manipulating the presence of such features as interactivity and communicability within the same site to assess their effects on web site experiences and evaluations would be a worthwhile future research endeavor.

Mixed-Media Advertising Strategy

Surprisingly, although many advertisements included a URL in the print advertisement, few actively promoted the site in the print ads. That is, most of the URLs were listed on the periphery of the print ad, without any specific reference to the specialized features of the web site. Moreover, although the sites contained detailed information beyond what was available in the print ad, for the majority of advertised web sites, locating the product within the web site was difficult. In fact, some of the products advertised in the print ads could not be found anywhere in the web site. If the print ad is successful in stimulating interest in the advertised product, then listing a URL that links directly to a web page without reference to the advertised product defeats the purpose of listing the URL in the print ad, as well as defeats the purpose of having detailed product information in the web site beyond what is available in the print ad.

This is particularly true when navigational tools such as a search engine are absent.

Why Are Online Companies Disillusioned?
Some Preliminary Answers

It is possible that companies are disillusioned with advertising on the Internet because their strategies preclude them from the benefits attainable through having a web site. In the sample of commercial sites examined here, the sites did not include many of the features allowing them to benefit from having a web site. Moreover, they had few navigational tools, making it difficult for visitors to realize all of the features of the site. Although these businesses employed a mixed-media advertising strategy by advertising their URL in another medium, few actively promoted the site and its features. In addition, the products advertised in print were often difficult to find online.

It appears that many of these weaknesses are caused by applying traditional advertising strategies to a dynamic environment, hence ignoring the unique features possible through the interactive nature of the medium. One example from this research is the failure to allow customers to customize the information (e.g., by including information at various levels of technicality). There is no need for the online advertisement to streamline the information for only one type of customer. Because the Internet has no limits in the amount of information provided in an online commercial exhibit, the web site can provide information to meet the majority of consumers' needs and interests. In addition, given the interactive nature of the medium, the web site can tailor the information for each consumer's needs (e.g., by providing an online form asking consumers what information they are looking for and how they would like the information presented), or consumers can select the information suiting their own needs (e.g., by selecting information that is designed for a younger or older market, toward those interested in testimonials versus product specifications, toward those willing versus unwilling to wait for elaborate graphics to download).

In addition, by transplanting traditional marketing strategies to a web site, one also ignores the unique problems posed by the Internet. Examples of problems specific to the Internet include encouraging people to visit the site and encouraging those who visit to return. One method of encouraging people to visit a site is by listing the site's URL in a print ad. Yet, listing the company's URL as if it were an 800-number or address is likely ineffective. The unique features of the site should be highlighted within the ad. For instance, food distributors could entice consumers to visit their web site by advertising in print that the site contains recipes for various events (e.g., the Super Bowl) and diets. Without such enticements, consumers may have little motivation to visit the site. This will likely become especially true as more companies go online, thereby reducing the novelty of merely having a web site. Moreover, as this study suggests, listing only the URL is ineffective in guiding the consumer to online product information. An inability to find the online product information will likely dissuade rather than persuade the consumer to purchase the product (and revisit the site).

Recommended methods of encouraging repeat visits include making the site interactive and updating the site frequently (Egan & Pollack, 1995; Sadikin, 1995). Both of these interactive features are unique to the Internet, and as this study suggests, are largely ignored by online advertisers. Hence, although current commercial sites appear to be making the site informative (e.g., by providing detailed product descriptions), this is likely insufficient to encourage repeat visits; the site will need to be entertaining as well (e.g., by having such interactive features as online discussions and product simulations).

In creating an online commercial site, it is important to recognize that the Internet requires different marketing and advertising practices than those used in traditional media and that mixed-media advertising requires coordinated efforts between those designing the web site and those designing advertisements for other media.

REFERENCES

Achieving coolness on the web. (1995, September 4). *Advertising Age* [Online]. Available: <http://www.adage.com/bin/viewdataitem.cgi? opinions & opinions75. html>.

Anderson, C. L. (1995). Computer as audience abstract. In C. S. Madden (Ed.), *Proceedings of the 1995 Conference of the American Academy of Advertising*, 23-25.

Badgett, T. (1995). *Welcome to. . . the Internet* (2nd ed.). New York: MIS Press.

Bayers, C. (1996, April). The great web wipeout: The World Wide Web drowns in a sea of red ink. *Wired*, 125-128.

Brueckner, R. (1994, July/August). You have a future in advertising. *Internet World*, 65-67.

Coalition for Networked Information. (1994, September). *Electronic billboards on the digital superhighway* [Online]. Available: <http://www.cni.org/projects/advertising/www/adpaper.html>.

Cronin, M. J. (1994). *Doing business on the internet.* New York: Van Nostrand Reinhold.

Egan, J., & Pollack, K. (1995, November 13). Gold rush in cyberspace. *U.S. News & World Report, 119*(19), 72-83.

Gray, M. (1997). *Measuring the growth of the web.* [Online]. Available: <http://www.netgen.com/info/growth.html>.

Gupta, S. (1995). *HERMES: A research project on the commercial uses of the World Wide Web.* [Online]. Available: <http://www.umich.edu/~sgupta/ hermes>.

Hodges, J. (1996, January 15). Words hold the key to Web ad packages: Sponsoring search terms becomes a popular option. *Advertising Age* [Online].Available: <http://www.adage.com/bin/viewdataitem.cgi? opinions&opinions149.html>.

Hodges, J. (1996, Feb. 12). It's becoming a small World Wide Web after all: Publishers, advertisers regionalize content services. *Advertising Age* [Online].Available: <http://www.adage.com/bin/viewdataitem.cgi? opinions&opinions 149.html>.

Hoffman, D. L., Novak, T. P., & Chatterjee, P. (1995). Commercial scenarios for the web: Opportunities and challenges. *Journal of Computer-Mediated Communication* [Online]. Available: <http://shum.huji.ac.il/jcmc/vol1/issue3/hoffman.html>.

Huffenberger, K., Kanfer, A., Schlosser, A.E., & Ryan, A. (1998). The diffusion of advertising URLs in magazines. [Online]. Available: <http://www.ncsa.uiuc.edu/edu/trg/urlgrowth>.

Jennings, R. (1996, February). *Brand with the new technology: Part II.* Paper presented at the Retail Advertising Conference, Chicago, IL.

Kanfer, A., Schlosser, A. E., & Ryan, A. (1996). [The growth of online advertising in print media]. Unpublished raw data.

Krugman, D. M., Reid, L. N., Dunn, S. W., & Barban, A. M. (1994). *Advertising: The role in modern marketing* (8th ed.). Fort Worth, TX: The Dryden Press.

Levine, R., Sun Microsystems, Inc. (1995). Guide to web style. [Online]. Available: <http://www.sun.com/styleguide>.

Magazine Readership. (1979/1980). *Encyclomedia, 2*(3), 139-161.

Network Wizards. (1998). *Internet domain survey.* [Online]. Available: <http://www.nw.com/zone/WWW/top.html>.

Petty, R., & Cacioppo, J. (1981). Self-persuasive approaches. *Attitude and persuasion: Classic and contemporary approaches.* Dubuque, IA: Brown, 213-225.

Pratkanis, A., & Aronson, E. (1991). Self-sell. *Age of propaganda: The everyday use and abuse of persuasion.* New York: Freeman, 123-127.

Raman, N. V., & Leckenby, J. D. (1995). Advertising on interactive media: Some issues, some suggestions. In C. S. Madden (Ed.), *Proceedings of the 1995 Conference of the American Academy of Advertising*, 247-251.

Richmond, A. (1995). The Web Developer's Virtual Library: Developing a High-End Web Site. [Online]. Available: <http://www.charm.net/~web/ Seminars/Style>.

Sadikin, P. (1995). *Advertising on the Internet: When can it bring leverage to the business?* [Online]. Available: <http//web.city.ac.uk/~dd559/int-adv.html>.

Serafin, R., & Ralston, J. (1995, September 4). Carmakers steer for interactive: Auto marketers rally behind media following sales acceleration. *Advertising Age.* [Online]. Available: <http://www.adage.com/bin/viewdataitem.cgi?opinions&opinions76.html>.

Snyder, J. (1996, April). Good, bad, and ugly pages. *Internet World, 7,* 26-27.

Solomon, S. D. (1995). Staking a claim on the Internet. *Inc. Technology, 16*(13), 87-92.

Sussman, V., & Pollack, K. (1995, November 13). Gold rush in cyberspace. *U.S. News & World Report, 119*(19), 72-80.

Thorell, L. (1994, July/August). Doing business on the Internet: Case studies: DEC, Silicon Graphics, and Sun. *Internet World,* 52-63.

Unger, R. (1996, February). *Brand with the new technology: Part I.* Paper presented at the Retail Advertising Conference, Chicago, IL.

Wilkie, W. L. (1994). *Consumer behavior* (3rd ed.). New York: John Wiley & Sons, Inc.

Williamson, D. A. (1995a, October 9). Web searching for a yardstick: Counting encounters on the Internet isn't as easy as 1-2-3. *Advertising Age*. [Online]. Available: <http://www.adage.com/bin/viewdataitem.cgi?opinions&opinions94. html>.

Williamson, D. A. (1995b, October 16). Inching toward web measurement. *Advertising Age*. [Online]. Available: <http://www.adage.com/bin/viewdataitem.cgi?opinions &opinions 96.html>.

The World Almanac and Book of Facts: 1995 (1994). New York: Press Publishing Co.

4

"New and Improved!" Advertising in Cyberspace: Using Specific Conduits to Access Browsers and Seekers

David R. Fortin
University of Canterbury, New Zealand

The World Wide Web has seen exponential growth over the last two years in terms of the number of users navigating the network and of the sites open for information access. It brings along new capabilities for information retrieval and exchange in a boundless universe. This paper attempts to identify how users might respond to advertisements on the Web based on two segments identified as *Browsers* and *Seekers*. Four advertising conduits are examined in a comparative approach and guidelines are proposed to improve communication efficiency.

One could argue that the World Wide Web is simply another medium, employed like television, radio, print, and so forth, to convey information and commercial communications. However, as we have seen in previous chapters, many researchers and marketers believe that the interactive nature of the Web and hence, the ability for the user to respond and react, creates a totally new environment that changes the traditional parameters of mass communication (Hoffman & Novak, 1996). This *one-on-one relationship* has the potential to increase consumer involvement with the medium and ultimately with the organizations resident on the network. If we think of information as text, it then becomes a structure of relations in which the line between author and reader slowly disappears.

This new approach clearly differs from the traditional model of mass communication where one source transmits to many receptors in a one-to-many fashion without reciprocity, e.g., the traditional advertising model (Venkatesh, Dholakia, & Dholakia, 1995). The traditional model derives its logic from the intrusive nature of advertising and the passive response from the viewer.

However, in the context of an interactive medium, these assumptions do not hold true.

Because of its unique interactivity and potential for navigation, the Web is labeled as a "many-to-many" channel where the emitter and receptor contribute to the information being exchanged (Hoffman & Novak, 1996). As with the introduction of any new product or service, a large proportion of web users are still in the exploration mode. New user trials can be characterized as "experiential" and over time become more "goal directed" (Hoffman & Novak, 1996). The purpose of this chapter is to understand the underpinnings of communication flow in a computer-mediated environment (CME) as regards advertising attempts currently on the Web. This chapter is based on the premise that two basic user profiles with distinctive behaviors can presently be found on the Web: Browsers and Seekers. The chapter concludes with an examination of specific advertising conduits available on the Web and their expected efficiency in light of the exposed framework.

THE SEARCH FOR INFORMATION

One of the most obvious features of a Cyberspace environment is its ability to access, sort, organize, and display enormous quantities of information. Because the information is indexed and retrievable, a logical assumption is that any individual using the network will be involved in some form of search activity. Given that search intensity is a trade-off between search costs and perceived incremental benefits, some studies have found very little evidence to support extensive search behavior under high-cost conditions (Wilkie & Dickson, 1985). However, search costs are drastically reduced in a Cyberspace context resulting in a greater likelihood that search processes will occur. Bloch, Sherrell, and Ridgway (1986) identified two types of search: prepurchase and ongoing. This is equivalent to Hoffman and Novak's (1996) terminology of goal-directed and experiential search:

> Goal directed activities . . . are instrumental and utilitarian in nature, extrinsically motivated, characterized by situational involvement and result in directed search and learning. In contrast, experiential activities are ritualistic and hedonic, intrinsically motivated, characterized by enduring involvement and result in non-directed search and learning.

The parallel of Cyberspace navigation with shopping behavior is strikingly similar. Prepurchase search is actively focused towards the immediate outcome, whereas ongoing search serves as an accumulation of information for potential (not absolute) future use. As retail shoppers "browse" through physical stores, Cyberspace users "surf" the Web leaving trails (bookmarks) or recording information (in print or electronic form) as they go along.

UNDERSTANDING BROWSERS AND SEEKERS

This dichotomy of user profiles has been observed by a number of researchers (Catledge, 1995; Gupta, 1995; Hoffman & Novak, 1996). The distinction is likely to be context sensitive, meaning that an individual user *may* be in a browsing mode in one situation and in a seeking mode in yet another. Given this apparent reality, firms advertising on the Web must first understand which segment they are targeting and adjust their message style and format accordingly.

Indeed, certain sites may draw more browsers than seekers given the mission and/or configuration of the sites. *Browsers* display serendipitous navigation patterns and hence do not actively search for information; the end-result is not as critical as the entertainment and hedonic nature of the process itself for these people. Clearly, dedicated web sites and search engine ads may be less effective than "cool sites" ads for these users. *Seekers,* on the other hand, use a directed search approach where the ultimate goal is known *a priori.* In this case, dedicated web sites providing added value, and search engine ads tied-in with the researched topic, will be more effective.

In terms of time constraints (or *perceived* time constraints) from a user standpoint, both segments may face some degree of frustration. Browsers are more likely to want to spend less time reading an ad that appear and will often "click-through" given that they navigate in a serendipitous sequence and that they are not pressed to find a particular piece of information. Similarly, with the introduction of search engine frames where ads appears first, the increased waiting period may be frustrating for the seeker, whose probability of click-through is very low. The same argument can be made for the presence of graphic intensive sites that deplete critical downloading time. Seekers are more likely to be annoyed by the presence of large graphic files if the purpose is strictly information-based.

In summary, there is a definite need for advertisers to understand the navigation objective of their communication target before they make decisions about advertisement design and placement. The next section deals with four different conduits that can serve as carriers of such advertisements.

ADVERTISING CONDUITS IN HYPERSPACE

In a context where information is ubiquitous and a multitude of conduits is available for similar information displays, some form of competition for access or "hits" naturally occurs. The classic model of attention-interest-desire-action (AIDA) is appropriate here as the major hurdle for commercial sites on the Web is the attention (awareness) stage. In fact, individual sites might never be accessed if not properly indexed in various search engines. Setting up a site is like having a billboard in your basement. The gateway for web site traffic is maximum exposure through both search engines and/or external advertising sources.

One strategy for maximal exposure is to offer content that will be cross-referenced with many keywords in various categories. It is kind of a "bait-and-switch" tactic, which assumes that once the user is inside the page, he or she will stumble on the commercial portion of the site (i.e., UC-Irvine bookstore and Ragu web sites). The medium is such that it allows one-to-one, many-to-one or many-to-many communications with the possibility of simulated experience through virtual reality; advertising then operates metanymically in this virtual environment (Venkatesh, Dholakia, & Dholakia 1995).

TABLE 4.1
Comparative Analysis of Advertising Conduits

Conduits	Advantages	Disadvantages
Dedicated Web Site	Control over content and context Extensive information Ability to re-route browsers and seekers	Building site awareness Inducing repeat visits is difficult Limited frequency
Host Web Site	Increased reach and frequency at traffic sites Opportunity to advertise in related context Ability to embed ad in Text Click-through	Pricing structure not yet resolved Low click-through levels No control over context at host site
Search Engine	Heavy traffic builds reach and frequency Opportunity to pop-up based on query Click-through	Pricing structure not yet resolved Most likely to reach seekers Increased download time may cause frustration
Screen Saver	Incidental exposure Part of updated content Click-through Passive and interactive	Configured for network, office use Download time is long Less involvement with the context

As observed in Gupta (1995), traditional media (i.e., magazines, newspapers, television) are still the prime source of web site address diffusion. Firms such as Magnavox in the United States advertise their web page address in their television executions in order to cross the awareness threshold. As part of a communication campaign, the opportunity for the consumer to access additional information and to communicate with the advertiser is a new feature that transforms the nature of the advertiser-receptor interaction.

Currently, four conduits for advertising on the Web are available:

Dedicated Web Sites: Designed and maintained for the purpose of providing information about a company or a line of products.

Host Web Sites: Specific ads appear imbedded in the text or as an icon that can be clicked for further information. Such an ad may appear in any web site and may not necessarily be linked with the content.

Search Engines: Similar to host web sites but with the opportunity to display an ad based on the topic researched by the user, which allows for tighter targeting strategies.

Screen-saver Ads Imbedded in Content: This conduit replicates the traditional advertising model of intrusiveness and passive viewing but also integrates an interactive component for the user to access further information.

Table 4.1 presents some of the advantages and disadvantages of these four advertising conduits in cyberspace. As the number of web sites increases over time, both potential users and typically consumers will not physically have the time to access all web sites for all products or services they consume. To achieve exposure, advertisers will need to rely on more intrusive forms of advertising outside their own proprietary home pages.

"NEW AND IMPROVED" FORMS OF ADVERTISING IN HYPERSPACE

Strategically, every marketer has specific goals for advertising on the Internet, and recently, large consumer packaged-goods firms such as Procter & Gamble have entered this new medium (*Marketing News*, May 20, 1996). Essentially, there are two common themes: to enhance brand or corporate image and/or to provide a targeted set of consumers with extensive product information in the hope of generating sales and maintaining loyal customers (Schwartz, 1996). The level of information and entertainment has to be carefully balanced according to the expected browsing or seeking profile of the user. The following nonexhaustive list offers guidelines for advertisers wishing to go online:

1. Offer an easy, fast-access entry page where browsers and seekers can be re-routed to proper destinations.
2. Try to embed ads within content for seekers, avoid delayed information access.

3. Avoid lengthy download times in initial pages (usually due to graphic intensity).
4. Use more than one execution on rotation to show that the information is "fresh."
5. Forget business card ads; bring value to the message by triggering interest.
6. Configure specific versions of the same message to be directed at either browsers or seekers.

The screen-saver approach developed by The PointCast Network <http://www.pointcast.com> is the first to incorporate the traditional model with the new interactive world. It strategically uses "downtime" as a conduit for information and advertising; its intrusiveness is mediated by a personalization option to limit information overload. As a result, it allows smaller firms or non-top-of-mind brands to achieve some form of exposure in a controlled intrusive fashion. The potential for this new conduit is quite promising especially in small and medium-sized business environments where local area network (LAN) links allow for frequent updates of information without user intervention.

CONCLUSION

As various sites continue to pop up everyday on the Web, network navigation will evolve and expand to new horizons. For marketers in this new environment, the potential for two-way communications creates a disruption in the traditional model of communication; if the potential is harnessed, firms may reach new heights in their ability to generate and sustain customer relationships. The converse is also true because consumers now have the ability to manage and control the information available in cyberspace. It is still to be determined what type of communication model will the ultimate user be most likely to respond to; all traditional mass media have relied on passive exposure to build frequency. In this new environment, advertisers may get only one chance, in that the latter has the power to never return to that particular location. Firms that are able to generate repeat visits through content updates and enhancements will have a better chance to succeed; to do so means merging information and entertainment into new *infotainment* forms (Dholakia, Mundorf, & Dholakia, 1996). Reaching specific clienteles means understanding how users access and register information. This chapter offers some guidance for advertisers wishing to embark in the cyberspace adventure.

REFERENCES

Bloch, P. H., Sherrell, D. L., & Ridgway, N. M. (1986, June). Consumer search: An extended framework. *Journal of Consumer Research, 13*, 119-126.

Catledge, L. (1995). Characterizing browsing strategies in the World Wide Web. *Graphic, Visualization, & Usability Center*, <URL:http://www.cc.gatech.edu/gvutop.html>.

Dholakia, R. R., Mundorf, N., & Dholakia, N. (1996). *New infotainment technologies in the home.* Mahwah, NJ: Lawrence Erlbaum Associates. In Schwartz, E. (1996, February). Advertising Webonomics 101, *Wired*, 4.

Gupta, S. (1995). *The Fourth WWW consumer survey.* University of Michigan. <http://www.umich.edu/~sgupta/survey4/>.

Hoffman D., & Novak, T. P. (1996). Marketing in hypermedia computer- mediated environments: Conceptual foundations. *Journal of Marketing, 60*, 50-68.

P&G ventures into Internet advertising (1996, May 20). *Marketing News, 30*(11), 12.

Schwartz, E. I. (1996, February). Advertising Webonomics 101, *Wired*, *4*(2), [Online]: <http://www.wired.com/wired/archive/4.02/webonomics.html>

Venkatesh, A., Dholakia, R. R., & Dholakia, N. (1995). New visions of information technology and postmodernism: Implications for advertising and marketing communications. *RITIM Working Paper No 95-05,* University of Rhode Island.

Wilkie, W., & Dickson, P. (1985). Shopping for appliances: Consumers' strategies and patterns of information search. *MSI Working Paper*, Marketing Science Institute, Cambridge, MA.

Part 2

Structure, Function, and Effectiveness

5

Children, Advertising, and the Internet: An Exploratory Study

Lucy L. Henke
University of New Hampshire

Displacement of Media Use and Nonmedia-Related Activity by New Technologies

Many studies have examined the potential for new communications media to displace established media (Henke & Donohue, 1986; Henke, Donohue, Cook, & Chung, 1984; Krugman & Rust, 1987; Lasswell, 1949; Rubin, 1983). By delivering services and content more efficiently or effectively, new media may threaten to capture the audiences and advertisers of existing media, thereby causing existing media to redefine themselves to survive. The emergence of radio - and then television - as mass media, and the introduction of cable television, videotext, teletext, the VCR, and digital cable radio have each caused researchers to speculate about whether new technologies would displace existing media or have a synergistic effect. Because new media have the potential to disrupt existing audience structures, advertisers must constantly assess the ability of various media to deliver appropriate target markets and attempt to integrate new technologies into marketing communications campaigns.

A related issue is the question of whether new communications media displace other activities besides media use. McLuhan's admonition that "the medium is the message" reminded media researchers that societies may be affected by the medium - what they communicate with - at least as much as they are affected by the content of the mediated message (McLuhan & Fiore, 1967). Time spent watching television, for example, is time not spent engaged in other activities. The question of nonmedia-related displacement is significant as a marketing or advertising issue, as well as an issue of broader social concern: What happens if broadcasting a local football game results in decreased attendance, or if the opening of a video store results in less business for local restaurants? Viewed from the social perspective, what if the introduction of a

73

new medium results in a net decrease in diversity of activities for the user? Perhaps it is no coincidence that the term *couch potato* has emerged in the age of proliferation of cable channels and television talk shows.

The Internet and Displacement

The introduction and tremendous growth of the Internet and the World Wide Web have raised questions about the impact of these new technologies on media use as well as nonmedia-related activities. The number of web sites is reported to have jumped from 23,500 in June 1995 to 90,000 in January 1996, just six months later (Internet Marketing & Technology Report, 1996). The number of Internet subscribers, reported to be roughly 11 million in January 1996, is expected to reach 27 million by the year 2000 (Hong & Leckenby, 1996), although some analysts predict the crash of the Web in the next decade (Bayers, 1996). Speculation about the impact of the Web covers the spectrum, with implications for everything from advertising, marketing research, and communications media to the nature of interpersonal relationships and the structure of political and social systems (Burke, 1996; Turkle, 1995, 1996).

The Internet and the Youth Market

Of particular interest to marketers, parents, and educators is the question of what impact the Internet will have on the youth market. As many researchers have documented, children have an increasing influence on consumer spending, both their own and their parents' (McNeal, 1990, 1992). Children are reported to spend $7.5 billion per year and to influence $132 billion of their parents' spending (Webster, 1995). Specifically, children ages 9 to 11 alone are reported to spend $2.8 billion of their own money and to influence $65 billion of their parents' spending (Stipp, 1993).

Second, children have access to and facility with computers and online services. A 1993 Simmons study indicated that 68% of children use a personal computer at home or at school, and about 20% had used an online service in the past week (Webster, 1995). In addition, children have demonstrated that they are "hip to technology" and easily master the new technologies as soon as they become available (Webster, 1995).

Finally, many researchers have investigated how children's perceptions of advertising affect their susceptibility to advertising claims. Studies have shown that the ability to identify the persuasive intent of advertising increases with age and cognitive development (Belk, Bahn, & Mayer, 1982; Meyer, Donohue, & Henke, 1978; Ward, Reale, & Levinson, 1972), can be taught in formal instruction (Donohue, Henke, & Meyer, 1983), and is related to skepticism about advertising claims (Bever, Smith, Bergen, & Johnson, 1975). Whether children identify commercial messages on the Internet as persuasive in intent may affect the perceived credibility of Internet advertising to the youth market.

STUDY FOCUS

The present study, an exploratory investigation of children's perceptions of advertising on the World Wide Web, examines the potential for displacement of media and of nonmedia-related activities by the WWW. The study assesses children's perceptions of the persuasive intent of favorite web sites and identifies their preferences for net surfing versus other favorite media-related and nonmedia-related after-school activities. Based on previous research, the following questions are addressed in the study:

1. Does the World Wide Web have the potential to displace other advertising media used by children ages 9 to 11?
2. Does the World Wide Web have the potential to displace other non-media related activities for children ages 9 to 11?
3. Do children ages 9 to 11 demonstrate the ability to identify the persuasive intent of advertising on the World Wide Web?

METHOD

Procedure

In December 1995, fourth graders from a local elementary school visited the authors' University to "surf the Net" under the guidance of three undergraduate facilitators. The field trip included a pretest questionnaire, an introductory hands-on session with the Internet, and a posttest questionnaire.

Before the Internet Session. Prior to surfing, each child filled out a questionnaire entitled "Facts About Me," which assessed favorite after-school activities, previous experience with computers including online services and the Internet, age, and other classification data. Following administration of the "pre-surf" questionnaire (and a 30-minute break for pizza and drinks), the children were led to one of the University's computer clusters, where they were seated in pairs at IBM-compatible 75 MHz pentium processors equipped with Netscape 1.1 and connected to the University's Internet server.

The Internet Session. The project directors gave a brief summary of what the Internet was, how it worked, and what sites would be visited during the children's field trip. Children were given a worksheet that included a list of five bookmarked sites and several other sites of potential interest. The computers had been bookmarked with five sites that represented a broad range of content types: the home pages of Toys R Us Toy Stores, Ben & Jerry's Ice Cream, the Museum of Science in Boston, *Foster's Daily Democrat* (a newspaper in New Hampshire that had recently gone online), and CNN television network.

The Sites. The Toys R Us site contained information on their newest toys and the top ten toys currently available, and provided the opportunity to send e-mail to Geoffrey, the store's giraffe mascot. The Ben & Jerry's site contained descriptions of current and previously used flavors and offered the chance to participate in contests or send e-mail to Ben and Jerry. Foster's and CNN both offered a variety of the day's national and international news and sports stories. CNN's site, in addition, offered entertainment news. The Museum of Science site offered a preview of the movie "Stormchasers," which was showing in the Omni theater.

Other sites listed on the worksheet included: the "Batman Forever" movie site, which showed movie clips, posters, information on all the movie characters, and also offered the opportunity to send e-mail to the movie's stars; the White House, which offered the opportunity to e-mail President Clinton; and home pages for ESPN, MTV, and Ticketmaster.

Sample

The participants in the study ranged in age from nine to eleven years. The convenience sample of 23 fourth graders attended a public school in a small town outside of Portsmouth, New Hampshire. Twelve were girls.

Variables of Interest

Favorite After-School Activities. In the presession questionnaire, children were asked to identify their favorite after-school activity by circling the item from a list which included: play a sport; play a musical instrument; do homework; watch TV; play video games; read; visit and play inside with friends or siblings; visit and play outside with friends or siblings; use the computer; play with toys by myself; do art work; or other (a blank was left for specification of favorite items not listed). They were also asked to identify their second-favorite and third-favorite activities, and to identify the things that they never did after school.

Previous Experience With Computers and Online Services. The children were asked whether they have a computer at home, and if so, how often they used the computer at home. They were further asked whether they have CompuServe, America Online, Prodigy, or Internet access at home, whether they have learned about computers at school, and if so, how long ago they learned, and whether they have learned about the Internet.

General Perceptions of the Internet. Questionnaires administered after the Internet session asked the children to identify how much they enjoyed using the Internet using a scale of 1 to 5 and whether using the Net was harder or easier than expected. Furthermore, they were asked whether using the Net was more or less fun than expected, and what was the biggest problem with using the Net.

Perceptions of Persuasive Intent. Children were asked which site they liked most, and were asked to identify whether the purpose of their favorite site was to give you information, entertain you, or advertise things so you will buy. They were also asked which site they liked least, and what was the purpose of the least-favored site.

Internet Versus Favorite After-School Activity. Project directors transferred each child's favorite, second-favorite, and third-favorite activities, which they had identified in the presession questionnaire, to three blank spaces for comparison with the Internet in the postsession questionnaire. Children were asked to choose, for each activity, whether they would prefer to engage in the activity or surf the net.

Analyses

Data were summarized and cross-tabulated to identify perceptions of the Internet, understanding of persuasive intent of web sites, and preferences for surfing the Net versus other favorite after-school activities. The small sample size prohibited extensive data analysis.

RESULTS

Regarding previous experience with computers and online services, a majority of the children in the study (69%) said they have a computer at home, and about half (51%) use it "very often." Only 26% said they have an online service at home, such as CompuServe, America Online, Prodigy, or Internet access. About half (51%) have learned about computers at school, primarily by the second grade. Most (69%) said they had not yet learned about the Internet. Teachers confirmed that the Internet had not been used in the school.

There was no consensus regarding favorite after-school activity. Watching TV, reading, and playing outside with friends or siblings were each chosen as the favorite, second-favorite, or third-favorite activity by 39% of the children.

Playing alone with toys was cited least often as one of the top three favorite activities (22%).

Children in the study gave the Internet session high marks. Most (74%) said they enjoyed using the Internet (a 4 or 5 on the scale of 1 to 5), and 51% gave the Internet a 5 for enjoyment. Using the Internet was about as easy or difficult as expected (43%) but was more fun than anticipated (74%).

Asked to identify their favorite web site in the study, 74% of the children named a commercial site, specifically Toys R Us or Ben & Jerry's. However, only 13% said the purpose of their favorite site was to advertise. Most (74%) thought the purpose of the sites was to entertain.

As regards net-surfing versus other favorite activities, a total of 39% of the children said they would prefer to surf the Net than to engage in their favorite after-school activity. The figure differs by activity, and assessing loyalty to each of the self-identified favorite activities separately yields interesting comparisons. Social activity was the favorite activity most likely to be abandoned in order to surf the Net.

Children in the study were most willing to give up playing with friends or siblings, inside (79%) or outside (89%), in favor of surfing the Net. Interestingly, loyalties to TV viewing and to doing homework were equivalent to each other: 67% of the children who named TV viewing as one of their favorite activities would prefer to surf the Net than to watch TV. The same percentage of children who named homework as a favorite activity would be willing to give it up in favor of surfing the Net. Children who were least likely to give up their favorite activity were those who cited reading or playing a musical instrument as their favorite: Only 33% and 38%, respectively, would give up those activities in favor of surfing the Internet.

DISCUSSION AND IMPLICATIONS

Though exploratory in nature, the study identifies several issues worth examining in future research. Which advertising media - or activities - are most likely to be displaced by the Internet for the youth market, and why? Although the novelty effect may temporarily increase the appeal of the Internet relative to other activities, findings suggest that the Internet will have an impact on both media and nonmedia activities. The present preliminary investigation suggests that television viewing is not as appealing as surfing the Internet, at least for new users. About 7 in 10 children would opt to surf the Internet rather than watch TV, even though they identified TV viewing as a favorite after-school activity. For these new users, social activity also loses out to the Internet. They appear to be more interested in checking out new toys, sending e-mail to their favorite movie characters or the White House, or viewing a video of the burning of the American flag on CNN's homepage than play outside or inside with friends and siblings.

Furthermore, marketing communication on favorite web sites is more subtle and difficult to identify than marketing communication in other media. Previous research indicates that even very young children can identify the persuasive intent of television advertising when age-appropriate methodologies are used (Donohue, Henke, & Donohue, 1980; Donohue, Henke, & Meyer, 1983; Henke, 1980). However, the present study finds children as old as nine have difficulty identifying the persuasive intent of commercial web sites targeted toward them. Although a majority of children in the study identified a commercial site as their favorite (74% named Toys R Us or Ben & Jerry's), only 13% thought the purpose of their favorite site was to advertise. Most (74%) said the purpose of the site was to entertain. Whether it is the "soft-sell" nature of the communication or the novelty of the medium that contributes to the lack of understanding among fourth graders is a subject for future research on children's perceptions of the Internet.

Finally, the results of the study point to the broader question of how the Internet can be effectively integrated into marketing communications campaigns, and what impact that integration will have on the concept of advertising. Early studies of the Internet show that, as with direct marketing, consumers are reluctant to use the Internet for direct purchase of goods and services. As hard-sell advertising of specific goods and services gives way to relationship marketing and integrated marketing communications, the distinction between advertising and editorial content is increasingly blurred. Advertisers who sponsor sites on the World Wide Web may only further blur the distinction by providing information, entertainment, and services of value to consumers, rather than advertising specific products and their attributes and benefits.

REFERENCES

Bayers, C. (1996). The great Web wipeout. *Wired* (April), 126-128

Belk, R. W., Bahn, K. D., & Mayer, R. N. (1982, June). Developmental recognition of consumption symbolism. *Journal of Consumer Research, 9,* 4-17.

Bever, T., Smith, M., Bengen, B., and Johnson, T. (1975, November/ December). Young viewers' troubling response to TV ads." *Harvard Business Review, 53,* 109-120.

Burke, R. R. (1996, March/April). Virtual shopping: Breakthrough in marketing research. *Harvard Business Review,* 120-131.

Donohue, T. R., Henke, L. L., & Donohue, W. A. (1980). Do kids know what TV commercials intend? *Journal of Advertising Research, 20*(3), 51-58.

Donohue, T. R., Henke, L. L., & Meyer, T. P. (1983). Learning about television commercials: The impact of instructional units on children's perceptions of motive and intent. *Journal of Broadcasting, 27*(3), 251-261.

Henke, L. L. (1980). *A nonverbal assessment of children's perceptions of television advertising.* Unpublished doctoral dissertation, University of Massachusetts, Amherst.

Henke, L. L., & Donohue, T. R. (1986). Teletext viewing habits and preferences. *Journalism Quarterly 63*(3), 542-553.

Henke, L. L., Donohue, T. R., Cook, C., & Cheung, D. (1984). The impact of cable on traditional television news viewing habits. *Journalism Quarterly, 61*(1), 174-178.

Hong, J., & Leckenby, J. D. (1996). Audience measurement and media reach/frequency issues in Internet advertising. *Proceedings of the 1996 American Academy of Advertising Conference,* Vancouver, B.C. *Internet Marketing & Technology Report.* (1996), *2*(2), 1-4.

Krugman, D. M., & Rust, R. T. (1987). The impact of cable penetration on network viewing. *Journal of Advertising Research, 27*(5), 9-13.

Lasswell, H. D. (1949). The structure and function of communication in society. In S. N. Katz (Ed.), *Mass communications.* Urbana: University of Illinois Press.

McLuhan, M. & Fiore, Q. (1967). *The medium is the massage: An inventory of effects.* New York: Bantam Books.

McNeal, J. U. (1990, September). Children as customers. American *Demographics, 12*(9), 36-39.

McNeal, J. U. (1992, February). The littlest shoppers. *American Demographics, 14*(2) 48-53.

Meyer, T. P., Donohue, T. R., & Henke, L. L. (1978). How Black children see TV commercials. *Journal of Advertising Research, 18*(5), 51-58.

Rubin, A. (1983). Television uses and gratifications: The interactions of viewing patterns and motivations. *Journal of Broadcasting, 27*(1), 37-51.

Stipp, H. (1993, August). New ways to reach children. *American Demographics, 15*(8), 50-56.

Turkle, S. (1995). *Life on the screen,* New York: Simon & Schuster.

Turkle, S. (1996, Winter). Virtuality and its discontents. *The American Prospect, 24,* 50-57.

Ward, S., Reale, G., & Levinson, D. (1972). Children's perceptions, explanations, and judgments of television advertising: A further exploration. In E.A. Rubinstein et al. (eds.) *Television and Social Behavior, Volume 4.* Washington, D.C.: Government Printing office, 468-490.

Webster, N. C. (1995, February). Marketing to kids. *Advertising Age,* 13, S1-S2.

6

Effectiveness of Internet Advertising by Leading National Advertisers

Judy Foster Davis
Eastern Michigan University

Businesses are increasingly flocking to the Internet for a variety of marketing purposes, including research, publicity, sales, and advertising. By April 1996, about 256,000 commercial domains were registered on the Internet with spending on Internet advertising expected to grow from $74 million in 1996 to $2.6 billion by the year 2000 (Narisetti, 1996). At the beginning of 1996, more than 50 of the Leading 100 National Advertisers (LNAs) had established corporate homepages (sites) on the Internet's World Wide Web ("Big biz," 1995). Although many large advertisers and their agencies have been criticized for being slow to embrace marketing on the Web, many LNAs on the Web have incorporated state-of-the-art features into their sites, creating addresses laden with graphics, company, product, and service information, links to related web sites, embedded e-mail, interactive games, and so on (Beatty, 1995, 1996b; Goldman, 1995a; Hodges, 1996; Rigdon, 1995). Trade reports indicate that moving into interactive/multimedia advertising dominates advertising agency future expansion plans (Beatty, 1996a).

Adoption of the Web by LNAs serving as models for other companies is important for two reasons. First, promotional strategies used by the LNAs are often imitated by others, thereby creating industry standards. Second, many LNAs can afford to experiment with marketing tactics on the Web, the results of which may be valuable for other companies interested in establishing or modifying web sites in ways that enhance the effectiveness of this new interactive medium.

PURPOSE

This study takes the perspective of the college student, and examines the effectiveness of advertising placed on the World Wide Web by several LNAs. Diffusion of innovation and cultural selection theories, along with demographic information on Internet users, suggests that college students may serve as influential cultural gatekeepers responsible for filtering and spreading information and ideas about Internet content to the broader society (Burn, 1996; Layne, 1995; Rogers, 1962; Solomon, 1988). Therefore, appealing to college students is believed to be important to the broader societal acceptance and potential success of web advertising.

LITERATURE REVIEW AND PROPOSED MODEL

Internet Advertising: Challenges to Effectiveness

Much of the effort directed at current web marketing is considered experimental, as the advertising industry grapples with issues of what is, and what is not, effective for the Web.   Firms have entered the world of web marketing anticipating big payoffs, including online browsing and shopping by consumers, the opportunity to build relationships with consumers and enhance databases, and greater profits (Plotkin, 1996; Raman & Leckenby, 1995; Shermach, 1995; Williamson, 1995). Presently, the medium is so new and unproven that there are few rules or standards about what tactics may produce desired results.

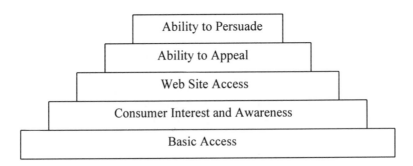

Fig. 6.1. Elements essential to effective internet advertising

There are a number of challenges to effective advertising on the Internet, or any interactive medium, which require promotional professionals to carefully develop appropriate content. Figure 6.1 depicts a model that identifies elements that may be essential to effective Internet advertising. Discussion of the model describes consumer, technological, and content factors that impact upon effectiveness.

Basic Access. In order for Internet advertising to be effective, at the most fundamental level consumers must have access to hardware and software permitting Internet entry. There are at least 40 million users of the Internet in the U.S. (Romei, 1998). The National Telecommunications and Information Administration (1997) estimates Internet access from home at about 18.6%. It is estimated that there are from 13.5 to 24 million users of the Internet (Hodges, 1995; Rigdon, 1996). Women account for about 34% of Internet users and the most popular Internet access places are work (66%), home (44%), and school (8%; Hodges, 1995).

Consumer access to the Internet from home has been slowed by the price of the technology, with computers considered the most expensive consumer purchase after a home and a car. To address the hardware cost issue, the computer industry has proposed the development of inexpensive machines primarily suited for access to the Internet (Hill, 1995; Johnson, 1996). Another hindrance to Internet use from home is the potentially high cost associated with connect rates to commercial online services (such as America Online and CompuServe), which may charge hourly rates. Many consumers have opted for flat rate service programs or have signed up with lower-cost Internet service providers (Sandberg & Ziegler, 1996). Modem speed has been cited as another hindrance to home Internet use, with slow modem speeds criticized for elongating graphic and information downloading times, producing consumer frustration. It is predicted that cable modems, rather than telephone modems, will offer a fitting solution to downloading time at home (Cleland, 1996b).

Consumer Interests and Awareness

Other elements likely related to the effectiveness of Internet advertising are consumer interests related to Internet usage and awareness of specific web sites. Surveys indicate that consumers are primarily interested in using the Internet for personal reasons, such as sending e-mail, for gathering news and general research information, and for entertainment purposes ("Internet buffs," 1996; Williamson, 1994.) Using the Internet to receive advertising on demand and to conduct product purchases have ranked at or near the bottom of consumer interest in the Internet (Miller, 1995; Williamson, 1994). Furthermore, a 1994 study showed more than 65% of consumers to be openly resentful of the idea of advertising on interactive media (Fawcett, 1994). Thus, encouraging consumers to visit specific advertising sites appears to be a difficult challenge to marketers. Judson (1995) suggested that advertisers enhance their ability to draw prospects to sites by including Internet addresses in all advertising, participating in electronic shopping sites with other marketers, and establishing hypertext links from editorial sites.

There are no published studies indicating consumer awareness of specific web sites, yet many marketers are actively publicizing their Internet addresses in traditional advertisements and articles. An industry study showed that only 23% of Internet users had visited more than 100 web sites in any depth, that web users had little recall of what they had seen, and that they did not recall brands seen ("Internet buffs," 1996). A report by PC Meter, an Internet tracking service, indicated no marketing site among the top 50 visited by consumers (Cleland, 1996a).

Web Site Access

On the surface, this may appear to be a minor issue, yet digital access to specific web sites can be problematic for two reasons. First, many Internet addresses are arcane and unwieldy, meaning that they are difficult for consumers to remember and may be lost forever if not documented and stored (Donaton, 1995). Another problem is that some sites appear to be ephemeral - there one day and seemingly gone another - creating consumer puzzlement and frustration. The site may be undergoing modification, there may be heavy traffic to the site, or there may be some other reason why the site is not accessible, yet a consumer encountering a "HOST NOT FOUND" message may be discouraged from returning to the site at some future time.

Ability to Appeal

Perhaps the biggest challenge to effective Internet advertising is the ability to appeal to consumers once they have encountered the site. A study of Internet users indicates that they spend an average of 68 minutes per session and about 25% of users log in daily ("Internet buffs," 1996). Time spent on an Internet site may be as long or as short as consumers prefer as they are in total control of their exposure to the content. Actively accessing advertising via the Internet is a new behavior for most consumers, who are traditionally accustomed to being exposed to advertising in a passive manner. Given that exposure to Internet advertising requires inherently more effort on the part of the consumer, many believe that it is imperative to design Web content that is attractive and appealing to consumers. Opinions on designing appealing Web content have focused on producing material that is interesting, informative, and entertaining to consumers. Much of the recent creative emphasis has been on developing arresting graphics, linking advertising with related editorial content, and incorporating interactive games, contests, sweepstakes, and other promotions into the content (Hodges, 1996; Plotkin, 1996).

Some creative efforts, such as linking content to popular events like the Super Bowl, or to popular TV programs, have been praised (Supple, 1996). Yet, the creative effort exhibited on many Web sites has been criticized. A common complaint is that content is allowed to become stagnant as sponsors fail to update/modify the site regularly. Another criticism is that some advertisements are essentially uninspired banners, low-quality brochures, or digitized print ads (Supple, 1996; Waltner, 1996). Even sites that are graphics-laden have been criticized, as their download time is lengthy at slower modem speeds. Some practitioners suggest that the Internet is inappropriate for a hard-sell marketing approach, and that advertisers should instead focus on providing product information or other material that has practical purposes (Loro, 1996; Shermach, 1995). Skuba (1996) suggested that a truly interactive and meaningful web site must involve the consumer in a deep, protracted session in which the consumer plays an active role. The session should deliver not only a brand message, but should also provide some measure of good information, utility, entertainment, and opportunity for feedback. To this end, it is believed that consumer interests, attitudes, and beliefs about the brand and/or category should be the guiding forces in interactive creative strategy (Skuba, 1996).

Ability to Persuade

As with traditional advertising, the ability to persuade is perhaps the most difficult effect for Internet advertising to achieve, be it prompting consumers to think more favorably about a company/brand or inspiring some sort of action. Raman and Leckenby (1995) suggested that interactive advertising may be useful in enhancing brand equity if consumers are provided the opportunity to engage in self-persuasion by, for example, participating in interactive games or contests in which consumers engage in biased information search. With respect to Internet advertising, one dimension of persuasive effectiveness is the extent to which consumers would be interested in returning to a site. Industry observers suggest that site designers encourage repeat visits by providing an incentive or reward that the consumer would value (Plotkin, 1996). Regularly updated content is also considered critical in encouraging people to return to sites (Skuba, 1996). Another measure of persuasive effectiveness may be the extent to which the consumer might encourage other people to visit a marketer's web site, as such interpersonal communication is regarded as highly credible and robust (Berkman & Gilson, 1986).

**Internet Advertising: College Students
as Early Adopters and Opinion Leaders**

For an innovation like the Internet, college students may act as early adopters of the technology and opinion leaders about Internet content. Diffusion theory indicates that early adopters of innovations, although typically constituting a small percentage of the total population, are instrumental in introducing innovations to broader society (Rogers, 1962). Technological innovations, such as computers and the Internet, place behavioral demands on consumers, who typically exhibit varying degrees of acceptance of the new behavioral requirements. Solomon (1992) suggested that in order for an innovation to be accepted, it should be compatible with consumers' lifestyles. For many students today, the use of computers and the Internet are compatible with their lifestyles. Studies show that the greatest proportion of Internet users (31%) are under age 30, which correlates directly with the age group of traditional college students; another 27% of Internet users are ages 30 to 39 (Fawcett, 1994; "Internet buffs," 1996). Other research shows that the younger age segments are comfortable with technology and consider it a normal part of their lifestyles (Burn, 1996; Layne, 1995; Ritchie, 1995). Also, many of the approximately 14 million college students in the U.S. today have free Internet access through their schools (Goldman, 1995b).

Innovations introduced to society are often filtered through informal opinion leaders, such as friends, family members, neighbors, and colleagues (Solomon, 1988). Ram and Jung's (1994) research on innovation in product usage indicated that early adopters are often more involved with products than the early majority and are more active in terms of information search, product usage, and opinion leadership. Chan and Misra (1990) suggested that opinion leaders are characterized, not only by familiarity and involvement with products, but also by willingness to transmit their opinions. Opinion leadership plays a critical role in new product adoption and diffusion. Young adults are important opinion leaders with respect to new technologies.

Generation X researcher Ritchie (1995) noted that young adults maintain a large network of contacts with relatives and friends and that many are consulted for advice about computers and their applications. In addition, Burnett and Smart (1994) documented a trend of young adults who remain in or return to the parental home after reaching adulthood. These young adults tend to exhibit interest in technology-based products and also influence household consumption decisions. In that college students possess access, demographic, and lifestyle characteristics consistent with Internet usage, and given the nature of their interpersonal relationships, they represent an important group to marketers seeking to develop effective advertising for the Web.

METHOD

Respondents and Procedure

Students enrolled in upper-class business courses at a large Midwestern university were asked to voluntarily participate in the study and were provided an incentive for their participation. The makeup of the student body at the university consists of a substantial number of commuter students and slightly older, nontraditional students. The university provides free Internet access to all enrolled students and has several computer labs on campus available to students.

The volunteers were randomly assigned to access one of eight preselected corporate sites on the World Wide Web. On access, participants were required to complete a questionnaire soliciting their opinions about the web site's appeal and to indicate basic demographic characteristics and Internet usage habits. The data were collected over a one-week period in February 1996.

Web Site Material

Web sites were selected from those established by companies included in the list of the 100 LNAs published by *Advertising Age*. The selected sites were chosen from four business categories characterized by heavy spending on consumer advertising: automotive, food, retail, and personal services. Two sites were chosen from each category. The selected web sites and a description of their features are reported in the Appendix.

RESULTS

The research procedure netted 272 usable questionnaires. As expected, the vast majority (84.1%) of the sample was in the 21 to 29 year age range. The sample was 39.2% male and 51.7% female. (The gender percentages do not total 100 due to item nonresponses.)

Basic Access

Table 6.1 provides a summary of respondents' Internet usage habits. As expected, these results indicate that basic access to the Internet is not a problem for college students. Also, more than 40% spend 1 hour or more online each week.

Student Interests and the Internet

Table 6.2 indicates students' main reasons for using the Internet. Consistent with other consumer studies, the result show that students are most likely to use the Internet for information/research purposes, and are far less likely to use it to obtain product and service information. About one third of the sample indicated that they were "least likely" to use the Internet to obtain product or service information. "Other" reasons for Internet use were: e-mail to family/friends; job search; "kill" or "waste" time; and to explore.

TABLE 6.1
Internet Usage Habits by College Students

Use Internet at:*	N	Percentage, %
Home	74	27.3
Work	34	12.5
School	209	77.1

Time spent online each week:**	N	Percentage, %
Less than 1 hour	132	48.7
1-3 hours	59	21.8
4-6 hours	30	11.1
7-10 hours	20	7.4
More than 10 hours	6	2.2

*Multiple responses were allowed to this item.
**Percentages not totaling 100 are due to item nonresponses.

TABLE 6.2
Students' Primary Reason for Using the Internet

Reason Ranked Number One:	N	Percentage, %*
Education/Study/Research	134	49.4
Entertainment/Recreation	61	22.5
Work-Related Duties	19	7.0
"Other"	19	7.0
Product/Service Information	15	5.5

*Percentages not totaling 100 are due to item nonresponses.

Student Awareness of Specific Company Web Sites

Students were asked whether they had prior awareness of the web sites indicated, the source of that awareness, and whether they had ever accessed those sites previously. Table 6.3 summarizes the responses to those items. There were small percentage attributions of awareness to traditional media, yet most awareness appeared to come from "other" sources, including word-of-mouth "at school," from "friends," and "family."

TABLE 6.3
Student Awareness Levels of Web Sites

Web Site	% Indicating Prior Awareness of Site	Perceived Sources of Awareness (%)	% Prior Access to Web Site
Ford	4.8	Television – 0; Radio – 0; Newspaper – 0; Magazine – 0 Other - 8.0	4.8
Saturn	24.3	Television - 8.1: Radio – 0; Newspaper - 0; Magazine - 10.8; Other - 13.5	5.6
Frito-Lay	9.7	Television – 0; Radio – 0; Newspaper –0; Magazine - 3.2; Other - 12.9	6.7
Hershey	.0	Television – 0; Radio – 0; Newspaper – 0; Magazine – 0; Other - None	.0
Target	13.9	Television - 2.8; Radio - 2.8; Newspaper - 2.8; Magazine - 8.3; Other - 16.7	2.8
Wal-mart	6.1	Television - 3.0; Radio – 0; Newspaper- 0; Magazine – 0; Other - 6.1	.0
AT&T	9.1	Television - 11.8; Radio - 2.9; Newspaper - 5.9; Magazine - 5.9; Other - 5.9	9.1
MCI	3.6	Television – 0; Radio – 0; Newspaper – 0; Magazine – 0; Other - 13.8	.0

Web Site Access Attempts

Once logged on to the Internet, most respondents (69.7%) were able to access the site on the first attempt. Yet, a few problems with access were noted. The access attempts by the sample for each web site are detailed in Table 6.4. In particular, many had difficulty accessing Ford Motor Company's site. Scaled mean responses to a survey item stating, "I had an easy time accessing this web site," ranged from 5.4 to 6.4 for seven of the eight web sites, where a score of 7 meant that the sample "strongly agreed" with the statement. For the Ford site, however, the sample provided a numerical mean response of 2.9, indicating a significant level of difficulty in accessing the site. As a result, the number of students who were able to access this site was significantly smaller than for the other companies. (This data is reported in Table 6.7.) Some apparently gave up the access attempt in frustration.

TABLE 6.4
Access Attempts by Web Site

| Web Site | Access Attempts | | | |
	One (%)	Two (%)	Three (%)	Four + (%)
Ford	33.3	14.3	9.5	42.9
Saturn	87.9	12.1	0.0	0.0
Frito-Lay	90.0	10.0	0.0	0.0
Hershey	71.0	22.6	0.0	6.5
Target	85.7	14.3	0.0	0.0
Wal-Mart	83.9	12.9	3.2	0.0
AT&T	69.7	21.2	6.1	3.0
MCI	82.1	10.7	7.1	0.0

Time Spent on Site by Students

In general, once the sites had been accessed, 38.8% of the sample spent between 1 and 5 minutes exploring the site, and 27.3% spent between 6 and 10 minutes. Nearly 15% spent 11 to 15 minutes on the site, and 5.9% spent more than 15 minutes. There was variation between the time spent at each web site, as is reported in Table 6.5. Correlation analysis on time spent at each web site with various attitudinal measures of effectiveness suggested weak to moderate ($\pm$ .29 to .44) relationships between the variables.

Extent of Appeal to and Persuasion of Students

Students recorded their opinion to ten different statements designed to measure their attitudes toward the web sites' content appeal in terms of interestingness, liking, relevance, and ability to persuade. The attitude items were measured on a 7-point, Likert-type scale where 1 = *strongly disagree* and 7 = *strongly agree*. The mean responses to these statements in general and for each web site are summarized in Table 6.6. Then, *t*-tests were conducted to determine whether the differences between the grand mean and the individual web site mean for each attitude statement were statistically significant, significantly different mean scores indicating greater levels of effectiveness for each attitude item are shaded in the table. A one-way ANOVA also indicated whether statistically significant differences among web sites were present for the attitude items (see Table 6.6).

TABLE 6.5
Time Spent at Each Web Site

Web Site	1-5 min. (%)	6-10 min. (%)	11-15 min. (%)	15 + min. (%)
Ford	43.8	43.8	6.3	6.3
Saturn	38.2	32.4	23.5	5.9
Frito-Lay	46.4	39.3	7.1	7.1
Hershey	40.6	18.8	31.3	9.4
Target	45.7	34.3	8.6	11.4
Wal-Mart	58.1	22.6	16.1	3.2
AT&T	51.6	35.5	12.9	0.0
MCI	33.3	33.3	22.2	11.1

Four web sites produced scores indicating significantly greater levels of effectiveness: Saturn, Frito-Lay, Hershey, and MCI, on 9 of the 10 measures produced a statistically significant difference with respect to the web sites' ability to appeal and persuade. The only measure that did not produce a significant difference between web sites was related to relevance of the content. The sample was neutral (i.e., "neither agree or disagree") as to whether the content was relevant to their needs. In general, the results suggest that the content appeal was somewhat high on perceptions of informativeness, liking, and interestingness. In contrast, the sample tended to disagree that the content was boring or a waste of time. The persuasion scores were not as strong as the appeal scores, having a tendency to hover in the neutral range. However, persuasion scores between web sites were statistically significant for each of the persuasion measures.

TABLE 6.6
Attitude Means toward Web Site Content ($N = 253$)

Attitude Statements: Measures of Appeal

Companies (Number of subjects)	I think this web site is interesting.	This web site is very informative.	I like this web site.	This web site is relevant to my needs.	I am bored by this web site.	This web site is a waste of time.
Ford (21)	4.8	5.0	4.6	4.0	3.3	3.7
Saturn (37)	5.0	5.6	5.0	3.9	3.4	2.8
Frito Lay (30)	5.5	5.0	5.6	3.7	2.5	2.5
Hershey (33)	5.7	5.6	5.5	4.0	2.3	2.8
Target (36)	4.8	4.9	4.8	3.4	3.5	3.1
Wal-Mart (33)	3.9	5.0	3.9	3.4	4.4	3.6
AT&T (34)	4.7	5.1	4.7	4.0	3.4	3.1
MCI (29)	5.2	5.7	5.1	4.3	2.9	2.5
Grand Mean	4.8	5.3	4.9	3.9	3.2	3.0
F-value	4.45*	2.33**	4.24*	1.18	4.87*	2.43**

Attitude Statements: Measures of Persuasion

Companies (Number of subjects)	"I would visit this web site again."	"After seeing this web site, I have a more favorable view of the brand/ company."	"This web site would help convince me to buy this brand."	"I would tell someone else about this web site."
Ford (21)	3.7	3.5	3.3	4.4
Saturn (37)	4.1	4.7	4.0	4.9
Frito Lay (30)	4.7	4.9	4.4	4.7
Hershey (33)	4.8	4.7	4.6	4.8
Target (36)	3.8	4.5	3.7	3.9
Wal-Mart (33)	2.9	4.1	3.2	3.9
AT&T (34)	4.2	4.0	3.9	4.2
MCI (29)	4.4	4.8	4.0	4.5
Grand Mean	4.1	4.4	3.9	4.3
F-value	3.17**	3.49*	3.38*	2.83**

Means are measured on a 7-point scale where: $1 = strongly\ disagree$; $2 = disagree$; $3 = disagree\ somewhat$; $4 = neither\ agree\ or\ disagree$; $5 = agree\ somewhat$; $6 = agree$; $7 = strongly\ agree$. $*p < .01$; $**p < .05$.

CONCLUSIONS

This study suggests that determinants of effectiveness of advertising on the Internet need to be looked at broadly, from issues ranging from basic access to the Internet to concern for the ability to appeal to and persuade different consumers. A substantial number of college students have adopted the Internet into their normal lifestyles, yet using the Internet to access marketing and advertising content does not appear to be a key motivation. Awareness of corporate marketing sites on the Web appears to be relatively low, with awareness primarily generated from interpersonal sources and, to a lesser extent, traditional media. Basic questions of access to web sites must also be addressed, as difficulty in accessing specific sites creates problems and frustration for both consumers and marketers. Once students have accessed corporate marketing sites, attitudes toward the appeal of the content appear to be somewhat favorable, with the best-liked sites providing interesting graphics, information, and opportunities for interaction.

The results suggest that the most persuasive content is that which includes more than just product information, but also gives the participant something to do, such as enter a contest, make a recipe, order a brochure, join a club, and so on. To this extent, opinion leadership may be fostered if the sites give the participants something to talk about – that is, interesting information and/or experiences. This study suggests that marketers need to expend more effort in designing appealing web content and should provide content that offers interesting and/or entertaining experiences worthy of conversation. Marketers might also design content that is specifically relevant to certain groups. For example, AT&T's site was updated to add a "College Network" to its web site, which links students to job, research, and service information.

REFERENCES

Beatty, S. G. (1995, December 27). Cyberagencies invade the Web, leaving old-line shops off-line. *Wall Street Journal*, p. B-18.

Beatty, S. G. (1996a, April 1). Big ad agencies continue buying spree. *Wall Street Journal*, p. B-7.

Beatty, S. G. (1996b, February 2). Poppe Tyson leads the charge of agencies signing on Internet. *Wall Street Journal*, p. B-11.

Berkman, H. & Gilson, C. (1986). *Consumer behavior: Concepts and strategies*, Boston: Kent Publishing

Big biz hits the Web, slowly. (1995, November 20). *Advertising Age*, p. S-11.

Burn, E. (1996, February). Back to school: The benefits of selling to the college market. *Direct Marketing*, *58*(10), 31-33.

Burnett, J., & Smart, D. (1994, May June). Returning young adults: Implications for marketers. *Psychology and Marketing*, *11*(3), 253-269.

Chan, K. K., & Misra, S. (1990). Characteristics of the opinion leader: A new dimension. *Journal of Advertising*, *19*(3), 53-60.

Cleland, K. (1996a, March 11). NPD's PC Meter tracks individual Web site visits." *Advertising Age*, 11, 20.

Cleland, K. (1996b, March 25). System operators tout speed to Web crawlers. *Advertising Age*, 24.

Donaton, S. (1995, January 23). Mucking up marketing on the 'net'. *Advertising Age*, 23.

Falling through the Net: New data on the digital divide (1997). National Telecommunications and Information Administration. <*www.ntia.doc.gov/ntiahome/net2/ falling.html*>, .

Fawcett, A. W. (1995, October 3). Interactive awareness growing. *Advertising Age*, 32.

Goldman, K. (1995a, February 2). Fresh alarm is sent over interactive age. *Wall Street Journal*, p. B-10.

Goldman, K. (1995b, August 18). On the World Wide Web, Sprint spins college student campaign. *Wall Street Journal*, p. B-3.

Hill, C. G. (1995, December 4). LSI to unveil chip design for building inexpensive machines to access Internet. *Wall Street Journal*, p. A-3.

Hodges, J. (1995, November 6). Internet World: AOL launches GNN. *Advertising Age*, 31.

Hodges, J. (1996, March 11). Marketers play Web games as serious biz. *Advertising Age*, 16.

Internet buffs average 6.6 hours of use a week. (1996, January 12). *Detroit Free Press*, p. 6-E.

Johnson, B. (1996, March 25). Will the Web win appeal worldwide. *Advertising Age*, 36.

Judson, B. (1995, August 7). Luring advertisers' prospects to Web. *Advertising Age,* 16.

Layne, B. (1995, November 20). Meet your future: Generation I. *Advertising Age*, p. S-12.

Loro, L. (1996, April 15). Grappling with cyber-consumers. *Advertising Age*, 12.

Miller, T. E. (1995, April). New markets for information. *American Demographics*, *17*(4), 46-54.

Narisetti, R. (1996, April 18). P&G steps up ad cyber surfing; Tide could have major effect. *Wall Street Journal*, p. B-10.

Plotkin, A. (1996, March 4). Online gold mine awaits exploitation. *Advertising Age*, p. S-4.

Ram, S. & Jung, H. (1994). Innovativeness in product usage: A comparison of early adopters and early majority. *Psychology and Marketing*, *11*(1), 57-67.

Raman, N. & Leckenby, J. D. (1995). Advertising on interactive media: Some issues, some suggestions. In C.S. Madden (Ed.), *Proceedings of the 1995 conference of the American Academy of Advertising*, 247-251.

Rigdon, J. E. (1996, March 13). Internet's no. 1 use: Information bureau. *Wall Street Journal,*p. B-1.

Rigdon, J. E. (1995, December 8). Web sites find niche in budgets ruled by TV, print campaigns. *Wall Street Journal*, p. B-6.

Ritchie, K. (1995, April). Marketing to Generation X. *American Demographics, 17*(4), 34-39.

Rogers, E. M. (1962). *Diffusion of innovations*. New York: Free Press.

Romei, L. (1998, January/February). The Internet: New apps, new traps. *Managing Office Technology*, *43*(1), 14-16.

Sandberg, J. & Ziegler, B. (1996, January 18). Internet's popularity threatens to swamp the on-line services. *Wall Street Journal*, p. A-1.

Shermach, K. (1995, February 13). Hype, hype, hooray for the info way. *Marketing News*, *29*(4), 8.

Skuba, C. (1996, Spring). Web site vs. Web session. *American Advertising*, *12* (1), 22-23.

Solomon, M. R. (1988). Building up and breaking down, the impact of cultural sorting on symbolic consumption. In J. Sheth and E. C. Hirschman (Eds.), *Research in Consumer Behavior*, Greenwich, CT: JAI Press.

Solomon, M. R. (1992). *Consumer Behavior*, Boston: Allyn and Bacon.

Supple, J. (1996, February 26). Of sod houses and dance hall girls. *Advertising Age*, p. S-14.

Waltner, C. (1996, March 4). Going beyond the banner with Web ads. *Advertising Age*, 22.

Williamson, D. A. (1994, January 9). New-media benefits still a thorny issue. *Advertising Age*, 25.

Williamson, D. A. (1995, November 20). Searching for a pot of gold. *Advertising Age*, p. S-2.

APPENDIX
Description of Corporate Internet Web Sites Included in the Study

Company and Web Site	Home Page Features
Automotive:	
Ford Motor Co. <http://www.ford.com>	Corporate logo prominently displayed. Blend of text and graphics with icon and text links to company, financial and product information. Links to historical information on Ford cars and Ford family. Visitors invited to complete a customer survey and join a research focus group. Embedded e-mail.
Saturn <http://www.saturncars.com>	Billboard-style graphic of Saturn car prominently featured. Blend of text and graphics. Links to brand information and retailer locations. Visitors may order a Saturn brochure online; become a member of the Saturn car club. May retrieve an 800-number to communicate with Saturn.
Food (snacks):	
Frito-Lay <http://www.fritolay.com>	Graphics-oriented; minimal text. "Chester" cheetah character corporate icon prominently featured. Visitors may click on various icons to enter a contest to win prizes, get recipes, and see company or specific brand information. Can wander a virtual "dream house" filled with Frito-Lay brands and enter "Chester's closet for amusement." Embedded e-mail.
Hershey <http://www.microserve.net/~ hershey/welcome.html>	Conservative graphics blended with text. Photo of company founder prominently displayed. Visitors may click on hypertext links to see company, founder, product, recipe and nutrition information. May order Hershey-theme gifts and collectibles. Includes information on Hersheypark and Hershey, Pennsylvania tourist attractions. Embedded e-mail.

Retail:

Target
<http://www.targetstores.com>

Billboard-style store logo with corporate sponsorship message prominently displayed. Graphics-oriented; minimal text. Visitors may click on icons for store location, baby gift registry information, and information on discounts for entertainment venues ("treatseats"). Click on text links for information on charitable and community activities. Visitors may "meet" a celebrity endorser and participate in entertainment product reviews.

Wal-Mart
<http://www.wal-mart.com>

Billboard-style store logo featuring photos of Wal-mart employees. Text-oriented; minimal graphics. Click on text links to retrieve store information, including Sam's Club; corporate information; vendor opportunities; and community service activities. May obtain free music concert tickets for a limited time. Embedded e-mail.

Services:

AT&T
<http://www.att.com>

Graphics-oriented featuring corporate logo and a variety of icons; minimal text. Icon and text links to information on a wide variety of consumer and business services and products. Embedded e-mail. (Site recently modified to feature more text than graphics; added a "College Network" with links to study and career information sites.)

MCI
<http://mci.com>

Billboard-style main graphic featuring a menu of options and photographs showing home and business activities. Substantial text with links to information on company networking, the Internet, and MCI corporation and service information. Embedded e-mail.

7

Interactive Media: A Means for More Meaningful Advertising?

Glen J. Nowak
Scott Shamp
Barry Hollander
Glen T. Cameron
University of Georgia

The past few years have seen tremendous interest on the part of marketers, media organizations, and advertising agencies in using computer-mediated interactive media to reach and communicate with consumers. The most popular methods involve the Internet, the World Wide Web, and online computer services. United States spending for online advertising is projected to grow from $1.3 billion in 1998 to $10.5 billion in 2003, with global spending for online advertising projected to reach $15 billion in 2003 (Mand, 1998). By February 1995, the number of registered commercial domains (i.e., Internet addresses) topped 32,000, with an estimated 1,500 new companies connecting to the Internet each month (Ellsworth, 1995). According to recent studies, marketers spent $351.3 million to advertise on the World Wide Web in the first six months of 1998, more than double the total 1996 spending (Mand, 1998). Major advertisers include more than 50 of the 200 largest U.S. consumer brands (Jaffee, 1996a).

In addition to using the Web to reach potential customers, a growing number of companies are working to make the Internet and other computer-mediated communication channels more accessible and usable for advertisers. Some, for example, are offering services designed to help advertisers reach specific target audiences (Cleland, 1996), while others are helping marketers determine when and where to run ads (Flynn, 1996).

With an estimated 57 million U.S. households expected to be online by 2002 (Mand, 1998), there is much optimism regarding consumer interest in web-delivered advertising and marketing information. While email and content browsing are usually the primary consumer uses of the Internet and online services (Cleland, 1995), creative and technological advances have increased the attractiveness and accessibility of advertising banners, Web sites, and search portals. According to recent surveys of online users, at least one third of interactive households use the web to investigate or buy products (Moran, 1997), with as many as 70% of regular Web users having made one or more online purchase (Magill, 1998). Other studies of Internet users have found that nearly 75% sign on to obtain information (Read, 1996), with about 40% using the Internet to seek out advertising and marketing-related information (Find/SVP, 1996). One study even found that 34% of interactive households think advertising on the Web is "effective and compelling" (Moran, 1997).

While Internet-related business and commerce is projected to increase from $1.9 billion in 1998 to around $4 billion by year 2000 (Jupiter Communications, 1998), actual consumer purchasing of products or services via Web-disseminated advertising remains relatively low. Most online consumer purchases are made via web pages or at Internet commerce sites (e.g., electronic book or music stores). In contrast, a 1998 survey of 1000 Americans found that only 1% of Web surfers click on banner advertisements – about half the success rate of direct mail advertising (Economist, 1998). Further, although some advertisers (e.g., Eastman Kodak, Saturn, AT&T) have found their web sites receiving over 100,000 "hits" each day (Read, 1996a; Taylor, 1995), other marketers have closed or considered closing their web sites due to lack of consumer interest and use (Aho Williamson, 1995).

Faith in the Web's potential, along with the forecasts of tremendous subscriber growth, will continue to foster marketer interest. For example, not only do surveys routinely show that consumer willingness to make online purchases in growing (Jaffee, 1996a), much research suggests online purchasing can become habit forming. One study found that, of those who reported buying online in the past year, the average shopper bought nine products and spent $475 (Magill, 1998).

Home Pages and Ad Banners

For many marketers, computer-mediated advertising involves homepages on the World Wide Web. Homepages, also known as web sites, are destinations for "travelers" (i.e., users) on the Internet. Along with verbal information about a company and its offerings, these sites typically use graphical and visual images (e.g., icons and banners) to attract user attention, organize information, and enhance the value or attractiveness of content. Homepages can range in length (or breadth of information) from one "page" (i.e., roughly equivalent to one computer screen of information) to thousands of pages (e.g., an Eastman Kodak contained over 20,000 pages; Read, 1996a). Unlike traditional media, the incremental costs incurred in adding information (i.e., pages) are generally much less than the initial startup expenses. This makes the Web doubly attractive from an advertising perspective. Not only does it enable advertisers to economically provide more information about their products or services, it improves their ability to respond to individual consumer needs. Homepages, thanks to their hyperlinked structure, enable marketers to organize information so that consumers can access only the specific topics and issues that interest them, and to avoid the rest (Emerick, 1996).

The organizational structure that increases advertisers' ability to provide information also gives rise to one of the major marketing challenges - attracting consumers to any given World Wide Web site. Not only do hyperlinks enable each consumer to select which elements of a web site to view, they place most of the control over the entire interactive experience in the hands of the user. Online users decide which web sites and home pages to visit, when those visits will take place, and what those visits will look like. As a result, in the interlinked computer world, it is consumers, more so than marketers, who make many of the important decisions regarding advertising homepage and information exposure. Thus, for a web site to become an effective marketing or advertising medium, one of the first issues facing an advertiser or an ad agency is finding online ways to attract consumers to their content (in addition to offline ways such as promoting the web site in other media or placing homepage addresses on product labels).

One popular, and general, online strategy for attracting users is using "banners" or "hot buttons" to promote or advertise one site on other popular and/or related web sites. This strategy often involves placing the links in electronic magazine/publisher web sites, other firm's web sites, or cyber-shopping malls (Aho Williamson, 1996b). In the first six months of 1996, marketers spent an estimated $66.7 million to place advertising "banners," or links, on World Wide Web sites and commercial online services (Aho Williamson, 1996b). When consumers click on (i.e., activate) a banner, they are instantaneously connected to the banner's destination (e.g., the marketer's homepage). On average, marketers pay web site content providers/publishers banner placement fees that range from $20 per thousand viewers to $150 per thousand viewers (Aho Williamson, 1996c).

A second general strategy, often used in conjunction with the first, is to use creative tactics and elements to attract consumers' attention. Many practitioner recommendations, for example, contend that effective interactive advertising requires the use of attention-getting devices, personalization, tangible rewards (e.g., coupons or price incentives), and other tactics that facilitate consumer involvement and/or immediate responses (Aho Williamson, 1996b; Fawcett, 1996; Judson, 1996). This is especially true for the banners and links that allow users to instantly go from one web site to another. As a result, much creative effort is expended designing attractive and enticing advertising banners.

Purpose of the Study

Significant numbers of online users frequently (i.e., 10%) or sometimes (i.e., 45%) look at advertising banners (Fawcett, 1996), but much uncertainty surrounds the use of advertising banners. Thanks in part to a relative lack of theoretical and empirical guidance, questions have been raised regarding: (1) the overall utility of advertising banners, (2) the creative characteristics of banners, and (3) viewer reactions to different types of advertising banners, particularly those that are data-driven. For example, some marketers question the ability of a banner format to achieve promotional objectives (Aho Williamson, 1996c), while others have debated the pros and cons of evaluating banner effectiveness (Ahl & Temes, 1996; Bush, Bush, & Harris, 1998).

The purpose of this study was thus twofold: One, to develop and put forward an information processing framework for examining issues related to advertising banners. Second, to use that framework in an exploratory study to examine consumers' attitudinal and intention reactions to an increasingly popular interactive advertising creative strategy - personalizing banners and/or messages by user or user group. Message personalization strategies involve varying the type and/or prominence of individual-specific consumer information in a message or advertisement (Nowak, Price, & Lewis, 1995). Because relatively little is known about the effects or effectiveness of different personalization strategies in computer-mediated environments, the conceptual framework developed here was used to examine two key, interrelated issues: (1) how to design promotional banners so that they attract consumers to marketing or advertising-related homepages; and (2) how consumers may respond to highly-targeted interactive advertising or promotion messages. Specifically, a literature review and an exploratory study using an interactive media lab were used to assess:

1. How might online users respond to highly targeted advertising banners? Would personalization of advertising banners increase the likelihood that online users will click-on the banner in order to access an advertising-related web site?
2. How might personalization of banners affect online users' reactions to an advertising-related web site?
3. What online user characteristics, if any, may be related to the accessing or use of a marketing-related web site?

MESSAGE PERSONALIZATION AND COMPUTER-MEDIATED ADVERTISING

In many respects, interactive advertising represents a hybrid form of product/service promotion that requires simultaneously utilizing elements from both image/brand advertising and direct response advertising. Marketers who invest in online technology and media typically rely on measurable behavioral responses, ranging from "hits" and "click-throughs" to merchandise orders, to assess the return on their advertising investment. At the same time, however, their interactive advertising needs to be interesting and engaging enough to attract Internet users' attention, and given the Internet culture's general disdain for explicit sales messages (Mehta & Sivadas, 1995), highly relevant to users' wants and needs. Even though this makes doing and using interactive advertising more complex, it also helps provide a foundation for assessing the value of computer-mediated advertising. For example, the hybrid nature of most web and online advertising means direct marketing practices, combined with academic research in advertising and consumer behavior, can be used to develop frameworks and measures for examining a range of cognitive, attitudinal, and behavioral effects (Hoffman & Novak, 1996).

An important similarity between direct response and web-based advertising is the need to elicit relatively immediate consumer responses. For many web-based marketers, this means finding creative strategies and devices that encourage or persuade consumers to click-on a banner that takes them to the marketing-related web site. According to one direct marketing consultant, "banners and links are like the outer envelope of a direct mail piece. . . If you have 2,000 people visiting a web site and you're only getting five clicks on your banner, something is wrong with the banner, not the site" [Roy Schwedelson, as quoted in Jaffee (1996b), p. 19]. The creative challenge is heightened further by the web culture's general disdain for blatantly commercial messages; a disdain that usually discourages marketers from indiscriminately sending e-mail advertisements to large numbers of online users.

Online users do appear to be interested and willing to receive personally relevant or meaningful marketing and advertising-related information. For example, Mehta and Sivadas (1995) found that although Internet users held a fairly negative attitude toward advertising, they were less averse to receiving targeted (vs. nontargeted) electronic communications from marketers. Studies involving electronic couponing have found personalization strategies that utilize household purchase information can increase redemption rates by 10% or more (Rossi, McCullough, & Allenby, 1994). In addition, many newspaper publishers have found that offering highly targeted computer-mediated advertising is one way to regain advertising revenue that has been lost to highly targeted, often personalized, traditional media such as direct mail (Nowak, Cameron, & Krugman, 1994). Not surprisingly, a growing number of Internet software companies are now offering technologies that enable marketers to personalize advertising appeals based on individual consumer profiles (McGinty, 1996).

In the case of web-based marketing, one way to accomplish this type of targeting is to use personalized or customized advertising banners to motivate or induce clicking responses to a marketing-related web site. Under such an approach, a marketer incorporates information into the advertising banner or message that recognizes individual consumer characteristics or differences. The degree of personalization can vary considerably depending on the type and/or amount of information that a marketer has (1) assimilated regarding individual consumers and (2) explicitly incorporates into a banner (McGinty, 1996). Highly personalized banners, for example, would attempt to address online users on a "one-to-one" basis by prominently and explicitly using words or verbal messages that acknowledge some unique consumer characteristic, interest, or past behavior. This can range from mention of the consumer's name to language that acknowledges a consumer's specific demographic characteristics, purchase motivations, lifestyle habits, previous purchases, or product category interests (Jones, 1990; Nowak, Price & Lewis, 1995). Conversely, nonpersonalized banners would use generalized verbal copy to direct a broadly targeted message to all potential users or viewers.

From an information processing perspective, message personalization is an execution cue that can be employed and manipulated to improve banner performance. Research involving direct response advertising has shown execution cues such as copy length (Beard, Williams, & Kelly, 1990), explicit mention of prices (Akaah & Korgaonkar, 1988), and gender-specific headlines (Holmes & Urban, 1989) can positively affect viewers' memory, ad evaluation, and behavior intention reactions. In addition to those studies, the integrative framework developed by MacInnis and her associates (MacInnis & Jaworski, 1989; MacInnis, Moorman, & Jaworski, 1991) provides a conceptual basis for suggesting that customizing or personalizing advertising banners should be an effective way to elicit favorable responses. According to these models, three factors most affect consumers' responses to advertising and promotional messages: opportunity, ability, and motivation.

Opportunity refers to the idea that consumer processing of information is often influenced by exposure conditions. For example, repeated exposures or nondistracting viewing conditions increase the opportunity to process, while cluttered environments decrease opportunity. However, successful information processing also requires having the skills or knowledge necessary to process the information (i.e., ability) as well as the desire to do so (i.e., motivation). Assuming that online advertisers appropriately target their banners (i.e., direct them toward audiences that have the ability to process them) and place them in appropriate places (i.e., ones that create the opportunity to process), the primary responsibility of creative executions, especially promotional banners, is to motivate responses.

In MacInnis et al.'s integrative model, creative devices such as message personalization represent execution variables that increase advertising effectiveness by enhancing viewers' information processing responses to an ad. The specific role of execution cues is twofold. One, they serve as a mechanism that attracts attention or increases the likelihood the consumer will attend to the ad. Two, they increase viewers' involvement with the advertising execution and/or motivation to process brand information. In low product involvement situations, the impact is primarily on attending to the ad and its execution elements (e.g., pictures, music, colors, etc.). In higher involvement situations, execution cues serve to facilitate (i.e., increase) brand processing, or the amount of attention and cognitive effort devoted to processing the primary advertising claim or message. To the extent that personalization devices are perceived as execution cues that enhance the relevance of the advertised brand, viewers should have greater motivation to process brand information from the advertising.

Based on the integrative information processing model, personalization strategies should be an effective way to attract online users to advertising and marketing-related web sites. At a minimum, personalizing an advertising banner with information that reflects the interests or characteristics of specific, known consumers should positively affect online users' awareness of the banner and motivation to click-on the banner in order to access the advertising-related web site. Perhaps more importantly, personalization also has the potential to increase viewers' involvement with the advertising-related web site. If personalization accomplishes that task, it subsequently would positively affect attitudinal and intention responses regarding the advertising-related web site and/or the marketer. This would most likely manifest itself in terms of attitude toward the web banner/advertisement, but may extend to attitude toward the advertised brand.

However, there are at least two factors that add uncertainty regarding the value of personalized advertising banners. First, the lack of significant online user acceptance of computer-mediated advertising may carry over to personalized advertising banners. Rather than perceiving such banners as providing personally relevant and meaningful information, online users may consider them intrusive and annoying. A 1996 Louis Harris survey, for instance, found most respondents concerned about online tracking for targeted marketing purposes (Harrison, 1996). If this is a common sentiment, personalized banners would be noticed, but motivation to access the sponsor's web site would be very low or nonexistent. Second, the use of personalized banners requires considerable preparatory work on the part of an advertiser. At a minimum, personalization requires gathering or accessing information on specific customers (either directly or indirectly via a secondary data source) as well as the technological capability to merge such information into the advertising banners. These significant incremental costs can only be justified to the extent that personalization increases advertising effectiveness (Hodges, 1996). Together, these two reasons suggest that exploratory research is a necessary precursor to the use of personalized ad banners.

RESEARCH METHOD

The exploratory study involved the creation and use of an electronic newspaper - the "Protopaper." Located on the World Wide Web, the Protopaper contained many of the media elements, content features, and advertising messaging options associated with commercial online and web-based ventures. Specifically, it included editorial copy, photographs, and graphics from three local publications (including the local daily newspaper) as well as audio news. Participants came to a university computer lab for two hour-long online sessions.

Study Participants. Thirty-two randomly recruited 22 to 40-year-old adults participated in the study. The participants were recruited using randomly generated phone numbers and were offered a $45 cash incentive for taking part in the study. Prospective participants were screened with respect to age, as the majority of Internet users are 45-years-old and younger. Full-time university students also were screened out of the study. Seventeen participants were female, and 15 were male.

Advertising Banners and Web Sites. Advertising banners and web sites were created for two product categories: restaurant dining (i.e., a site that promoted a nonexistent, local restaurant called "Signature Café") and music (i.e., a site that promoted a nonexistent, local music store called "Music World"). Although neither business existed locally, it was assumed most participants would believe these were actual establishments because of the constantly changing nature of the local area's dining and retail businesses. Dining and music were used because they readily lend themselves to the information-provision/browsing nature of the computer-mediated world. To strengthen comparability, the dining and music web sites were similarly designed. Each offered a menu of different content categories (i.e., the dining web site allowed users to examine American, Mexican, and Italian cuisine offerings, and the music site allowed users to examine country, jazz, and rock music offerings). Each content area, in turn, listed and described five specific offerings. Along with verbal descriptions, pictures and graphics were used to make both web sites user friendly.

Hypertext-linked banners were created to take and induce study participants to access (i.e., click-through to) the Signature Cafe and Music World web sites. These banners had two primary characteristics. First, the advertising banners underlined and highlighted the web site's name in blue to indicate that clicking on it would take the user to another World Wide Web document (i.e., the Signature Cafe or Music World site). Second, and more importantly, the banners were personalized using the participant's name as well as their primary music/cuisine preference. The headline announced their name (e.g., "Bob"), while a line of body copy mentioned their specific interest (i.e., "If Jazz music is your thing, check out the selection at Music World!"). Similar to the methods employed by a growing number of Internet software providers (McGinty, 1996), individual participant's product category preferences were obtained using a multisection pretest "Consumer Shopping Habit" questionnaire. Along with demographic, media, and computer-habit information, and entertainment/news preference measures, this survey assessed participants' product category preferences, habits, and involvement levels for restaurant dining, music, and car buying. Car buying served as a "foil product" (i.e., it was included to reduce attention to the test categories). Involvement levels were measured in order to assess the impact of a priori product category interest. Product category involvement was measured using a 10-item scale based on Zaichkowsky (1986). Participants were not told how, or whether, any of the pretest survey information would be used.

Study Design and Procedure. The study involved two hour-long sessions at a university media lab, with sessions taking place on different days. During the first one-hour online session, participants were given instructions in how to use the system and how to access web-based information. They were not exposed to any advertising banners nor told about the Signature Cafe and Music World web sites. Exposure to the advertising banners took place during the second online use session, which took place one to three days later. Each participant's online activity also was recorded and stored in a user log.

Rather than having a commercial message on screen at all times (as some online services do), this study employed an intermittent ad approach similar to the advertising model used in radio and TV broadcasting. An attempt was made, using computer software that tracked the number of user "hits" (i.e., information requests), to ensure that all participants were exposed to both personalized advertising banners. On an individual user's fourth and seventh hits, the program would access the database that contained the user's dining and music preferences. On the fourth hit, the banner promoting the Signature Cafe appeared at the top center of the computer screen (i.e., at the beginning of the article or information the user requested). On the seventh hit, the banner promoting Music World appeared at the top center of the computer screen. The position and prominence of the banners was constant for all participants.

As a result of an unanticipated participant behavior, the exploratory study employed a quasi-experimental design. In order for participants to be exposed to the personalized advertising banners, they had to request (i.e., access) current (rather than archival) Protopaper news/entertainment articles. To see the first banner, they had to request at least four current articles; to see the second banner, they had to request/access three more (i.e., a total of seven). As a result of this computer programming requirement, eight participants were never exposed to a personalized advertising banner (in effect, becoming an a unexposed "control" group). Figure 7.1 summarizes the final study design.

Dependent Measures. A range of attitudinal and intention measures was employed. Multi-item, seven-point semantic differential measures were used to assess attitude toward the advertisement, attitude toward the advertiser, and shopping intent. A personalization manipulation check measure was embedded in the semantic differential items (i.e., participants were asked to indicate where the ad fell on a 7-point "personal-impersonal" scale). Other dependent measures assessed participants': (1) interest in online advertising and product information, (2) likeliness to subscribe to, and pay for, an online computer service, and (3) privacy concerns.

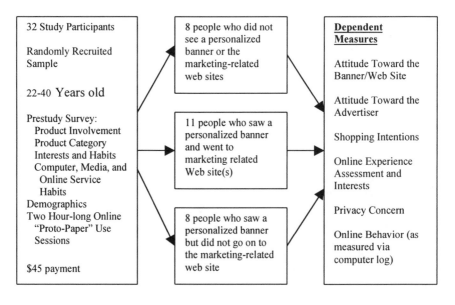

Fig. 7.1. Study design and overview.

RESULTS

Descriptive and comparative analyses were used to assess the impact of personalization on viewers' reactions to the personalized banners as well as to the marketing-related Web sites (see Fig. 7.2 for a summary of findings). In addition to comparing the responses of those who went to the marketing-related Web site to those who did not, pre- and posttest responses were examined to identify potential explanatory or predictive variables. Overall, the results suggested personalization increased the effectiveness of advertising banners and that some online user characteristics may, in fact, be positively correlated with clicking behaviors (please see Figure 7.2). In addition, the general pattern of results lent much support to the conceptual model.

Online Behaviors. In the course of the two online sessions, the 27 people who participated in both sessions generated 2,715 content-related hits, either of HTML pages containing text stories, links to text stories, or audio stories. Of these, 85% involved news-related content. Of the 19 people exposed to a personalized banner, 11 went on to view the marketing-related web site, with all but one person viewing both sites. Eight of the participants who were exposed to a personalized banner did not go on to either site, while an additional eight participants were never exposed to a personalized banner or the marketing-related web sites.

Advertising-Related Attitudes, Perceptions, and Shopping Intentions. The 11 participants who went to the marketing-related web sites after being exposed to the personalized advertising banner had generally favorable attitudes toward both banners/web sites (a combined measure). Overall attitude toward the Music World advertising banner and web site averaged 5.1 (with 7 representing the highest possible rating) on the 5-item measure, while attitude toward the Signature Cafe banner and site averaged 4.6. Importantly, the results also indicated that personalization did not appear to alienate those participants who saw the banner but did not go on to the Web site. For example, banner clickers and nonclickers perceived the two banners the same with respect to irritating-pleasantness (i.e., x = 4.7 on a 7-point semantic differential scale where 7 represented "pleasant"); cleverness (i.e., x = 4.8 on a 7-point semantic differential scale where 7 represented "clever"); personalization (i.e., x = 5.2 on a 7-point semantic differential scale where 7 equaled "personal"); and relevance (i.e., x = 5.1 on a 7-point semantic differential scale where 7 equaled "relevant to me").

The two sets of advertising banners/Web sites had similarly positive responses on viewers' attitude toward the advertiser and shopping intentions. In the case of the advertiser, attitude toward Music World averaged 4.9 (where 7 represented the highest rating), and attitude toward Signature Cafe averaged 5.0. In terms of purchase intention (i.e., intention to visit the store or restaurant), those who accessed the web sites tended to exhibit more positive inclinations. Participants who saw only the banner averaged 4.6 on the two-item intention measure (where 7 represented the highest likelihood), yet those who went on to the web site averaged 5.3. The difference, which approached statistical significance (i.e., $p = .08$), suggested personalization may have potentially positive carryover effects.

Online Experience. Relatedly, participants who clicked-on to the Music World and Signature Cafe web sites rated their online experience more favorably than participants who never went beyond the promotional banners. With respect to the online use experience, those who responded positively to the personalized advertising banners rated the *Protopaper* experience more favorably on 7-point semantic differential scales involving "unexciting-exciting" (i.e., $x = 6.2$ vs. 4.9, $p < .05$) and "difficult to use-easy to use" (i.e., $x = 6.5$ vs. 5.6, $p < .05$). Although the small sample size generally provided too little statistical power to detect other differences, the pattern of results for the other experience items did suggest those who visited the marketing-related web sites were more likely to perceive use of computer-mediated newspapers as "interesting," "fun to do," and "enjoyable."

Further evidence that personalized advertising banners likely have an overall positive impact, especially on motivation to process information, was provided by the posttest survey measures that attempted to capture participant's assessments of the online experience. Those who responded favorably to the advertising banners (i.e., clicked-on it to view the web site) had higher average scores on a 7-point "enjoyed doing--didn't enjoy doing" scale (i.e., $x = 6.7$ vs. 5.5, $p < .05$) as well as higher scores on two "use experience" indices. The first index, a 7-item semantic differential scale that involved bipolar adjectives, characterized the use experience. This index indicated that participants who responded to the banners characterized their use experience more positively than participants who did not click-through or see an advertising banner (i.e., $x = 6.4$ vs. 5.5, $p = .05$). Based on the scale items, those that clicked-on generally rated the experience quite favorably with respect to interesting, easy-to-use, fun-to-do, and pleasant. The second index, which involved nine bipolar adjectives that could be used to describe the *Protopaper*, resulted in average scores of 5.9 for those who clicked-on the banners versus 5.0 for those who did not. Based on the scale items, participants who accessed the restaurant and music store web sites were more likely to describe the *Protopaper* in such terms as "friendly," "appealing," "fast," "entertaining," and "informative."

Information and Online Interest. The pretest survey revealed relatively modest participant interest in having immediate, 24 hours per day to access product and service information, newspaper classified advertising, and local restaurant guides and menus (i.e., $x's = 3.2, 3.1$, and 2.6, respectively, on 5-point interest scales). However, after being exposed to and clicking-on the personalized advertising banner, participants' interest levels increased. Although the increase was not statistically significant for information about products and services (x = 3.6 vs. 3.2), it was significant at the p = .06 probability level for interest in newspaper classified advertising (x = 4.2 vs. 3.1) as well as restaurant guides/menus (x = 3.6 vs. 2.6).

Participants who clicked on to the Music World and Signature Café Club web sites also exhibited greater interest in online services than those who did not access those sites. These participants had a higher likelihood to subscribe to an online computer service (x = 3.6 vs. 2.4 on a 5-point likelihood scale) as well as to subscribe to an electronic newspaper (x = 3.9 vs. 2.1, $p's$ < .01). Most indicated they would even being willing to pay more for a subscription to an electronic newspaper than for a subscription to a printed newspaper (x = 2.7 vs. 1.8, p < .05). In addition, participants who viewed the two marketing-related Web sites indicated a greater likelihood to order a product or service that they saw advertised in an electronic newspaper than participants who did not access the sites (x = 3.4 vs. 2.4, p < .05).

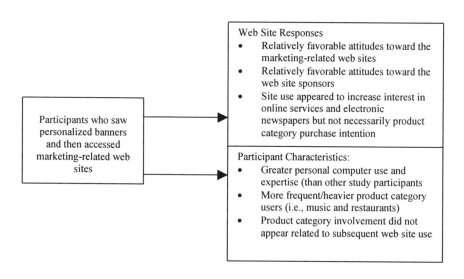

Fig. 7.2. Banner personalization summary findings.

Privacy Concern and Online Behavior. The study did not find differences between the two groups of participants with respect to privacy concern or global online behaviors (i.e., average length of time people in different groups spent using the various offerings). With respect to "concerned about the privacy issues associated with electronic newspapers," both groups of participants (i.e., those who responded favorably to the personalized banner and those who did not/did not see a banner) indicated they "neither agreed nor disagreed" (i.e., $x's$ = 2.8, 3.3 on a 5-point scale). Although a comparison of pre- and posttest privacy responses for those who responded favorably to the personalized banners did not achieve statistical significance, the possibility that personalization increases privacy deserves needs further examination. Average privacy concern scores after exposure were $\underline{x}$ = 3.9 (vs. 3.3), but the sample sizes in the study did not offer the statistical power necessary to adequately examine this issue. As for online behavior, the analyses of computer log data failed to reveal any differences between those who responded favorably to personalized advertising banners and the other study participants. For example, the total number of hits did not differ between groups nor did average number of sites visited.

DISCUSSION AND CONCLUSIONS

Advocates of online and marketing-related web sites frequently cite message targeting and personalization as significant advantages of computer-mediated media over traditional advertising media (Forrest, Kinney, & Chamberlain, 1995; Hoffman & Novak, 1996; McGinty, 1996). Although efforts to document and understand consumer processing and responses to computer-mediated advertising are just beginning, initial notions that marketing messages will need to move from "intrusive commercials" to "invited conversations" appear to have much merit. Thus, one of the main challenges facing online marketers is finding effective ways to "offer polite invitations" that initiate or foster dialogues with individual consumers (Schrage, Peppers, Rogers, & Shapiro, 1994).

Although the sample size in the present study precluded extensive data analyses, the fact that a number of statistically significant differences were detected with a randomly selected sample suggests message personalization is one useful approach. Further, along with documenting the utility of message personalization, this study's findings also lend insight into the conceptual underpinnings of such strategies in interactive media environments.

Participants' responses indicated that message personalization generally enhanced the effectiveness of web site banners. Personalization increased the likelihood that online users would access the marketing-related web site and appeared to contribute to favorable perceptions regarding both the web site and its sponsor. Importantly, neither of the personalized banners used in this study was viewed as intrusive or annoying. Rather, most of the participants who were exposed to a personalized banner rated them highly in terms of creativity and relevance.

Along with indicating that personalized banners facilitate positive responses toward the marketing web site and its sponsor, this study provided evidence that personalization may have significant carryover effects. In this case, these effects ranged from more favorable impressions regarding the online environment to poststudy increases in participants' interest in related information services. Compared to other study participants, those participants who utilized the personalized banners had more favorable impressions regarding the content provider (i.e., the Protopaper) and also exhibited higher posttest interest in online restaurant guides, classified advertising, and obtaining product/service information via an interactive medium. Overall, personalization also appeared to contribute to users' positive impressions regarding the ease, enjoyment, and utility of online advertising and interactive media information sources such as the *Protopaper*. Although the results do not shed light on the reasons for these impressions, the notion that personalization serves to make the online environment more "user friendly" and/or "meaningful" is worth further examination.

Consistent with MacInnis et al.'s (1989, 1991) integrative information processing framework, the impact of personalization was essentially twofold. First, it appeared using names and product category preferences provided execution cues that increased participants' motivation to attend to marketing-related information. In this case, over half the participants who were exposed to a personalized banner responded favorably. Second, the increased processing effects generated as a result of positively responding to a personalized banner appeared to be relatively modest. Rather than induce extensive brand processing, banner responders' attitudinal, intention, and interest responses reflected an overall response pattern indicative of low-level information processing. This pattern includes increased interest in the advertising medium as well as favorable attitudes toward the ad and advertiser, but little apparent impact on shopping or purchasing intentions (MacInnis & Jaworski, 1989). These findings suggest that while personalization can be an effective mechanism for inducing online users to access a marketing-related web site, it is not a strategy that is likely to predispose high involvement processing at the site. The level of processing that takes place once a user is at the web site appears to be primarily, if not exclusively, a function of the web site's structure, content, and features.

Based on the integrative framework, the results obtained here also suggest that attitudes toward a web site and its sponsor are influenced by favorable perceptions regarding the information environment or context. As in the case of television advertising, it appears there is significant potential for program and/or medium context effects to shape consumers' attitudes toward online advertising and advertisers. Unfortunately, this study's design precluded examining issues involving relative attitude strength (e.g., did exposure to the personalized banners affect nonresponders attitudes toward Signature Cafe or Music World?) or programming/editorial context. Thus, future studies need to address whether personalized banners, in and of themselves, have affective or cognitive effects (i.e., do they have effects independent of the web site?) as well as whether users' cognitive or emotional reactions to a particular online environment affects their responses to sponsor's advertising.

Figure 7.2 also illustrates that participant characteristics may play an important role when it comes to banner or message personalization in an interactive environment. This study's results suggest that advertising responsiveness, particularly with respect to accessing additional product information, is affected by a user's computer experience and product category behavior. Based on the results of the pretest consumer interest questionnaire, study participants who positively responded to the personalized banners were more likely to own a personal computer with a modem, more likely to subscribe to an online computer service, and be more frequent restaurant diners and music purchasers. Such a finding implies that banner personalization strategies would be particularly effective for products and services marketed toward "heavy" online users as well as "heavy" product category or brand users. It also suggests that consumers' media experience/expertise and product category experience may mediate their responsiveness to personalized banners or messages. In either case, the answers will only come through further research. This research is needed to examine the propensity of experienced online or product category users to positively respond to such messages as well as determine which has the strongest relationship - product category experience or interactive media experience. In addition, uncertainty remains regarding what relationships, if any, exist between product category involvement and personalized advertising messages.

In conjunction with identifying productive areas for future research, this study's findings raise important practical considerations regarding banner and message personalization. Despite their utility - and the high levels of support and enthusiasm engendered among online media and database technology providers - personalization strategies can have significant shortcomings. First, online marketers should remain cognizant of potential consumer privacy concerns. The data in this study, while statistically inconclusive, highlighted the possibility that personalized messages can increase privacy concerns - even among consumers who have a known product category interest. Until more extensive research is conducted, and more is known about the relationships between information use and privacy concerns, online marketers would likely benefit from adopting the information guidelines and practices utilized by responsible direct marketers. These include avoiding inappropriate use or disclosure of sensitive information (e.g., financial data), integrating consumer-relevant rather than irrelevant personal data into promotion messages or banners, and keeping consumers informed regarding information attainment and use (Nowak & Phelps, 1995). Although many of the consumers in this study did not appear to be inherently or automatically averse to banner or message personal-ization, the lack of widespread consumer acceptance of online advertising and promotion suggests online marketers should be very selective with personalized messages.

Relatedly, online marketers should carefully consider which consumer information is integrated into personalized banners or messages. Some personalization strategies, particularly those that utilize immediately recognizable information (e.g., names) may facilitate attainment of some advertising goals (e.g., attract attention) while simultaneously hindering attainment of other objectives (e.g., more extensive information processing). As direct mail industry practitioners can attest, simple personalization strategies, while often effective at attracting immediate attention, frequently provide only a temporary novelty effect. The strongest and most enduring personalization effects are likely to result from the meaningful use of behavioral and lifestyle data. Some of the personalization effects found in this study may have resulted from utilizing both name and consumer preference data. It thus would be useful to undertake studies that assess the independent contributions of the two approaches. Although fewer online users may notice and respond to banners that utilize only behavior or lifestyle data (i.e., they are less obviously recognized as being personalized), over the longer term, marketers who employ such a strategy may accrue at least two significant advantages. First, better prospects – that is, consumers who are responding to a banner as a result of actual product or service interest. And second, better marketing communications - that is, customized banners and messages that are more reflective of, and relevant to, the personalized, interactive nature of the Internet.

REFERENCES

Ahl, L D., & Temes, P. (1996, July 22). Evaluating web banner advertising. *Direct Marketing News, 18*, p. 16.

Aho Williamson, D. (1996a, January 22). Marketers link up to tune of $54.7 million. *Advertising Age*, 28.

Aho Williamson, D. (1996b, October 21). A banner year: What Web ads need to Succeed. *Advertising Age*, 1,43-44, 46, 48-51.

Aho Williamson, D. (1996c, November 4). Banners to bots, publishers vie for right model. *Advertising Age*, p. S6.

Aho Williamson, D. (1995, November 20). Searching for a pot of gold. *Advertising Age*, p. S2, S4.

Akaah, I. P., & Korgaonkar, P. K. (1988). A conjoint investigation of the relative importance of risk relievers in direct marketing, *Journal of Advertising Research, 28*(4), 38-45.

Beard, J. D., Williams, D. L., & Kelly, J. P. (1990, Winter). The long versus short letter: A large sarnple study of a direct mail campaign. *Journal of Direct Marketing, 4*, 13-20.

Bush, A.J., Bush, V. & Harris, S. (1998, March/April). Advertiser perceptions of the Internet as a marketing communications tool. *Journal of Advertising Research, 38*(2), 17-27.

Business: Caught in the net. (1998, September). *Economist, 34*(80), 87.

Cleland, K. (1995, November 11). E-mail offered for free. *Advertising Age*, 1,6.

Cleland, K. (1996, November 4). Web narrows gap between ads, editorial. *Advertising Age*, p. S3,S14.

Demo. (1996, February). How big is the net. *American Demographics, 18*(2), 8.

Ellsworth, J. H. (1995, June). Boom Town. *Internet World*, *6*, 33-35.

Emerick, T. (1996). Media and marketing strategies for the Internet. In E. Forrest & R. Mizerski (Eds.), *Interactive media: The future present.* Lincolnwood, IL: NTC Publishing, 174-214.

Fawcett, A. W. (1996, October 14). Online users go for facts over fun. *Advertising Age*, 46,51.

Find/SVP. (1996, January 15). Net population: 'The latest numbers," *Advertising Age*, 15, 38.

Flynn, L. J. (1996, February 13). Start-ups plot to make the Web comfortable for advertisers. *New York Times*, p. D3.

Forrest, E., Kinney, L., & Chamberlain M. (1996). The impact of interactive communication on advertising and marketing. In E. Forrest & R. Mizerski (Eds.), *Interactive marketing - The future present.* Lincolnwood, IL: NTC Business Books, 135-148.

Harrison, D. (1996, October 14). Consumers oppose online tracking for targeted marketing. *Direct Marketing News, 16*, pp. 1,50.

Hodges, J. (1996, August 26). Only for you: Web publishers get personal. *Advertising Age*, 17.

Hoffman, D., & Novak, T. P. (1996, July). Marketing in hypermedia computer-mediated enviromnents: Conceptual foundations. *Journal of Marketing, 60*, 50-68.

Holmes, J. H., & Urban, W. A. (1989, Spring). Selected effects of headline gender and spokesperson gender in direct response advertising. *Journal of Direct Marketing, 3*, 6-14.

Jaffee, L. (1996a, January 29) 12.4 million in Web ads in 4Q '95. *Direct Marketing News, 18*, 10.

Jaffee, L. (1996b, May 27). Ad banners, links and tracking build list company's Web services. *Direct Marketing News, 18*, 19,21.

Jones, S. K. (1990). *Creative strategy in direct marke ing.* Lincolnwood, IL: NTC Publishing.

Judson, B. (1996*). NetMarketing: How your business can profit from the online revolution.* New York: Wolff New Media.

MacInnis, D. J., & Jaworski, B. J. (1989, October). Information processing from advertisements: Toward an integrative framework. *Journal of Marketing, 53*, 1-23.

MacInnis, D. J., Moorman, C., & Jaworski, B. J. (1991, October). Enhancing and measuring consumers' motivation, opportunity, and ability to process brand information from ads. *Journal of Marketing, 55*, 32-53.

Magill, K (1998, August 3). Merchants – not consumers – are blocking e-commerce, study says. *Direct Marketing News, 20*, 19-20.

Mand, A. (1998, September 14). Actng up. *Mediaweek, 8*(34), p. S32.

McGinty, R. (1996, November 4). The online marketer's killer app: Personalization. *Direct Marketing News, 16,*39.

Mehta, R., & Sivadas, E. (1995). Direct marketing on the Internet: An empirical assessment of consumer attitudes. *Journal of Direct Marketing, 9*(3), 21-32.

Moran, C. (1997, January). Web trek. *Potentials in Marketing*, 22-25.

Nowak, G. J., & Phelps, J. (1995). Direct marketing and the use of individual-level consumer information: Determining how and when "privacy" matters. *Journal of Direct Marketing, 9*(3), 46-60.

Nowak, G.J., Cameron, G.T. & Krugman, D.M. (1993). How local advertisers choose and use advertising media. *Journal of Advertising Research, 33*(6), 39-49.

Nowak, G. J., Price, P., & Lewis, P. (1995, March). Let's get personal: The cognitive and attitudinal effects of "personalizing" print ads. Paper presented at the 1995 conference of the American Academy of Advertising, Norfolk, VA.

Read, B. B. (1996a, February 12). Mainstream alternative for advertisers. *Direct Marketing News*, 2.

Read, B. B. (1996b, March 25). Net result: Consumers will control electronic marketing. *Direct Marketing News*, 1,46.

Read, B. B. (1996c, August 26). Web ad sales double; IBM, Microsoft, Netscape lead. *Direct Marketing News*, 19.

Rossi, P. E., McCullough, R.E., & Allenby, G. M. (1994). Is household-specific targeting worth it? *MSI Report No. 94-118*, Cambridge, MA: Marketing Science Institute.

Schrage, M., Peppers, D., Rogers, M., & Shapiro, R. D. (1994). Is advertising finally dead? Part 2. *Wired Magazine, Issue 2.02*, pp. 22-26.

Taylor, C. (1995, May 29). Slow lane: Anatomy of an interactive ad. *Media Week*, 10-13.

Web ad revenues. (1998, April 6). Jupiter Communications, press release.

Zaichkowsky, J. L. (1986). Conceptualizing involvement. *Journal of Advertisng, 15*(2), 4-14,34.

8

Sophistication on the World Wide Web: Evaluating Structure, Function, and Commercial Goals of Web Sites

Charles Frazer
University of Oregon

Sally J. McMillan
Boston University

In the mid-to late-1990s, the World Wide Web (web) exploded into public consciousness. But while the early growth was fast, it was not certain. For example, in 1996, estimates of Internet audience ranged from 5.8 million to 24 million (Johnson, 1996). But difficulty in estimating audience size was just one of the problems that plagued web researchers. Equally important concerns were the characteristics and purposes of marketing-oriented web sites.

Another significant concern of early web-based researchers was evaluation of the extent to which commercial web sites were designed to take advantage of the unique characteristics of this emerging medium. Had marketers escaped what Rogers (quoted in Weinberger, 1996) and Rust and Oliver (1994) called "the mass-marketing mind-set?" Some web site developers argued that Internet culture dictates a different form and level of address from that of traditional advertising (Bray, 1995). Had developers heeded this admonition? Upshaw (1995) suggested that the Internet and other interactive media offer an advanced form of relationship marketing that focuses on brand-building rather than price-cutting. Had online commercial sites taken advantage of brand-building opportunities?

Exploration of these questions presented a challenge. By 1996, *The New York Times* (Gabriel, 1996) estimated the web might contain between 90,000 and 265,000 sites. This study aimed to examine the uses that marketers made of the web in the first year of commercial access to this computer-mediated communication technology. Rather than seeking to sample from an unknown number of sites, only some of which would be commercial in use, the research-ers chose to examine sites that had received news coverage in *Advertising Age*, a leading advertising and marketing publication with a circulation of 86,000 (Braun, 1996). *Advertising Age* began publication of web addresses in November 1994 and has since served as a visible source of ongoing coverage of issues related to online marketing and marketing communication.

REVIEW OF LITERATURE

Because of the rapidly evolving nature of the Internet and the explosion of commercial activity on the World Wide Web, numerous topics related to computer-mediated communication (CMC) and online marketing communi-cation often receive coverage in both traditional media and online sources. This paper seeks to establish a baseline for discussion of web advertising by examining five key topics: the structure of commercial web sites, functional interactivity within the sites, commercial goals of online communication, analogies to other types of marketing communication, and the types of businesses that have developed a commercial presence on the Internet.

Structure

Much of the literature contrasts the structure of the World Wide Web with other more traditional media types. For example, Strangelove (1994) suggested that the Internet is "first and foremost an oral culture . . . . Sensitivity to Internet culture will define success for any business entering into this global matrix" (p. 4). Hoffman and Novak (1995) identified the unique characteristics of the web as computer-mediation, hypermedia, machine-interactivity, network navigation, and telepresence. Rheingold (1993) suggested that as communication becomes digitized, it can carry "everything that humans can perceive and machines can process - voice, high-fidelity sound, text, high-resolution color graphics, computer programs, data, full-motion video" (p. 75).

Neuman (1991) suggested that interactive, computer-mediated communi-cation has the potential to break down distinctions between print and broadcast media and empower individuals to choose media modalities that are most conducive to individual learning styles and entertainment preferences. Negroponte (1995) stated that computer-mediated communication facilitates personalization of media messages. Text, graphics, motion, and sound can all be brought together into a customized form of communication that he characterizes as *The Daily Me*. He extends this concept to commercial messages as he stated that "advertising will be so personalized that it is indistinguishable from news. It *is* news" (p. 170).

Analysts seem to agree that the structure of the Internet is marked by media diversity. It is characterized as multimedia. December (1996) described the Internet as a range of media rather than a single medium. It integrates capabilities of many existing media into a highly flexible and personalized communication tool.

The characteristics of flexibility and personalization are an important element of this new medium. However, neither the trade nor academic literature offers much specific guidance on how to structure sites to facilitate this flexible personalization while also taking full advantage of mutlimedia capabilities of the Web.

The foregoing suggests that the Web offers a vast array of capabilities for commercial communication. The extent to which these structural capabilities are designed into commercial web sites is a matter of considerable interest because it may provide indications about more effective implementation.

Function

A primary function of CMC is its capacity for interactive communication. Rafaeli (1988) defined *interactivity* as recognizing three pertinent levels: "two-way (non-interactive) communication, reactive (or quasi-interactive) communication, and fully interactive communication" (p. 119). Morris and Ogan (1996) suggested that interactivity can be variable in nature, "increasing or decreasing with the particular Internet service in question" (p. 46). And December (1996) suggests that interaction may occur either in "real time" or through the use of on-demand retrieval systems.

Dorsher (1996) noted that "unlike the one-way communication of other mass media, which have many message receivers and relatively few senders, computer networks let every user be a receiver and a sender. The Internet allows two-way mass communication, from the many to the many" (p. 11). Hoffman and Novak (1995) suggested that the interactive capabilities of CMC offer a radical departure from traditional marketing environments. The many-to-many communication model of interactive communication enhances the persuasion function of marketing communication by enabling a two-way flow of communication between producers and consumers. Grunig and Hunt (1984) also emphasized the importance of two-way communication in building long-term relationships between organizations and publics.

Rust and Oliver (1994) portrayed this new world of interactive commercial communication as having potentially positive impacts on both producers and consumers. "The information superhighway will become the global electronic supermarket of the 1990s, uniting producers and consumers directly, instantly, and interactively. Advertising will be transformed from *involuntary* (and necessarily intrusive) to *voluntary* (and sought out)" (p. 73). Lappin (1995) warned that interactive marketing could take a less idealized form:

> What if a decade or so from now, we wake up to find that the digisphere has been overrun by swarms of inane mass marketers - people who believe that "interacting" is something you do with a set-top box that provides only an endless stream of movies-on-demand, bargains overflowing from virtual shopping malls, and spiffy videogames? (p. 176)

Lappin's pessimism is based on a noninteractive view of the Web's development. The promise and power of commercial CMC is based on the view that it can transcend traditional marketing communication tools through the promise of full interactivity. Thus, the extent to which interactivity is achieved by contemporary marketers is important. Examination can indicate the direction of future evolution of the Web.

Commercial Goals

What are the goals of marketers in the multimedia, interactive environment of the Internet? Although an examination of the full range of marketer goals is beyond the scope of this study, one distinction can be readily examined: the extent to which price promotion is emphasized over brand building.

Andersen Consulting has started to experiment with the use of interactivity to address a price sensitive market. The company's BargainFinder instructs the virtual shopper to "Just type in the artist and album name of a rock or pop CD. Then sit back as your agent gets prices from nine virtual retailers" (Andersen Consulting, 1996). The company is also conducting an online survey that includes a question about user acceptance of advertising to support price-oriented online shopping. As of April 1996, the company reported that 26% of survey respondents "would like stores to use online advertising to let them keep service up while keeping prices down."

Online retailers seem to be less than enthusiastic about automated price shopping. In a sample search, three of the nine virtual music stores that were searched by BargainFinder returned the message that the store is blocking out search agents.

Upshaw (1995) suggested that price-oriented messages are less appropriate in interactive media than are brand-building communications. He indicated that buyer action in the interactive marketing environment establishes a connection between the buyer and the brand. CMC offers the potential to strengthen and intensify brand relationships and involvement.

The extent to which CMC can be used to develop or reinforce brand equity is a vital area of exploration for marketers. If it is used simply as a form of discounting or price promotion, the Web is unlikely to have profound impact on marketing practice.

Internet Marketing Typology

Hoffman, Novak, and Chatterjee (1995) proposed a typology of commercial web sites based on analogies to traditional forms of marketing communication. They suggested six functional categories of commercial web pages: online storefront, Internet presence, content, mall, incentive site, and search agents.

Online storefronts offer direct sales via an electronic catalog or other more innovative format. Marketing communication in these environments may resemble point-of-purchase sales promotions. This model combines elements of direct marketing with in-store shopping and it "has the potential to be vastly more efficient than either." However, it is currently inhibited by the slow transmission of online communication and by marketers' lack of knowledge about online shopping behavior.

Internet presence sites may take the form of flat ads with simple nonlinked information, image sites that have an emotional appeal to the consumer, or information sites that provide detailed rational information about the firm and/or its offerings. Flat ads resemble magazine advertising. Image sites combine the kind of entertainment and corporate message that might be associated with corporate sponsorship of sporting events. Information sites often resemble corporate brochures. Hoffman, Novak, and Chatterjee (1995) suggested that the primary purpose of Internet presence sites is to build a relationship with the consumer even before the need to purchase a product arises. However, they noted that one of the biggest challenges for these types of sites is developing an appropriate application for the online medium.

Content sites can be fee-based, sponsored, or searchable databases. Content sites most closely resemble our current notions of traditional media -- virtual equivalents of newspapers, magazines, radio, and television - all live online. Marketers can profit from these sites either through subscription fees or the more traditional purchase of an advertising message that supports the site. One of the primary challenges identified for this type of site is the question of how to measure and optimize consumer response to advertising in sponsored content sites.

Mall sites are typically a collection of online storefronts. Virtual mall managers provide many of the same marketing communication services of their real-world counterparts - traffic development, joint promotions, and so on. Incentive sites are a unique form of advertising that attracts a potential customer to a site. These types of sites may be used in settings like malls to increase traffic to other types of commercial sites.

Finally, search agents are designed to identify other web sites through a keyword search of a database that extends throughout the Web. Hoffman, Novak and Chatterjee (1985) suggested that search agents offer novel ways to generate traffic to commercial sites, but they also note that the proliferation of commercial sites might limit the effectiveness of search agents for generating traffic to any specific site.

The Hoffman, Novak, and Chatterjee (1985) typology suggests a wide range of commercial activity on the Web. It would be useful for both marketing and academic research purposes to understand the relative size of each of the categories as an assessment of their significance.

Business Types

As of April 12, 1996, there were 26,012 firms listed in Open Market's (1996) commercial sites index. This lists almost twice as many Net sites as Hoffman, Novak, and Chatterjee (1995) found in a similar search just seven months earlier. In the same time period, the Yahoo *Business and Economic Directory* (1996) listing for companies increased from 23,540 to 63,422. Table 8.1 presents the 20 product and service categories with the highest number of listings in the Yahoo directory as of April 12, 1996.

TABLE 8.1
Top 20 Categories in Yahoo Product and Service Directory (Total = 63,422)

Category	Number of Sites	Percentage	Category	Number of Sites	Percentage
Apparel	2,270	3.58	Entertainment	300	0.47
Travel	1,650	2.60	Automotive	172	0.27
Magazines	1,589	2.51	Advertising	150	0.24
Computers	1,150	1.81	Animals	142	0.22
Food	1,060	1.67	Get Rich Quick!	136	0.21
Busi. Opport.	872	1.37	Security	120	0.19
Health	765	1.21	Financial Services	109	0.17
Drinks	569	0.90	Religion	107	0.17
Sports	562	0.89	Children	95	0.15
Personals	356	0.56	Education	91	0.14

The Internet is in its infancy and marketers have yet to determine what products and services are best served by the web. Williamson (1995) suggested that "companies - especially major marketers - that went up because it was the trendy thing to do will undoubtedly look back on the hundreds of thousands of dollars they spent and not know what they are getting for it" (p. S2). Williamson noted the importance of developing a business plan to determine if a particular product or service is suited to web marketing.

METHODOLOGY

The study described here examined the content of web sites that have received news coverage in *Advertising Age,* a leading advertising trade magazine that began publication of web addresses in November 1994. All web sites listed in *Advertising Age* for a one-year period from November 1994 through October 1995 were examined. Overall, 201 sites were found; 156 (78%) of those sites were functioning at the time of the study. A full list of the sites is available from the authors. Seven coders were trained to use a content analysis form, and coders spent a total of about 30 hours examining the sites. Holsti's intercoder reliability formula yielded a score of 88.1% for the 10% of sites that were cross coded.

Research Questions

Three research questions guided this study:

1. What structural elements define these sites and how is structure related to the Internet marketing typology used in the site and the business type of the site sponsor?
2. How have these sites implemented interactivity with potential consumers and how is the interactive function related to the Internet marketing typology used in the site and the business type of the site sponsor?
3. What is the balance of price-oriented versus brand-building messages in these sites and how are these commercial goals related to the Internet marketing typology used in the site and the business type of the site sponsor?

Operationalizing Variables

Coders were instructed in categorizing sites both in terms of Internet marketing types and business types. The list of business types was based on the most common categories to emerge during pretesting. Because neither the Internet marketing types nor the business types are mutually exclusive, coders were allowed to classify a site using one or more of these categories.

Structure of the sites was operationalized by creating an index that measures whether sites include multiple media (text and graphics) as well as other common structural elements: a "table of contents," hypertext links within the site, a menu bar at the bottom of the first page, a menu bar on subsequent pages, and a mechanism on secondary pages that provides quick return to the first page. The scale ranges from 0 to 7 with a score of 0 indicating none of these structural features are included in the site, and a score of 7 indicating a site includes all these structural features. Cronbach's alpha for this index is .52.

Function was operationalized by creating a 4-point scale based on inclusion of interactive elements: e-mail hot link, toll-free phone number, online-ordering capability, and online customer support. Cronbach's alpha for this index is .36. Selling presentation was operationalized by the coders' report of whether the site had no selling message, a price-based message, a brand-building message, or a mixed price/brand message.

RESULTS

Because of the relatively small sample size, some of the Internet marketing types and business types were collapsed for the sake of analysis. The Internet marketing types identified by Hoffman, Novak, and Chatterjee (1995) were grouped into the following eight categories (numbers in parentheses are number of sites coded as having characteristics of this Internet marketing type): Internet presence - information (97), Internet presence - image (51), content - sponsored (20), storefronts and online malls (17), content - fee based and searchable (13), search agents (11), and other Internet marketing types - including flat ads (11).

The business types were grouped into the following 11 categories (numbers in parentheses are number of sites coded as representing each type of business): clothing and entertainment (35), online media (31), other business types (28), computer-related (22), advertising and public relations (18), automotive and financial (14), telecommunications and travel (14), food and beverage (13), interactive design (13), directories and malls (12), and sports (10).

Three of these groupings require additional explanation. Clothing and entertainment were grouped together because both of these categories represent relatively low-cost products and services that could be impulse purchases. By contrast, automotive and financial categories were grouped together because they represent higher-cost products and services that are more often a considered purchase. Finally, telecommunications and travel were grouped together because each had relatively few examples in this sample and because both represent a product or service that has high potential for utilizing the unique capabilities of CMC. Travel-related sites could have a high level of interactivity by allowing consumers to customize travel arrangements and eliminate the need for travel agents. Telecommunication functions are central to the current operation of computer-mediated communication.

The business types used in this study do not exactly parallel the most common categories of product/service listings in the Yahoo directory (see Table 8.1); however, there is a high degree of similarity. The top six categories from Table 8.1 are all included in this list. Thus, *Advertising Age* coverage of commercial sites seems representative of major categories of products and services marketed on the Internet.

Structure

These sites lack multimedia characteristics. Overall, 72% of the sites used only two types of content - most often text and still graphics. Only 10% added audio communication and 14% included moving video.

Tables 8.2 and 8.3 report the relationship between the structure index (which measures the number of structural elements that help guide a user through the site) and the categories of Internet marketing types and business types. For each category, two-tailed t tests were used to determine if there is a significant difference in the mean structural index score for sites coded as members of the category and all other sites.

TABLE 8.2
Analysis of Structure Index and Internet Marketing Types

	Items in Category			Not in Category			
	Mean	N	SD	Mean	N	SD	t
Search Agent	6.55	11	.69	5.55	145	1.36	2.39*
Presence/Image	5.78	51	1.22	5.54	105	1.41	1.10
Presence/Information	5.75	97	1.26	5.41	59	1.48	1.50
Content/Sponsored	5.70	20	.98	5.61	136	1.40	.36
Storefront/Mall	5.59	17	1.06	5.63	139	1.39	-.13
Incentive Site	5.50	10	1.18	5.63	146	1.37	-.33
Content/Fee Based							
& Search	5.46	13	1.61	5.64	143	1.33	-.38
Other	5.27	11	1.62	5.65	145	1.33	-.75

$p < .02$, $N = 156$, Scale = 0-7, Index Mean = 5.62, $SD = 1.35$

The positive relationship between the structure index and search agents indicates that these sites use a greater number of organizational tools than do other sites. The positive relationship between the structure index and automotive/financial and directory/mall sites in Table 8.3 suggests that these two business types are also likely to use a high number of organizational tools.

Function

These sites are relatively low in their utilization of the interactive potential of CMC. Of the sites, 50% used one or none of the four interactive capabilities measured by this study. E-mail was the interactive element most often included (in 75% of the sites) followed by toll-free phone numbers (35%), online ordering (27%) and online customer support (24%).

TABLE 8.3
Analysis of Structure Index and Business Types

	Items in Category			Not in Category			
	Mean	N	SD	Mean	N	SD	t
Automotive/Financial	6.36	14	.84	5.55	142	1.37	3.20**
Directory/Mall	6.25	12	.87	5.57	144	1.37	2.48*
Sports	6.20	10	1.03	5.58	146	1.36	1.79
Computer-Related	6.05	22	1.33	5.55	134	1.35	1.61
Telecommunication/							
Travel	5.86	14	1.03	5.60	142	1.38	.87
Online Media	5.84	31	1.27	5.57	125	1.37	1.05
Clothing/Entertainment	5.69	35	1.83	5.60	121	1.40	.35
Food and Beverage	5.54	13	1.51	5.63	143	1.34	-.21
Other	5.32	28	1.49	5.69	128	1.32	-1.20
Interactive Design	5.31	13	1.38	5.65	143	2.68	-.86
Advertising/PR	5.11	18	1.45	5.69	138	1.33	-1.60

** $p < .01$, * $p < .05$, $N = 156$, Scale = 0-7, Index Mean = 5.62, $SD = 1.35$

Tables 8.4 and 8.5 report relationships between the function index (which measures the number of interactive elements in the site) and categories of Internet marketing types and business types. For each category, two-tailed t tests were used to determine if there is a significant difference in the mean function index score for sites coded as members of the category and all other sites.

Search agents emerge in Table 8.4 as the strongest in implementing multiple ways for viewers to contact the organization. Storefront/mall, and content (fee-based and sponsored) sites also show a strong positive relationship with the function index indicating that all of these types of sites provide multiple opportunities for interactivity.

Table 8.5 suggests that advertising and public relations sites are significantly lower than the average on the function index. The mean number of ways that these organizations provide for interaction with possible customers is less than one. This shows that some sites provide no mechanism for two-way communication. Findings reported in Table 8.3, suggest that advertising and public relations sites also have fewer structural elements than other types of sites, although that negative relationship is not statistically significant. These findings may suggest that many advertising and PR agencies are creating web sites without careful consideration of how they will be used.

By contrast, directory/mall sites have a significant positive relationship with the function index reported in Table 8.5 as well as the previously noted significant positive relationship with the structure index (see Table 8.3). Thus, one might conclude that directory/mall sites represent some of the more sophisticated sites in this sample.

TABLE 8.4
Analysis of Function Index and Internet Marketing Types

	Items in Category			Not in Category			
	Mean	N	SD	Mean	N	SD	t
Search Agent	2.55	11	1.04	1.54	145	1.02	3.11**
Storefront/Mall	2.35	17	1.00	1.52	139	1.02	3.25**
Content/Fee Based & Search	2.23	13	1.09	1.55	143	1.03	2.15
Content/Sponsored	1.70	20	.92	1.60	136	1.07	.16
Presence/Information	1.61	97	1.04	1.59	59	1.09	.14
Other	1.54	11	1.13	1.61	145	1.05	-.19
Presence/Image	1.49	51	.97	1.67	105	1.09	-1.03
Incentive Site	1.20	10	1.23	1.64	146	1.04	-1.10

** $p > .01$, * $p < .05$, $N = 156$, Scale = 0-4, Index Mean = 1.61, $SD = 1.05$

TABLE 8.5
Analysis of Function Index and Business Types

	Items in Category			Not in Category			
	Mean	N	SD	Mean	N	SD	t
Directory/Mall	2.67	12	1.23	1.52	144	.99	3.14**
Computer-Related	1.95	22	.95	1.55	134	1.06	1.67
Sports	1.90	10	1.29	1.59	146	1.04	.75
Automotive/Financial	1.86	14	.86	1.58	142	1.07	1.10
Clothing/Entertainment	1.71	35	1.10	1.58	121	1.04	.65
Interactive Design	1.62	13	1.04	1.61	143	1.06	.02
Online Media	1.61	31	1.02	1.61	125	1.06	.02
Other	1.57	28	1.07	1.62	128	1.05	-.21
Food and Beverage	1.46	13	1.05	1.62	143	1.05	-.53
Telecommunication/ Travel	1.29	14	.99	1.64	142	1.05	-1.27
Advertising/PR	.83	18	.71	1.71	138	1.05	-3.44**

** $p < .01$, $N = 156$, Scale = 0-4, Index Mean = 1.61, $SD = 1.05$

Commercial Goals

Price-based selling messages do not seem predominant in this sample of commercial web sites. Only 3% of the sites use a price-based selling message as contrasted with 56% that focus on brand-building. Of the sites, 19% utilized a mixed price/brand strategy and coders indicated that the remaining 23% of the sites contained no selling message.

Tables 8.6 and 8.7 report relationships between the type of selling message used at sites and categories of Internet marketing types and business types. Each category was cross-tabulated with type of selling message; chi-square statistics were used to test for significance. Because of the relatively low number of cases in some of the cells, these tests should be considered as an early baseline that needs further analysis with a greater number of cases.

The strong dominance of brand-building messages is evident in this analysis. Brand-building was more frequently used than price-cutting even at the directory/mall business type sites and the storefront/mall marketing communication-type sites. However, these sites were also the most likely of any in the sample to utilize price-based selling appeals.

TABLE 8.6
Analysis of Selling Message and Internet Marketing Types

	Percent Sites with Selling Message					
	Price	*Brand*	*Mixed*	*None*	*N*	*Chi-Square*
Storefront/Mall	17.6	17.6	29.4	35.3	7	24.30**
Presence/Image	0.0	70.6	19.6	9.8	1	10.75*
Other	0.0	27.3	18.2	54.5	1	7.11
Content/Fee Based & Search	0.0	30.8	30.8	38.5	3	4.54
Presence/Information	1.0	58.8	19.6	20.6	7	3.57
Search Agent	0.0	54.5	36.4	9.1	1	3.32
Content/Sponsored	0.0	45.0	20.0	35.0	0	2.50
Incentive Site	0.0	50.0	10.0	40.0	0	2.09

** $p < .01$, * $p < .05$, $df = 3$

The selling message of Internet presence/image sites is strongly brand oriented. This finding is consistent with the definition of an image site. Advertising and public relations businesses are also likely to focus on a brand building message. A fairly strong (though not statistically significant) use of brand-building messages was also found for food and beverage and computer-related sites.

Finally, the "other" category for business types shows a statistically significant level of sites with no selling message. It is this lack of selling message that relegated many of these sites to the "other" category. Although these sites did appear in the *Advertising Age* sample, many of them do not have a strong marketing orientation. See for example, Amtrak at <http://www.amtrak.com> or Women's Web at <http://www.womweb.com>.

TABLE 8.7
Analysis of Selling Message and Business Types

| | Percent Sites with Selling Message | | | | | |
	Price	Brand	Mixed	None	N	Chi-Square
Directory/Mall	16.7	58.3	16.7	8.3	2	11.35**
Other	0.0	35.7	14.3	50.0	8	14.39**
Advertising/PR	0.0	83.3	0.0	16.7	8	7.44*
Clothing/ Entertainment	2.9	60.0	25.7	11.4	5	4.05
Telecommunication/ Travel	7.1	57.1	7.1	28.6	4	2.55
Food and Beverage	0.0	69.2	23.1	7.7	3	2.43
Interactive Design	0.0	46.2	15.4	38.5	3	2.13
Automotive/ Financial	0.0	57.1	28.6	14.3	4	1.74
Online Media	0.0	54.8	22.6	22.6	1	1.33
Computer-Related	0.0	63.6	18.2	18.2	2	1.21
Sports	0.0	50.0	30.0	20.0	0	1.13

** $p < .01$, * $p < .05$, $df = 3$

Additional Measures

The structure scale and interactive function scale were correlated to determine if there is any relationship between sites that provide multiple structural elements to help guide the user and sites that have a high number of interactive elements. No significant correlation was found ($r = -0.07$).

Finally, the Internet marketing types were cross tabulated with business types. Only two significant relationships were found: Computer-related sites show a positive relationship with Internet presence/information ($r = 4.20$) and clothing/entertainment sites show a positive relationship with Internet presence/image ($r = 5.17$). These relationships are consistent with past marketing practices of the business types. The lack of correlation between other organizational types and the Internet marketing types suggests online venues may be leading to new marketing communication practices, even for highly advertised brands such as automobiles, thus eliminating any clear pattern between business type and Internet marketing type.

DISCUSSION

Future research should examine developments in multimedia to determine if the possibility for a new form of commercial communication is evolving within the structure of computer-mediated communication. Similarly, other general functions of web sites, such as providing a "space" for online community, might be identified and measured to build additional scales for function. A larger sample might also yield more statistically significant analysis of the types of selling messages used in web sites.

Additional research should select sites purposefully to increase total number of cases in each categorical variable. Our analysis is of a relatively small sample but the universe expands daily. Conclusions are also hampered by low coefficients of significance. However, indications from this exploratory study suggest confirmation of the opinions of informed observers.

Sites tended to include many (mean of 5.6 on a 7-point scale) structural elements to ease audience use. Advertising and public relations sites scored lowest on this index. Functions that allowed contact with the site sponsor had a mean of 1.6 of a possible 4, indicating that few sites offer a full array of contact options. Once again, advertising and public relations sites offer fewest contact options with a category mean of .83 on a 4-point scale. Most of the sites in the sample as a whole focus on brand-building rather than price cutting; advertising and public relations sites provide leadership in this regard as one the strongest brand-oriented categories.

Finally, expected relationships were found between some business types and the Internet marketing types. Computer-related sites correlated with information-intensive Internet marketing communication types, and clothing and entertainment sites correlated with image-based Internet marketing communication.

These data suggest that indices of sophistication seem a productive avenue for exploration and analysis. So far, it does not seem that many web marketers are taking full advantage of the interactive capabilities in this form of marketing communication.

The explosive growth of the World Wide Web as a commercial environment commands attention from researchers in both business and academic realms. This study, although limited in size and scope, provides a snapshot view of early commercial developments. More systematic study is needed to analyze strategies for fully utilizing the interactive capabilities of the Web as a form of marketing communication and for assessing its effectiveness in building brand equity.

REFERENCES

Andersen Consulting (1996). BargainFinder agent prototype [Online] Available: <http:// bf.cstar.ac.com/bf/>.

Braun, G. (Ed.). (1996). Gale directory of publications and broadcast media. New York: Gale Research.

Bray, P. (1995, April 24). Selecting a web provider. Speech at COMDEX, Atlanta, GA [Online] Available: <http://cybersight.com/cgi-bin/cs/s? comdex.gmml>.

December, J. (1996). Units of analysis for Internet communication. *Journal of Communication, 46*(1), 14-38.

Dorsher, M. (1996, March). Whither the public sphere: Prospects for cybersphere. Paper presented at the conference of the Mass Communication and Society Division of the Association for Education in Journalism and Mass Communication, Grand Forks, ND.

Gabriel, T. (1996, February 12). The meteoric rise of web site designers. *The New York Times*, p. C-1.

Grunig J. E., & Hunt, T., (1984). *Managing public relations.* New York: Holt, Rinehart & Winston.

Hoffman, D. L., & Novak, T. P. (1995, July 11). Marketing in hypermedia computer-mediated environments: Conceptual foundations. [Online] Available: <http://www 2000.ogsm.vanderbilt.edu/cmepaper.revision.july11.1995/cmpepaper.html>.

Hoffman, D. L., Novak, T. P., & Chatterjee, P. (1995). Commercial scenarios for the web: Opportunities and challenges [Online]. *Journal of Computer Mediated Communication, 1*(3). [Online] Available: <http://www.usc.edu/ dept/annenberg/ vol1/issue3/hoffman.html>.

Johnson, B. (1996, March 25). Will the Web win appeal world wide. *Advertising Age*, 36.

Lappin, T. (1995, May). Deja vu all over again. *Wired*, 174-177, 218-222.

Morris, M., & Ogan, C. (1996). The Internet as mass medium. *Journal of Communication, 46*(1), 39-50.

Negroponte, N. (1995). *Being digital.* New York: Knopf.

Neuman, W. R. (1991). *The future of the mass audience.* Cambridge, MA: Cambridge University Press.

Open Market. (1996). Commercial sites index [Online] Available: <http://www. directory.net>

Rafaeli, S. (1990). Interacting with media: Para-social interaction and real interaction. In B.D. Ruben & L.A. Liverouw (Eds.), *Mediation, Information and Communication: Information and Behavior, Volume 3.* New Brunswick, NJ: Transaction Publishers, 125-181.

Rafaeli, S. (1988). Interactivity: From new media to communication. In R. Hawkins et al., (Eds.) *Advancing communication science:* Merging mass and interpersonal processes, 110-134. Newbury Park, CA: Sage.

Rheingold, H. (1993). *The virtual community:* Homesteading on the electronic frontier. Reading, MA: Addison-Wesley.

Rust, R. T., & Oliver, R. W. (1994). The death of advertising. *Journal of Advertising, 23*(4), 71-78.

Strangelove, M. (1994). *How to advertise on the Internet.* Ottawa, Canada: Strangelove Internet Enterprises, Inc.

Upshaw, L. B. (1995). *Building brand identity.* New York: Wiley.

Weinberger, D. (1996, March). One-on-one with One-on-Ones's Martha Rogers, *Wired, 4,* 153.

Williamson, D. A. (1995, November 20). Searching for a pot of gold; Profiting on the Net is still a long-term bet for online marketers, and a risky one as well. *Advertising Age,* S2.

Yahoo (1996). *Business and economic directory* [Online] Available: <http:// www.yahoo.com>.

9

Scaling the Web: A Parasocial Interaction Scale for World Wide Web Sites

John Hoerner

University of Alabama

This study examined the feasibility of parasocial interaction between visitors to commercially sponsored sites on the World Wide Web and the hosts or personalities of those sites. Although most studies have focused on parasocial interactions between television personalities and viewers using the Parasocial Interaction (PSI) scale developed by Rubin, Perse, and Powell (1985), a variation of the PSI scale was employed in this study to examine parasocial interaction with web site personae. Research participants examined four web sites using the PSI-Web scale. They determined the parasocial signals generated by the personae were well-received, and there were strong correlations between the parasocial indicants and the value of the web site visit, as well as the intention to visit the site again - information useful to commercial web site developers.

The explosive growth of the World Wide Web has been difficult to quantify accurately. The popular search engine *Lycos* indexes the number of unique URLs whenever a search is initiated. On October 7, 1995, *Lycos* indexed 8.54 million URLs (Hoffman, Novak, & Chatterjee, 1995). Just six months later, *Lycos* indexed 37.6 million unique URLs during a search. By late 1997, there were an estimated 200 million URLs. The number of users accessing the Web has shown similar growth. In 1997, there were an estimated 35 million users in the U.S., with that number expected to increase to nearly 136 million by 2002 (International Data, 1998). Worldwide, there are currently less than one billion Internet addresses, although that number is expected to increase to more than seven billion by 2002 (Steinert-Threlkheld, 1998).

As more commercial web sites like these begin operation daily, advertisers seek new and different ways to make their web sites distinctly different, yet user-friendly. The frequency of visits to an advertiser's site is one indicator of web site appeal. Although the Volant TurnPike site was receiving more than

85,000 visitors, or "hits" in one day (Volant TurnPike, 1995), more recent numbers far in excess of that have been reported for special-event web sites. The promotional site for the movie "Showgirls" received more than 1.5 million hits a day, and the site for Super Bowl XXX received more than 6 million hits on game day (Snider & Maney, 1996). With more than 17 million people currently using the Web (Hoffman, Kalsbeek, & Novak, 1996), daily hit numbers such as these in the millions have become more common. On the day Netscape made the latest version of its highly popular Navigator software available for downloading (February 13, 1996), Netscape's site logged more than 40 million hits (Snider & Maney, 1996).

For most sites, the number of hits may not be a true indicator of the number of visitors, as one visitor can generate up to 30 hits in the process of downloading text, video, graphics and audio files (Snider & Maney, 1996). The software on computers used as servers for the web sites cannot distinguish how many hits are first-time visitors or repeat visitors that day, nor can it determine the length of a site visit. In fact, one study suggests as many as 90 percent of the hits at a particular site are repeat visitors (Volant TurnPike, 1995). Recent surveys of the amount of commercial business conducted on the internet (the so-called e-commerce) showed growth that was nothing short of explosive. In 1998, 27.6 million U.S. users purchased goods and services on the Web valued at $32.5 million. By 2002, this e-commerce is expected to grow to more than $425 million annually (Headcount, 1998). Worldwide, the projections for 2002 are as high as $250 billion in e-commerce (Steinert-Threikheld, 1998).

How does a commercial web site sponsor capture a sense of this exploratory consumer behavior as a means to better allocate advertising expenditures? Although the number of hits per day may be an indicator of a site's initial appeal, sustaining appeal as well as measuring the number of repeat visitors may be a more challenging task. Some sites use various registration techniques to track repeat visitors, although many web users may find having to log in somewhat of an annoyance.

A Yankelovich Partners survey of online users described the behavior of typical "cybercitizens" as seeking information from a commercial web site 71% of the time (Yankelovich, 1995 Cybercitizen Survey). They used the Web for entertainment 16% of the time, which, when added to the time spent "surfing" (8%), and learning and exploring (8%), means information- and entertainment-seeking behavior occupied nearly one third of the time spent on the Web. Another survey reported "browsing" (27%) and entertainment (22%) as the most common uses of the Web (Pitkow & Recker, 1994). The subsequent version of the same survey reported much higher browsing activity (71%), and entertainment (63.6%) as the primary uses of the Web. Shopping represented just over 11% of the Web usage, up 3% from the earlier survey (Pitkow & Kehoe, 1996). The 1998 survey found shopping behaviors, especially for computer-related products, were much stronger, with more than 75% of the respondents seeking information on computer hardware and software. More than 60% of the respondents reported seeking information on books, travel arrangements, and music (Kehoe, Pitkow, & Rogers, 1998).

PARASOCIAL INTERACTION

Designers for several of the commercial web sites have developed fictional characters as a means of generating continued visitor interest in those sites. Some of the characters are carryovers from television commercials, but others may have been created especially for web sites. The desire to "get to know" these fictional characters may be a method of capturing the exploratory behavior of the web-browsing public and holding on to it for advertising purposes. Although such characters are more typically found in noncommercial web sites where the visitor can initiate interactions and carry on chatroom conversations, they exist in a few commercial sites as well. Even if there is not a host character at a particular web site, the site can have a personality by virtue of its graphic design, writing style, and treatment of information. A brief comparison of a reader's initial impressions of *People* and *U.S. News & World Report* magazines would produce widely divergent descriptions of those magazines' personality and character. A web site could have a personality in a similar manner.

Several commercial web sites feature hosts that could be categorized as "personae," stemming from the description Horton and Wohl (1956) first gave to television personalities who have a carefully developed broadcast "persona" designed to appeal to viewers. This persona can take on many of the characteristics of a companion, including regular and frequent appearances, a sense of immediacy (by appearing live on television) and the feeling of a face-to-face meeting.

Parasocial interaction, often called "intimacy at a distance," is based on this frequent and consistent appearance of the persona, or mediated personality. The "illusion of intimacy" (Horton & Wohl, 1956), as well as the persona being friendly, attractive, trusted, and unchanging are key to the development of a one-sided, parasocial interaction. Viewers of television soap operas (Rubin & Perse, 1987a) and news programs (Koenig & Lessan, 1985; Levy, 1979) engage in parasocial interactions, as do fans of the more-recently developed cable television home shopping channels (Grant, Guthrie, & Ball-Rokeach, 1991). The informal living room sets and chatty style of the home shopping channel hosts (Grant et al., 1991) as well the blurring of boundaries between the show and the home audience (Horton & Wohl, 1956) can certainly foster parasocial interaction. The frequent telephone interaction between the host and viewers further strengthens parasocial interaction, as most of the newscasters (Levy, 1979; Rubin & Perse, 1987b) and soap opera characters (Rubin & Perse, 1987a) studied previously were not able to respond directly to the viewers.

Horton and Wohl (1956) first posited the concept of parasocial interaction in terms of television viewing behaviors, when audiences began developing a sense of intimacy and friendship with mediated television personalities who they had never met in person. A more contemporary conceptualization of parasocial interaction has been described as the interpersonal involvement of the media user with the media being consumed (Rubin et al., 1985). This particular definition may be more suited for an examination of World Wide Web sites, since a Web site, albeit one with a host, is not a true persona or mediated personality in the sense used in previous parasocial interaction research. However, a web site could be construed as a persona because of the parasocial signals it can generate.

Although a newscaster can speak directly to the camera in warm, conversational tones and engage in casual interactions with other members of the news team (Levy, 1979) to generate parasocial signals, a web site does not have this advantage of a live performance. However, the parasocial signals generated by the host of a web site might possibly parallel those of a newscaster on broadcast television. These signals could include a casual, conversational tone of the narrative text made up of clever monologues, as well as in-depth character development of the persona and opportunities for electronic mail interaction with the persona.

All of these signals, whether generated by a fictional or real-life persona, are designed to encourage computer-mediated parasocial interaction. Being able to analyze and evaluate these signals will require a new measure of parasocial interaction designed expressly for web sites.

THE PARASOCIAL INTERACTION SCALE

To develop the original scale used to measure parasocial interaction, research participants responded to a series of statements that focused on the various components of parasocial interaction - notably empathy, perceived similarity, and physical attraction. Other components included friendliness, companionship, and identification with the persona (Levy, 1979; Nordlund 1978). These statements were based on suggestions by Horton and Wohl (1956) that parasocial interactions were reminiscent of face-to-face interpersonal interactions. Rubin, Perse, and Powell (1985) refined these statements to formulate a 20-item Parasocial Interaction scale (PSI). The PSI scale has since been shown to be reliable and internally valid (Auter, 1992; Rubin & McHugh, 1987).

The questions in the original 20-item scale, and in the later, abbreviated 10-item scale were directed towards news programs, newscasters, and soap operas. The shortened scale has been used for research in soap opera characters (Perse & Rubin, 1987a), favorite TV personalities, and local TV news involvement (Perse & Rubin, 1987b). A slightly modified, 14-item PSI scale was used to investigate television shopping channels (Grant et al., 1991). The objective of this investigation was to develop a new parasocial interaction scale (PSI-Web) that could be used to evaluate web sites for parasocial interaction signals.

The elements that encourage parasocial interaction are grouped in four categories: attitudinal perceptions and dispositions (e.g., affinity, empathy, humor, reality, and human quality or perceived similarity); sense of involvement including level of intimacy and knowledge of details about the characters (Auter, 1992); the degree to which media presentations are consistent, resemble interpersonal interactions (Horton & Wohl, 1956), and focus on qualities of friendship (Rubin et al., 1985); and behavioral dispositions (e.g., talking back to a television program, seeking more information about it, or making viewing that program part of a regular routine). These factors work together to make a persona the perfect friend - dependable, discreet, and uncritical (Horton & Wohl, 1956), as well as non-threatening and a perfect role partner for the viewer (Rubin et al., 1985). As ideal as a relationship with this type of persona might be for some people, some researchers have suggested that parasocial interaction could become a functional alternative to real interpersonal relationships (Rubin & Rubin, 1985).

The Parasocial Interaction Scale for Web Sites

Examining the 20 items in the original Parasocial Interaction scale (Rubin et al., 1985), several are directly related to the physical appearance and announcing delivery style of the newscaster, or to the news in general, and are not applicable to an investigation of web sites. These include statements such as "I like hearing the voice of my favorite newscaster in my home," I find my favorite newscaster to be attractive," and "My favorite newscaster keeps me company when the news is on television" (Rubin et al., 1985). The remaining items required some modification to be indicants of parasocial interaction, versus additional scale items that reflect web browsing activity would have to be created. Fifteen items were developed and incorporated into a new scale called the Parasocial Interaction Web Site Scale (PSI-Web). The scale items are described in Table 9.1.

Although these statements are framed in the parasocial interaction tradition, they also delve into the advertising realm. Plummer (1971) described seven dimensions of response to television commercials that have some relevance to investigations of web sites, especially the commercial ones. These dimensions are entertainment, irritation, familiarity, empathy or gratifying involvement, confusion, informativeness or personal relevance, and brand reinforcement (Plummer, 1971). Certainly these dimensions could be applied to web site content analysis, and most are reflected in the PSI-Web scale items.

The uses and gratifications literature also has a bearing on web site interactions. In a recent investigation of web sites by Eighmey & McCord (1995), two factors, identified as Continuing Relationship and Personal Involvement, showed important differences among the web sites. Continuing Relationship was important in terms of the site's ability to attract and hold audiences, and Personal Involvement was described as one of the most differentiating dimensions in web site evaluations and accounted for the largest amount of variance. Other factors that showed some importance included Clarity of Purpose, Information Involvement and Entertainment (Eighmey & McCord, 1995). Attention to these factors was given in the PSI-Web scale as well to ensure all the relevant dimensions of a web site interaction experience were measured.

Responses on the PSI-Web scale were made exactly the same as on the original PSI scale, with respondents indicating their agreement with the items on a 5-step Likert scale that ranges from *strongly disagree* (1) to *strongly agree* (5). Means and standard deviations were then determined. The 15 items on the PSI-Web scale were analyzed and evaluated for accuracy of dimension measurement by a panel of five, experienced web users.

TABLE 9.1
Parasocial Interaction Web Site (PSI-Web) Scale
(Descriptions in parentheses used for data reduction)

---

1. This web site adds credibility to the information it provides me. (INFORMAT)
2. I would tell my friends about this web site. (FRIENDS)
3. I feel sorry for this web site when there are mistakes or problems with it. (EMPATHY)
4. This web site is interested in my opinions and comments. (FEEDBACK)
5. I feel as if I am part of a close-knit group when I visit this web site. (GROUP)
6. Visiting this web site helps me form opinions about the topics and issues presented at this site. (OPINIONS)
7. I would visit this web site again. (VISIT)
8. The personality of this web site is friendly and down-to-earth. (PERSONAL)
9. I can trust the information I get from this web site. (TRUST)
10. Visiting this web site made me relax and have fun. (FUN)
11. I wanted to say something to this web site. (SAY)
12. I got mad at this web site when it didn't work properly. (MAD)
13. The personality of this web site makes me feel comfortable, as if I am with friends. (COMFORT)
14. I felt the time I spent visiting this web site was worth it. (VALUE)
15. This web site was considerate and didn't overload my computer's technical capabilities. (CONSIDER)

METHOD

Four commercially sponsored web sites were used for this experiment. Two sites featured host personalities that represented consumer products, while the other two sites presented consumer products in a straightforward manner with no host or spokesperson. The sites with personae were for a brand of Italian sauces and home appliances, and the straightforward web sites were for a brand of bicycles and athletic shoes.

At the Italian sauces site, a visitor arrived in the kitchen of a stereotypical Italian mother, "Mama." Various phrases, such as "So, how come you only stop by when you're hungry?" were used as mock conversational ploys. The visitor could see what was cooking on the stove (new sauces), ask Mama for recipes, learn to speak Italian from the "Professore" (with sound files) or win a trip to Italy. Visitors could also send Mama e-mail, to which real employees would reply. There were more than 30 episodes of a humorous serial story called "As the Lasagna Bakes," with new installments posted each week.

The home appliance site used a cartoon likeness of the real-life advertising repairman personality, to bring visitors back to the site on a regular basis. The repairman, seen in many television commercials, had a key place on the home page and his own chatroom where electronic mail interaction was encouraged. Even though the appeal of this site to college-age research participants may have been limited, it was included because the persona, the repairman, was necessary to provide participants with two web sites that featured personae.

The athletic shoe site was described as place the "Cyberpark, a serious playground for serious athletes," with fitness, running, and health pages. Detailed fitness workouts for upper and lower body, information on staying healthy and preventing injury were just a few of the Web pages. For runners, separate pages provided training secrets, marathon information, running tips and interviews with well-known runners. There was also a gift shop, as well as detailed information on all the athletic shoes.

The bicycle site offered a variety of information, including a message from the company president, the company's history and philosophy, product descriptions of its bicycles, and various racing activities. One page featured updates of the web site information and late-breaking "news" (competitive riders who won on this brand of bike). There was a written tour of the company's factory, an interactive list of dealers, and links to a number of bicycle-related web sites. One page even featured an online club of the friends of this brand.

A total of 57 research participants were drawn from introductory mass communication classes at a large southern university. Of the group, females represented 56.2%, a disproportionate population compared to the 43% of typical web users in the 1995 Yankelovich Partners survey. A more recent data reanalysis of the CommerceNet/Nielsen Internet Demographics Study suggested that women represent less than 22% of regular or hard-core web users (Hoffman et al., 1996). The sample for this experiment was a convenience sample, and did not approximate actual web user demographics; however, it does approximate the U.S. population distribution of 52% females.

All participants were asked about experience with the Web prior to exposure. Those expressing a lack of experience were given brief instruction in the use of the Netscape Navigator web browser software prior to visiting the web sites. Each participant was asked to review the PSI-Web scale items to become familiar with the type of responses expected. They were then asked to spend a minimum of 10 minutes examining each site. The four sites were bookmarked, so even those participants relatively unfamiliar with browser operation would not have any difficulty locating the sites. General comments about the sites were also solicited on the survey form.

RESULTS

Data reduction involved principal axis factor analysis to identify associations among the PSI-Web scale items, and to determine which factors generated the strongest parasocial interactions. The first factor analysis identified five statements that did not contribute to measures of parasocial interaction, as the loadings on Factor 1 were less than .45 following Varimax rotation see Table 9.2).

These items included the following: "I feel sorry for this web site when there are mistakes or problems with it" (Empathy), "This web site adds credibility to the information it provides me" (Informat), "I got mad when this web site didn't work properly" (Mad), "I can trust the information I get from this web site" (Trust), and "This web site was considerate and didn't overload my computer's technical capabilities" (Consider). Although the first item mirrored the Rubin et al. (1985) original scale item, it did not seem as relevant for web sites. The remaining items reflected information seeking, or more of the technical aspects of visiting a web site, rather than parasocial interaction, and were not included in further data analysis.

Two statements with high factor loadings that were not related to parasocial interaction were regrouped with the "attitudes" factor. They were "I would visit this web site again" (Visit), and "I felt the time I spent visiting this web site was worth it" (Value).

The second factor analysis on the remaining 10 items showed Comfort accounted for the largest proportion of the variance (38.8%), while Feedback contributed an additional 11.9% of the variance (see Table 9.3). The remainder of items in Factor 1 seemed to support parasocial interaction, while the Factor 2 items appeared to reflect feelings.

TABLE 9.2
Parasocial Interaction Web Scale Items: First Factor Analysis

Rotational Loadings

Variable	Factor 1	Factor 2	Factor 3
Comfort	.6978	.1994	.2108
Friends	.7398	.2103	-.1987
Fun	.8104	.2370	-.0460
Group	.6607	.2142	.1024
Opinions	.5097	.4512	-.1476
Personal	.5867	.3415	.0112
Say	.5604	-.1291	.1256
Feedback	.4921	.2234	.2701
Value	.8216	.2626	-.1619
Visit	.8281	.1652	-1947
Consider	.0523	.7562	.1415
Informat	.3483	.6606	-.0201
Trust	.2341	.7788	-.0763
Empathy	.0466	.1989	.7834
Mad	-.0769	-.3794	.5633

TABLE 9.3
Parasocial Interaction Web Scale Items: Second Factor Analysis

Rotational Loadings

Variable	Factor 1	Factor 2
Comfort	.7734	.1174
Feedback	.5572	.1571
Friends	.7154	-.1633
Fun	.8229	-.0499
Group	.7460	-.0046
Opinions	.6402	-.2007
Personal	.7100	-.1154
Say	.4617	.2182
Empathy	.1637	.7215
Mad	-.2201	.7215

An index representing the means of the eight parasocial interaction scalar items was calculated by site and gender, along with the means of Value and Visit. Correlations were computed from these means (see Tables 9.4, 9.5).

Although the means suggested certain preferences, the correlations were better indicators.

Examination of the correlations among these means clearly showed the women's preference for Site 2, and further delineated the men's preferences. The men felt Site 2 was worthwhile, but would prefer to visit Site 1 again. This may not be surprising, considering the site's content. There was a higher correlation for the combined genders at Site 2 for Value and Visit, although the Index mean for the combined genders suggested Site 4 was preferred.

TABLE 9.4
Means of Selected Variables By Gender and Site

	Site 1	Site 2	Site 3	Site 4
Female Index*	24.31	28.75	23.91	28.19
Femaile Value	2.75	4.00	2.94	3.56
Female Visit	2.34	3.94	2.75	3.69
Male Index*	25.08	24.60	21.76	26.00
Male Value	3.28	3.28	2.40	3.16
Male Visit	3.04	3.24	2.24	2.92
Combined Index*	24.65	26.93	22.96	27.23
Combined Value	2.98	3.68	2.70	3.39
Combined Visit	2.65	3.63	2.53	3.35

*Index represents the mean of responses for eight scalar items excluding Visit, Value, Consider, Empathy, Mad, Trust, and Informat.

TABLE 9.5
Correlations Between Index and Selected Variables By Site and Gender

	Site 1	Site 2	Site 3	Site 4
Female Value	.73	.78	.64	.60
Female Visit	.61	.77	.72	.56
Male Value	.73	.86	.78	.84
Male Visit	.81	.78	.72	.76
Combined Value	.72	.84	.72	.72
Combined Visit	.70	.79	.73	.67

All correlations one-tailed significant at .001.

Both men and women were more attracted to the athletic shoe site, and the women wanted to visit it again, while the men would rather visit the bicycle site again. Although neither of these sites had personae, they had the highest correlations between the most important dimensions of parasocial interaction -

the index - and behavioral intent - the repeat visit. The informational content of the athletic shoe site may have been the driving force behind the site's perceived value and attractiveness for repeat visits. Although the women may have formed a parasocial relationship with this site, it was not with the site's persona, but with the mediated site itself (perhaps because the fitness information was directed primarily towards women).

For the Italian sauce site, there was a noticeable difference of opinion between females and males. Men had the highest index score for this site, and the second highest correlation for Value. The index for the women was also high, but the correlations painted a slightly different picture. The women's Value correlation for this site was the lowest of the four sites, suggesting the Italian persona may have had some influence on the men and their desire for parasocial interaction, but not on the women.

The home appliance site scored in the middle of the group, with women preferring it over the Italian sauce site according to the Value and Visit correlations. The site had valuable information if someone was shopping for a washer or dryer. The men felt the same way and the correlations showed they found the site more worthwhile than the women, yet it was their last choice for a repeat visit. The home appliance site did seem to generate the most empathy, perhaps because of the repairman character. More participants also expressed irritation with the site, possibly because the graphics were slower to load than the other sites. Also, there was no apparent explanation of how to participate in a featured contest.

The bicycle site did not perform as well as might have been expected among college students. The women generally were not interested in bikes, although the men wanted to visit it again. The write-in comments suggested that this site was too serious and only for real fans of mountain bikes. Also, the bikes were described in text, but there were no graphic illustrations of them.

DISCUSSION

Parasocial interaction with web sites does not appear to be dependent on the presence of a persona, as evidenced by the high correlations for the athletic shoe site. Even though the original hypothesis might have been that the Italian sauce site would outperform the other sites because of its strong persona, such was not the case. The desire for relevant information in a very palatable form outweighed Mama's clever antics in her kitchen.

More than the effects of the presence or absence of a persona, this study demonstrated the validity of the PSI-Web scale in measuring affinity for a web site and parasocial interaction with that web site. Forecasting consumer behavior, especially where new media are concerned, is not a simple process. Even the measurement of hits at a web site, data that is relatively simple to gather, is not an accurate gauge of interest, affinity, or intent to visit again. Yet, for commercial web sites, measuring the latter behaviors is certainly a valuable yardstick as evaluating concept or design performance.

Escaping from the strictures of the literal definition of a persona as envisioned by Horton and Wohl (1956) four decades ago, the Web persona has become a different creature. The literal, mediated personality from the newscast or soap opera of the past is gone. The design metaphor, flow of the web experience, and styles of textual and graphic presentations of the information all become elements of a web site persona and encourage parasocial interaction by the visitor/user with that persona. The broader description of parasocial interaction by Rubin et al. (1985) as "interpersonal interaction of the media user with the media being consumed" more succinctly describes the web site visit experience as measured by the PSI-Web scale.

With the traditional boundaries of the persona removed, future research into web site persona and parasocial interaction could progress in several directions. The flow experience of computer-mediated communication posited by Csikszenmihalyi (1988) could be used as a framework to examine elements of the persona that facilitate flow and presumably parasocial interaction. The forms in which information is presented, resulting in either experiential or goal-directed behaviors (Hoffman & Novak, 1995) could be investigated to see which form produces a higher level of parasocial interaction. The design metaphors, both conceptual and graphic, may be investigated in a similar manner, as a weakness in either could be a flow inhibitor. Finally, the PSI-Web scale, in conjunction with clickstream measurement techniques, could be used to more accurately predict consumer behavior in computer-mediated communications.

REFERENCES

Auter, P. E.. (1992). TV that talks back: An experimental validation of a parasocial interaction scale. *Journal of Broadcasting & Electronic Media, 36,* 173-181.

Commercial Sites Index. (1996). [Online] Available: <www.directory.net/ index>.

Csikszentmihalyi, M. (1988). The future of flow. In M. Csikszentmihalyi and I.S. Csikszentmihalyi, (Eds.), *Optimal Experience: Psychological studies of flow in consciousness.* New York: Cambridge University Press, 365.

Eighmey, J., & McCord, L. (1995, November). *Adding value in the information age: Uses and gratifications of the World-Wide Web.* Paper presented at the Conference on Telecommunications and Information Markets, Newport, RI.

Grant, A. E., Guthrie, E. K., & Ball-Rokeach, S. J. (1991). Television shopping: A media system dependency perspective. *Communication Research, 18,* 773-798.

Headcount (1998). [Online] Available: *<http://www.headcount.com/index/ httml>*.

Hoffman, D. L., Kalsbeek, W. D., & Novak, T. P. (1996). Internet usage in the United States: 1995 baseline estimates and preliminary market segments. *Project 2000 Working Paper.* [Online] Available: <http://www2000.ogsm.vanderbilt.edu/1995.internet.estimates.html>.

Hoffman, D. L., & Novak, T. P. (1995). Project 2000: Marketing in hypermedia computer-mediated environments: Conceptual foundations. [Online] Available: <http://www. 2000.ogsm.vanderbilt.edu/cmepaper.revision. july11.1995/cmepaper. html>.

Hoffman, D. L., Novak, T. P., & Chatterjee, P. (1995). Commercial scenarios for the Web: Opportunities and challenges. [Online] Available: <http://www.ascusc.org/ jcmc/vol1/issue3.hoffman.html>.

Horton, D., & Wohl, R. R. (1956). Mass communication and parasocial interaction, *Psychiatry, 19*, 215-229.

International Data Corporation (1998). [Online] Available: <http//www.idc. com>.

Kehoe, C., Pitkow, J., & Rogers, J. (1998). GVU's 9th WWW User Survey, [Online] Available: <http://www.cc/gatech.edu/gvu/user_surveys/survey-1998-04/>.

Koenig, F., & Lessan, G. (1985). Viewers' relationship to television personalities. *Psychological Reports, 57*, 263-266.

Levy, M. R. (1979). Watching TV news as para-social interaction. *Journal of Broadcasting, 23*(1), 69-80.

Nordlund, J. E. (1978). Media interaction. *Communication Research, 5*, 150-175.

Perse, E. M. (1990). Media involvement and local news effects. *Journal of Broadcasting and Electronic Media, 34*, 17-36

Pitkow, J. E., & Recker, M. M. (1994). *Using the Web as a survey tool: Results from the second WWW user survey.* [Online] Available: <http://www.cc.gatech.edu/gvu/ user_surveys/survey-09-1994/>.

Pitkow, J. E., and Kehoe, C. (1996). *GVU's 4th WWW User Survey.* [Online] Available: <http://www.cc.gatech.edu/gvu/user_surveys/survey-10-1995/>.

Plummer, J. T. (1971). A theoretical view of advertising communication. *Journal of Communication, 21*(4), 315-325.

Rubin, A. M. & Rubin, R. B. (1985). Interface of personal and mediated communications: A research agenda. *Critical Studies in Mass Communication, 2*, 36-53.

Rubin, A. M., & Perse, E. M. (1987a). Audience activity and soap opera involvement: A uses and effects investigation. *Human Communication Research, 14*(2), 246-268.

Rubin, A. M., & Perse, E. M. (1987b). Audience activity and television news gratifications. *Communication Research, 14*(1), 58-84.

Rubin, A. M., Perse, E. M., & Powell, R. A. (1985). Loneliness, parasocial interaction and local television news viewing. *Human Communication Research, 12*, 155-180.

Rubin, R. B. & McHugh, M. P. (1987). Development of parasocial interaction relationships. *Journal of Broadcasting & Electronic Media, 31*, 279-292.

Snider, M., & Maney, K. (1996, February 16). Getting stuck in Net's Web. *USA Today*, 1D-2D.

Steinert-Threlkeld, T. (1998). Wiring the world for a net economy. *Inter@ctive Week*, 5(47), 16.

Steinert-Threlkeld, T. (1998). [Online] Available: <http:www.zdnet.com/icom/e-busi-ness/1998/12/net.economy/index.html>.

Volant TurnPike. (1995). [Online] Available: <http://turnpike.net/index.html >.

10

CyberHate: Extending Persuasive Techniques of Low Credibility Sources to the World Wide Web

Megan McDonald

"WARNING! This site contains White nationalist views. If you do not have an open mind, do not enter." Anonymous

This warning device is something like what you might find when you open the homepage to one of a number of hate groups on the World Wide Web.

The Internet, and more specifically the World Wide Web, makes communication virtually unlimited for those who currently have access to and use a computer system connected to a phone line. Regardless of the criticisms, including the sometimes "slow" pace of the Web (the Web has not yet achieved the same status as a fast-food restaurant), it has the potential to change our lives in tremendous ways, adding to our entertainment and information resources. For all the people "quaking in their boots" over technological changes, it is important to point out that the proliferation of this source will not, in fact, pollute the air or the water. It will also likely reduce the use of paper in terms of magazines, faxes, memos, and so on. The groups that should be afraid of this new media are the competing companies that furnish entertainment and information on hard copy.

With this in mind, there is a rapidly growing number of web users taking advantage of the ease and accessibility of the facile nature of HTML language in order to get their "voices," their opinions, or a slice of their lives on the Web. This fluidity forecasts a great influx and transference of ideas, cultures, and so forth, but it also foreshadows sharing the Web with others that voice offensive and sometimes unacceptable ideas. The new legislature of the Telecommunications Act of 1996 addresses this issue at hand by attempting to block pornography on the Internet. The past debates over sex and violence on television and their accessibility to susceptible minors are extended to the Web. Accordingly, this study explores the landscape of hate group web sites in order to describe the types of persuasive techniques that these groups can use in order to gain attention and reach minors as well as adults.

ATTITUDE CHANGE

The Yale approach to social psychology hinges on four tenets that are essential to attitude change: attention, comprehension, acceptance, and retention (Zimbardo, Ebbesen, & Maslach, 1977). With attention, the first process, many web creators face the same challenges that the advertising industry has been surmounting for years: how to get the attention of viewers in an ever-growing and competitive market? For most web creators with a socially acceptable product, the question of attention finds its answer in basic advertising strategies (sex, vividness, etc.). However, for unacceptable products, persuasive techniques must be used in order to gain the attention needed to start the process outlined by the Yale Team.

Persuasive Techniques

Research done on "foot-in-the-door" techniques reveals a process in which compliance is gained by sequential requests, the first being less than a second request. If the first request is granted, the second request will more than likely be met with compliance as well. Beaman, Cole, Preston, Klentz, and Steblay (1983) revealed that this phenomenon appears more "complex than typically thought" and that new theoretical developments were needed to extend this area of research.

Freedman and Fraser (1966) pioneered research on this technique commonly observed in the sales world. They concentrated on the idea of external pressure and its relation to compliance gaining. They felt further research would be most beneficial if it specified "other manipulations which produce an increase in compliance without an increase in external pressure" (p. 202).

A review of hate groups on the Web reveals a variety of foot-in-the-door techniques used to gain the attention of browsers. There are: warnings, disclaimers, objectives/purposes, social approaches, and more sophisticated counterargument strategies. This continuum of sophistication reveals a hierarchy of savvy among these hate groups in their quest to enlist willing supporters and/or leave critics with a less negative impression. On one end of the continuum, some groups even term themselves as "in your face" while others prefer the "sustained, electronic 'guerrilla warfare,' 'hit-and-run' style, using short, 'self-contained' posts" as the basis of their struggle to propagate their groups' ideals.

The counterargument strategy, while not traditionally termed under foot-in-the-door techniques adds valuable insight in this area. Sternthal, Dholakia, and Leavitt (1977) tested the role of argumentation strategies as a factor in the determination of the effects of high and low credibility sources. They found that the source credibility had less effect than did the argumentative skill of the source, making argument an extremely important aspect of message response.

Munch, Boller, and Swasy (1993) also studied the effects of argument structure on product attitude formation. They discussed the role of arguments in forming "targeted beliefs about product claims" (p. 301). The rationale used to prove claims is key to creating a product attitude.

Hate groups, with their prior knowledge of their low credibility to a majority of people, may use a more sophisticated argument structure to refute negative message responses, at the very least. At the most, they can gain the support of web users open to the ideals set forth in their rationales, the argument structure being that much more effective in those cases.

Applications to Cyberhate Groups on the Web

This study employs a content analysis of 30 web sites belonging to hate groups. They are limited to rascist/nationalist groups. One can find compilations and links to most. The selected web sites were coded by the author and another coder using a questionnaire that tested for the five techniques outlined previously (i.e., warnings, disclaimers, objectives/purposes, social approaches, and more sophisticated counterargument strategies). The questionnaire also documents various technical aspects of the sites themselves including global/local links, word counts, and so forth. Most of the web sites were printed out with the date and time noted. A few of the technical questions had to be answered by getting back online and reentering the Web at a later time.

METHOD

Intercoder reliability was found to be low during the initial analysis of the data, so the questionnaires were examined in detail in order to compare answers. All disagreements were reconciled after thorough discussion between the coders.

After having run the data through "StatView," a computer software program, the results illustrate an interesting picture of hate groups on the Web. The sample size was originally 40, but it is difficult to pinpoint the total population of such web sites. These web sites appear to change frequently, become censored by their provider, and get "lost" on the Web. Perhaps the home computer that carried the web site was shut off or in the repair shop.

The number was initially narrowed to 35, but by the time the second coder began coding (only a few days' lapse), some of those web sites could no longer be found. The final sample was 30. Some of these disappearances reveal another problem due largely to the CDA and the new Telecommunications Act of 1996. Its "call to arms" for morality on this difficult-to-monitor medium has caused a great stir in the courts and in homes. The main problem is not the content as it is accessible to adults, but as it is accessible to minors.

Like bookstores, many providers such as Prodigy are creating a "brand" or a standard of the web sites they carry. They actively censor and remove sites that do not meet those requirements. However, magazines of an adult nature are covered in the store and not sold to minors. It is difficult at the moment to mimic this practice on the Web due to its technological limitations, though the filtering software challenges this viewpoint. This unstable situation created problems for this study because the sites were constantly changing. Nevertheless, it is an interesting to consider the Web activity for hate groups at one point in time.

RESULTS

Structural Elements

The nature of certain structural elements of interest was included in the analysis (see Table 10.1). It was discovered that 20% of the sample gave the warning "contents that may be considered negative or offensive." Eighty percent did not use such a straightforward approach. Ten percent gave a disclaimer of responsibility for the provider and only 3% disclaimed affiliation with a particular hate group. On the other hand, 73% gave an explicit affiliation with a particular group. None stated that the site was "official," but 13% stated that the site was "unofficial." Thirty percent were vague as to their affiliation.

Thirty-seven percent used a technique involving a "statement of objectives, standards, values, credo, or manifesto" of the group or person(s) involved with the web site. Twenty-four percent included a text description of the group's history, philosophy, and so forth..

Considering a "social approach," 13% specifically "invited" or "welcomed" netsurfers. However, 24% supported the atmosphere of the web page with additive text in the form of jokes, quotes, prayers, and so on. Another 52% supported the atmosphere with graphic elements like symbols, photos and cartoons that appealed to the social emotions. It is important to note that almost all of the Web sites used graphic elements, but this question attempts to distinguish mere use of graphics from use with the intention of creating a parasocial relationship.

Only 14% gave a text description of the leader(s) and/or prominent personalities affiliated with the group. Then, 7% gave a text description of the web page creators (and only one gave a photo of the creator). Further, 7% gave an events schedule of some sort. However, 79% of the web sites gave contact an events schedule of some sort. However, 79% of the web sites gave contact information for further communications either in the form of single/multiple addresses and/or e-mail addresses.

TABLE 10.1
Structural Elements

Structural Element	Type	Percentage
Warnings	Negative or offensive	20%
	Not negative nor offensive	80%
Disclaimers	Lack of responsibility on provider's part	10%
	Lack of Affiliation with particular hate group	3%
	Explicit affiliation	73%
Notification of status	"Official"	0%
	Unofficial	13%
	Vague affiliation	30%
Background provided	Statement of group's objectives and standards	37%
	Group's history and/or philosophy	24%
Social approach	Invitation/welcome	13%
	Additive Text	24%
	Graphic Elements	52%
Notification of leadership	Description of leadership	14%
	Description of web page creators	7%
Encouragement to become involved	Events schedule	7%
	Contact information	79%

Nature of the Content

The nature of the actual content of hate groups reveals some interesting findings (see Table 10.2). The last part of the continuum, "counterargument strategy" reveals results in terms of argument formation. Twenty-one percent state that "Hate Groups" in general, or theirs in particular, are "victims of intolerance" and subject to persecution or harassment. Twenty-five percent use moderating symbols such as poems, quotes, and sayings in defense of their arguments for their views. Twenty-one percent support their arguments with historical facts. Another 11% use legal facts/jargon in defense, and only 4% use scientific or biological facts to support their views.

TABLE 10.2
Nature of the Content

Content	Type	Percentage
Counterargument strategy	Victimization	21%
	Moderating symbols	25%
	Historical facts	21%
	Legal facts/jargon	11%
	Scientific/biological facts	4%
Language of warning	Positive	3%
	Neutral	7%
	Negative	10%
Appearance of warning	Within headline	10%
	Within body of text	10%
	Footnote	3%
Warnings in text versus graphics	Text only	10%
	Graphics only	0%
	Text and graphics	10%

Several other questions served to merely point out some basic characteristics of the web sites. A set of questions revolved around the warning and showed that 3% used "positive" language and diction in their warning. Another 7% used neutral language, but 10% used negative and forceful language to warn netsurfers of the content.

Ten percent of the warnings used a headline type of warning, making it a visible focus on the page, but 10% put a warning in the actual body of the text of the site. Another 3% included it as a footnote. There were several cases of double counting when web sites used a combination of more than one of the three kinds. An average word count of the warnings came out to 7 words per warning. The warning was also coded for its use of text and graphics. Ten percent used text only warnings. None of the web sites used symbols/graphics only for warnings, and 10% used text and symbols/graphics for their warnings.

Frequency counts of 15 different words were completed. Although some web sites seemed to use some of these words in great quantity, others did not use them at all or at least infrequently. "White" was the most frequently used word and had a count of 4 times per web site. "Black" was less than 1. "Nationalists" had a count of 1 to 2 times per site. "Race" was used 2 times per site. The following words were used less than once per site: "pride," "war," "kill," "party," "government," and "big brother." "Hate" was used almost once per site. The following were not used at all: "hell," "damn," "nigger," and "injustice."

Web Page Characteristics

Several characteristics of the sampled web pages were coded (see Table 10.3). The average number of links in from other sites was 35 to 36. Local links averaged out to 27. Global links to other sites came to about 12 to 13. Thirty-three percent (12) of the sites had their own domain name. Sixty-seven percent (18) of the sites were attached to a provider. None of the sites were ".org" sites or ".gov" sites. Two were ".edu," and an overwhelming 16 were ".com."

An "Individual group" created 24% of the sites, and an "individual person" created 24% of the sites. None of the sites were created by groups/individuals based in the Southwest, Southeast, or the West. Eight percent of the sites were based in the East. Another 8% were based in the South, and 23% were based in the North. Seventy-three percent were based outside the United States in countries like Denmark, Britain, Ireland, Canada, and so forth. There was one problem with this question. It did not include the Midwest, so a group like the Ku Klux Klan (KKK), which is based in Ohio, would have been included under the North.

CONCLUSIONS

It's interesting to note that the most prevalent foot-in-the-door technique used seems to be the Objective Approach (37%) with the Counterargument Strategy close behind at 25%. These results show a sophisticated use of persuasive techniques. The objective strategy usually involves stating the views of the group in a very straightforward neutral way. It does not incite nor does it insult. Groups using this technique gain the upper hand by appearing more rational than expected. Although they may not persuade as many people to "buy" their viewpoints of "White nationalism" or "racism," they clearly do not dissuade people from their viewpoints.

TABLE 10.3
Web Page Characteristics

Characteristic	Type	Number/Percentage
Linkages	Links In	35-36/site
	Local Links	27/site
	Global Links	12-13/site
Provider	Domain Name	33%
	Attached to a Provider	67%
Web Location	.org	0 sites
	.gov	0 sites
	.edu	2 sites
	.com	16 sites
Group versus Person	Created by a group	24%
	Created by a person	24%
Origination	West	0 sites
	East	8%
Origination (continued)	South	8%
	North	24%
	Outside United States	73%

The Counterargument Strategy, however, seeks to change the netsurfers' minds about nationalism/racism by using "moderating symbols" such as poems, quotes, sayings, and so on, as well as historical facts. They seem to use the legal facts/jargon less. One interpretation might be that most of these groups may not be as concerned with legalities. They also rarely use scientific or biological facts as the basis of their arguments. One might conclude that these types of facts have been widely used and publicly refuted to such a great extent in the past that they can not serve as a viable and substantive argument base.

Another technique, the Social Approach, seems to be used extensively. Even though an explicit welcome or other invitation is only used in 13% of the web sites, other parasocial techniques are used more frequently. Twenty-four percent of the sites use additive text in the form of quotes, jokes, prayers, and so on. Roughly half of the web sites use graphic elements to help create a parasocial atmosphere. These data suggest a heavy emotional appeal used by the web site creators as an effort to make contact with netsurfers. This can be compared to the salesperson's technique of shaking one's hand and conversing in an extremely friendly manner.

The warning is used by 20% of the web sites and does not seem to be as effective as the other techniques unless it is taken as insightful or as a curiosity. The warning may be enough to draw people in just to see what all the controversy is about. As far as the disclaimer is concerned, only 10% of the web sites included a disclaimer of provider and only 3% denied affiliation with a particular group. Disclaimers do not seem to be widely used by the cyberhate groups. It is possible that it doesn't work as a foot-in-the-door technique and is there merely to relieve certain parties from responsibility for the public's response to the content. It also builds a better relationship with providers in a time of increasing strain on the web site-provider relationship.

This study contributes to the further theoretical development of persuasive techniques as used in the perseverance of socially unacceptable web sites. It will contribute to the education of web users as they sift through and filter the Web. Web users may become more aware of foot-in-the-door techniques. This will serve to enhance judgment skills when forming attitudes and responding to messages on the Web. This judgmental approach to the Web will become more important as web users and parents of web users (in the case of minors) "hang ten" and incorporate filtering software into their systems. Choosing the size of the wave one wants to surf may be as important to information seekers as it is to any professional surfer honing her or his skills.

REFERENCES

Beaman, A. L., Cole, C. M., Preston, M., Klentz, B., & Steblay, N. M. (1983). Fifteen years of foot-in-the door research: A meta-analysis. *Personality and Social Psychology Bulletin, 9*(2), 181-196.

Freedman, J. L., & Fraser, S. C. (1966). Compliance without pressure: The foot-in-the-door technique. *Journal of Personality and Social Psychology. 4*(2), 195-202.

Munch, J. M., Boller, G. W., & Swasy, J. L. (1993, September). The effects of argument structure and affective tagging on product attitude formation. *Journal of Consumer Research. 20*, 294-302.

Sternthal, , B., Dholakia, R. & Leavitt, C. (1978, March). The persuasive effect of source credibility: Test of cognitive response, *Journal of Consumer Research. 4*, 252-260.

Zimbardo, P., Ebbesen, E., & Maslach, C.(1977). *Influencing Attitudes and Changing Behavior* (Second ed.) Reading, MA: Addison-Wesley.

11

Online Newspaper Advertising: A Study of Format and Integration With News Content

Ann M. Brill
University of Missouri

Advertising is the fuel of free enterprise and a free press
– pillar inscription, Lee Hills Hall
Missouri School of Journalism

It is no secret that newspapers, in a democracy, depend on advertising for their survival. In the absence of government control and ownership, newspapers have had to find a way to not only survive, but thrive. They quickly learned they could not count on subscribers to pay most of the bills, but they found willing patterns in the merchants of the day (Emery & Emery, 1988). The integration of editorial matter - "news" - and advertising has long been an accepted practice in the United States and much of the democratic world (Siebert, Peterson, & Schramm,1956). It also has been questioned by media scholars and consumers who often see a blurring between editorial material and news (Lacher & Rotfield, 1994; Soley & Craig, 1992). Consumers are caught in the middle of this debate: They want their information free from bias, they want the informational content of the advertising, and above all, they want inexpensive newspapers. It is a rare publication that can be supported only by subscription dollars.

THE SYMBIOTIC RELATIONSHIP BETWEEN ADVERTISING AND EDITORIAL MATERIAL

Advertising can be defined as "paid, professionally designed messages channeled through the media to potential consumers" (Thorson & Moore, 1996). The definition of "editorial material," usually referred to as "news," continues to evolve. At its most basic level, it is information that is both interesting and useful to the audience (Brooks et al., 1996).

Even in today's competitive media market, newspapers remain a strong industry and a reasonable channel for advertising. In the mid-1930s, newspapers had more than 45% of all advertising dollars. That dropped to 26 % by 1990 and has further eroded since then (Baskette, Sissors, & Brooks,1992; Emery & Emery, 1988). That figure, however, still represents the largest part of the advertising dollar spent in the United States. What are newspapers selling? Their audience as potential customers. Newspaper subscriptions pay less than 25% of the actual cost of publishing the newspaper. The revenue generated from advertising sales constitutes the majority of the actual cost of publishing most newspapers. The relationship between newspapers and advertisers, between editorial content and advertisements, is a symbiotic one. Advertising dollars pay most of the bills, but the editorial content lends credibility to the advertising (Cameron & Haley, 1992; Sandler & Secunda, 1993). Furthermore, although the idea of a newspaper creating an environment conducive to advertising may seem to fly in the face of an objective press, it nonetheless allows the free press to be affordable to more citizens. Meyer (1987) argued that the ideal situation for advertising is an objective press because the press attracts a larger audience and lends credibility to all content, including advertising.

There is no reason for the advertiser to exercise any control or influence over the editorial content. Indeed, to do so would be counterproductive, because it would undermine the independence that creates the trustworthy editorial environment that, in turn, gives the paper its influence (Meyer, 1987). Yet, as the literature shows, Meyer found many examples of advertisers who tried to dictate placement of their ads based on their perceptions of unfavorable editorial content.

The literature, and perusal of most newspapers, shows that advertisements often are placed adjacent to editorial content that would complement their product or services (i.e., travel agencies' "specials" in the travel section or film ads in the entertainment section). And although an observer may question the interplay between advertising and complementary editorial content on the same page, the fact remains that ultimately both have to answer to subscribers/consumers. If newspapers lose their readers, they have nothing to sell (McManus, 1994).

Advertisers may, according to the literature, exert two types of controls over news content: first, to select and attract the largest possible audience for their goods and services, and second, to create an atmosphere for those ads within the context of editorial content (Bagdikian, 1990; Turow, 1992). The online newspapers will face this same challenge.

In speaking of the interplay between advertising and editorial content, the editor of one newspaper said: "We're a business. [And] as newspapers change, there is a much closer interaction between ads and news than [there] used to be" (Lesly, 1991). It also should come as no surprise that ads for automobile dealers appear in a supplement dealing with automotive issues. The *Raleigh News and Observer* acknowledges that the whole idea behind such supplements is to generate income: "[The auto section is designed] to create a marketplace for advertisers. It doesn't make sense to do it [write critical articles] to piss off advertisers. . . . At this stage, there isn't a single bit of advertising that isn't important. As a group, auto dealers are our third-largest advertisers" (Singer, 1991). Into this symbiotic relationship comes a new version of the newspaper: the online, digital publication.

Still in its infancy, the online newspaper looks to its print counterpart not only for financial support, but for models of content, including advertising. The number of newspapers online has grown feverishly since 1994. With the rapidly growing number of newspapers online, according to *Editor & Publisher's* homepage on the World Wide Web, the industry has invested considerable resources in online products. *Editor & Publisher Magazine*, along with Jupiter Communications, Inc., monitors the number of newspapers online. According to their information, as of November 1, 1998, there were commercial newspaper online services operating throughout the world. That number is up from 750 at the beginning of 1996 and 100 at the beginning of 1995. *Editor & Publisher* reports that they receive notification of 5 to 10 new online ventures by newspaper companies every day (Outing, 1996). Nearly all of those newspapers are on the Web and nearly 75% of them are based in the United States.

What is motivating many of these newspapers to create an online version is fear and greed. The fear comes from seeing their circulation numbers stagnate among older readers and decline among younger readers. It is exacerbated by the idea that local advertisers may go online with another Internet provider, especially one as powerful as AT&T. "The fear comes from the threat to newspapers' advertising base, especially the classified advertisements" and the greed comes from the belief that ". . . if a system is ever invented that accurately counts and categorizes each visitor to a newspaper's web site, publishing on the Internet could become a profitable marriage of newspapers' advertising bases and franchise strengths" (Peterson, 1996). Publishers also hope that their new online ventures will aid newspapers struggling with an aging and declining readership and a corresponding decline in advertising dollars (Peterson, 1996). Yet, the industry readily admits it has more questions than answers at this point about its future. Those questions include the role that advertising will play and how it will fit with the editorial content online.

CREATING THE "NEWS HOLE"

The model for print journalism, especially newspapers, is that advertising not only is the major revenue source, it also dictates the "news hole" - the amount of space that can be supported, or the amount of news that can be used to fill in the rest of the page.

Advertising in newspapers takes two forms: classified and display. Classified advertisements consist of lines of text, arranged in categories that appear in segregated pages of the newspaper, usually in the last pages. They are less expensive than display ads and usually purchased by readers rather than businesses. Newspaper display advertisements contain larger typefaces, graphics, are sold by the column inch, and are placed on the same pages as editorial content. It is generally accepted that the types of advertising in the newspaper relate to the appeal to consumers: In display advertisements, the idea is to attract the newspaper reader who is perusing the editorial content. Classified advertising, however, is considered more of a "yellow pages" type of advertising where consumers are seeking out information. Display ads appear in various sections of the newspaper, although some placement is based on appeal to certain readers (i.e. restaurant ads in the lifestyle section or automotive repair in the sports section). Interestingly, although little about the use of display ads in print carries over to the online version, that difference is maintained online. This paper deals only with display advertising because, although classified advertising exists in many online newspapers, it follows the print model of no integration with editorial content.

Historically, advertising space was sold first, ads placed on the pages, and editorial content filled in the remaining space. As newspapers became more professional-looking, the advertisements filtered to the bottom of the vertical page where they anchored the editorial content (Baskette, Sissors, & Brooks, 1992).

Even with the advent of computer design of pages, and increased use of color and graphics, little has changed in the last century regarding the placement of advertising and news on the page. The "page," however, is part of the change that is taking place as newspapers publish online editions.

CYBERSPACE: TOO MUCH AND TOO LITTLE

Unlike its print counterpart, the online newspaper has virtually unlimited amount of space in which to publish information. The Internet, commonly called "the Net," was developed by the U.S. government more than 35 years ago as a data link among a handful of military installations and academic communities. Today, it connects an estimated 148 million sers worldwide (Nua, 1998; Global Internet Statistics, 1998). Reports from the Internet Information

Society estimate that it is growing at a rate of 150,000 new members every month. And, although it is still subsidized by the government, the Internet operates independently, with no owner or central management.

As a publishing opportunity, the newspaper industry cannot afford to ignore this new medium. Without production costs of ink, printing presses, and an antiquated delivery system, newspapers can substantially cut their overhead. Because many online newspapers also are producing what is called "shovelware," editorial content recycled from the print newspaper, they usually do not need to hire additional editorial staff. What they have found, however, is that display advertisements cannot move from print to online without major modifications (Harrison, 1996).

Although the Internet is thought to be virtually limitless in the amount of material it can contain, it is limited by the size of most computer screens. The screen limitation presents a major paradigm shift for advertising and page designers: One of the frustrations of designing computer-based advertising is the size of the screen, which typically measures from 8 to 15 inches diagonally. Even newspapers that use a tabloid format have a larger area in which to work, and because most newspapers still publish in a broadsheet format, based on a six-column grid, those ads cannot simply be reproduced on the screen. In addition, the format for print newspapers has long been vertical, not the horizontal format of the television or computer screen. Of course, this technology is a moving target and it remains to be seen what will emerge as the online newspaper of the future. Large screens would allow more information although it appears unlikely that today's consumers will want to "read" information on a large-screen format like that of a television. Some online newspaper have chosen to retain their vertical format, although they are finding consumers dislike having to spend so much time scrolling down screens (Laurel, 1992). Computer screens are different in more than how they look. They work differently than a newspaper page: They are interactive in ways we have yet to learn (Leary, 1990).

Let's Put On An Advertisement!

Webmasters often paraphrase the old Mickey Rooney/Judy Garland quote when they talk about people who have big ideas of what to put on a web page with little knowledge of how or why they are creating the site. That is a major concern as online newspapers try to figure out not only how to create advertisements and where to put them, but how to make money from them.

The professionals creating web sites, and in particular, web advertisements, do so as part of the total marketing plan. A company such as AT&T advertises in all media and it is no surprise to find it on the Web in various forms, both as ads/icons on others' pages and on its own web site. This idea of integrated communication helps explain why newspapers feel it is imperative that they establish an advertising base on the Web; it also may help them understand how this form of advertising might best be utilized and presented:

> The new challenge for clients is to find the most effective and efficient way to make use of the "new" marketing communication alternatives. The concept of integrated marketing communication is helping them meet that challenge, allowing them to strategically focus and coordinate their marketing communication programs in a way that will produce a synergistic effect, a result that can also help the bottom line. (Duncan & Caywood, 1996, p. 17)

As the studies of integrated communication discuss, there are three issues here: First, the mixture of media voices; second, the point of entry for the integrated campaign; and third, the conceptualization of the audience(s) (Thorson & Moore, 1996). Here, the mixture of media voices refers to the integration of advertising and editorial material; the point of entry is the web page/screen design; and the conceptualization of audience is the (limited) understanding we have of online consumer behavior. The first two issues will be explored in this and the following section and the third will be part of the discussion.

Although the concept of the mixture of voices has limited applicability to the integration of news and advertising on a single web page, it does help explain the motivation of companies such as AT&T and IBM. These companies have not only created their own web sites as part of their integrated marketing approach, they advertise those sites in online newspapers and other sites where they believe consumers will see their ads/icons. Again, their point of entry is the web site and specifically, the online advertisement. Where the ad is located is an integral part of screen design. What is particularly frustrating to online designers, however, is that consumers use different web browsers to view web sites. Because not all browsers recreate the image in the same way, pages can look and operate very differently from computer to computer. Also, the resolution of the screen can make a colorful, complex ad look primitive.

Perhaps the biggest frustration on the part of both viewer and designer is the amount of time those nice, fancy graphics take to download and show up on the screen. When that happens, users are likely to go to a display mode that only shows text - so much for the hard work of the page or advertising designer.

In addition to the hardware and software problems, there are psychology differences between print and online advertising. Display advertising executives say that print advertising does not translate into good web design (Covington, 1996; Peterson, 1996). On the computer screen, advertising cannot be directed at consumers as much as drawing them into the "real" ad. The idea is to get consumers to click on the ads and thus receive more information. Print ads are not designed for interactivity beyond cutting coupons. In fact, because one oft-cited problem with print newspapers is excessive ink ruboff, readers are usually careful not to touch the print newspaper too much!

What advertisers currently get for their money is an icon or listing in a directory or a banner on a newspaper's web page. That icon or banner is linked to the advertiser's own web site, usually created by another agency. One newspaper manager likened that to the practice of inserts in which the company may pay for an advertisement that says, "See insert in Sunday's newspaper."

If the consumer does pay attention to the online ad and clicks on the ad to actually go to the company web site, the advertiser may have lured the consumer away from the news content. In traditional media terms, it might be equivalent to a consumer reading an advertisement in the newspaper for Budweiser, putting down the newspaper, picking up a brochure for the beer, and perhaps even setting down that brochure to pick up yet another publication. It is difficult to imagine anyone sitting at home going through this physical process, yet it is the type of activity one might see in a bookstore or library - the World Wide Web just makes browsing that much easier and faster.

Floating Advertisements

The placement of advertisements in online newspapers is difficult to understand and the online managers freely admit they are still trying to determine effective placement. An analysis of online newspapers in early 1996 found that placement of advertising in the editorial sections followed three patterns: (1) ads that appear at the top of the screen as a banner, but did not infringe on the editorial material, (2) ads that were placed to the side or top of editorial material within the context of the page, or (3) ads that were located in the midst of a page, breaking into the editorial content. In some of these newspapers, advertising is integrated not only with section previews and indices, but with news stories. The newspapers are: *The New York Times, Raleigh News and Observer, Boston Globe, Virginia Pilot, San Jose Mercury News, Wall Street Journal. Colorado Springs Gazette*, and *Minneapolis StarTribune*.

The newspapers were not chosen as a representative sample, but rather for their representation of different lengths on time online, size of print counterpart, geographic variety, and, in most cases, because they were slated as participants in the Audit Bureau of Circulation's beta-test audits of web sites and were to be part of ABC's Interactive Auditing Service, which was to launch in June 1996 (ABC, 1996). Those tests should give advertisers and online newspapers a better understanding of their audiences and are discussed further later in this chapter.

Each of these newspapers also has available a print counterpart that could be used for comparison regarding ad placement. Because these newspapers have typically been online for less than a year at the time of this perusal and had just begun to accept advertising, what follows is largely a descriptive approach as the industry struggles to obtain and place advertising in its news pages.

Today's advertisements in online newspapers are in their infancy. By and large, they follow the familiar grid pattern of their print counterparts and are modular in design. Their size is significantly smaller, however, than most print display ads. For example, where Fidelity Investments might purchase one fourth-page to a full-page advertisement in *The New York Times*, in the online version, they settle for a small square icon that appear to the left of the news content. Fidelity cannot even tell where that ad will appears in the stack of three icons because, with the use of special software, the ads rotate placement from screen to screen. Prodigy pioneered the use of advertising on commercial online services, not without substantial complaints from their customers (Singer, 1995). Prodigy also gathered enough demographic information on their paid subscribers to be able to target their ads. For example, although information about sales of computers would appear on the bottom of every Prodigy subscriber's screen, only ads for men's shoes would appear on screens where a male owned the account. Prodigy also targeted advertising based on the ages of account owners.

Like their print counterparts, online advertisements seek either a mass or target audience. Advertisements in *The New York Times Electronic Edition* would appeal to a broader consumer market than ads on *HayNet*, a Web site about horses. Most of the advertising on the Web is targeted to a more defined audience; rather than a mass appeal, it is narrowcasting on a one-on-one basis. And although print newspaper readers cannot miss spotting ads on the page, just as they do on the online version, it takes another step to really see the ad, which resides on a different page of the Web.

A typical placement for the banner type of advertisement that appears in online newspapers is the top or bottom of the screen. Often, it overshadows the newspaper's own masthead. Sometimes, it can even be confusing to tell which page is the front page of the newspaper. The online versions of the *Boston Globe, San Jose Mercury Center*, and *The New York Times* all carry advertising on what looks like a front page. What viewers are actually seeing, however, is an index. In the case of the *Globe*, it is not even the index to the online newspaper, but a network called <boston.com>. This is one of the few pages that requires no scrolling, yet that "front page" typically has more than 25 elements or entry points that consumers can chose to click, including the *Globe*. "Page One" of the *Globe* reverts to the traditional newspaper pattern of advertising along the bottom of the page, although it is not really the bottom, because a rule separates the ads from links to other sections of the newspaper. Yet, the placement at the bottom of a row of bulleted headlines and story synopses leads the reader's eye to the advertisements.

The New York Times online also has two "front pages." What nonsubscribers see is the *Times* without the advertisements. After providing the user id and password (*The Times Online* is free during its initial stages of development), another site labeled "Front Page" appears, along with three ads that run along the left side of the screen. That left-side position is a valuable commodity because with some web browsers, the *Times'* design is too wide, which forces the page to wrap, moving the news sections down the screen. What the viewer sees at that point is only the ads; he or she must scroll down the screen to see the news. That trio of stacked ads appears throughout the sections fronts, except for two sections: The editorial and op/ed pages do not contain ads.

Curiously, though, the programming for the ads is in place, in that the outline of the ads appear, then disappear, but depending on the web browser, the top part of the screen is blank. Again, the reader has to scroll down to get to the editorial material. Yet because the screen design usually "paints" or appears onscreen in a pattern from top to bottom and left to right, readers are more likely to see those ads. They also may be more likely to wait for them to appear. Like all graphics on the Web, advertising icons can be turned off by the user. *The Times Online* advertising manager says software will eventually correct some of those problems, but they also are exploring new uses of advertising. Unlike the *Globe*, the *Times* also has advertising embedded in news stories, running smaller ads next to its masthead and at the end of the story. The *Times* has even placed an animated advertisement, next to its masthead, above a story.

The *Pilot Online*, counterpart to the *Virginia Pilot*, has been online for nearly two years. In addition to the newspaper, they operate InfiNet, a network that hosts more than 24 online newspapers (Kouba, 1996). The *Pilot* sells its valuable front page ad spots only to itself, with an ad for "Autopilot," a link to the newspaper's online automobile ads. The paper's online advertising manager says he believes there is more money in online classifieds, and he is concentrating on that area for now.

Like the *Pilot*, *The News and Observer* has been on the Web long enough to become a model for fledgling ventures. The front page does not host advertising, although some of the glitzier icons could be mistaken for ads. Section fronts usually have banner ads. *The News and Observer* claims to have had 6 million hits in the first week of 1996. It is one of the few online newspapers to publish a rate card, charging about $2,400 a week for putting an icon link from its top web page to an advertiser.

At the other end of that spectrum lies the *Minneapolis Star Tribune Online*, which has four horizontal ads/icons on its front page. Those ads appear on the first screen, above the newspaper's index, special sections, animated weather information, contest information, and a link to other newspapers in the Cowles chain. The advertising manager declined to explain how the hierarchy of the ads was determined or the philosophy of where to place ads, which do appear throughout the news pages in varying locations, often bouncing to the left side of the screen, but not to the bottom of the story.

The *San Jose Mercury Center* is the online flagship of the Knight-Ridder chain and considered the most successful online newspaper, with reports of making a small profit in 1995 (Auerbach, 1996). This online paper also charges a subscription fee and additional fees for services such a retrieving a story from its library. Further, the staff are proud of its masthead, a collage of people that the managing editor says is representative of the San Jose area (Koon, 1996). The online paper does not have an ad on the first screen, but as users scroll down to see what else is online that day, ads appear on the right margins. There are no advertisements on index pages, section fronts, or integrated with stories. However, San Jose has been able to sell a type of space usually only attractive on search engines: The Mercury Mall page hosts icons that lead to advertisers' own pages. Space on that page is unimaginative and unappealing. . . but not inexpensive. Industry analysts say each button earns San Jose about $3,000 a week. Advertising on the Web comes in two forms: Advertisers set up their own web pages or they buy space on someone else's. Many companies do both and so, as Microsoft buys a button/link from *San Jose Mercury Center*, it also wants to lure readers to its own site that contains editorial content as well as ads for other products (and NBC).

One of the newest major newspapers to launch a web site is one that has been online in one form or another for more than a decade. Dow Jones began its *Wall Street Journal Interactive* site on April 28, 1996. In addition to the mass marketed *Journal*, subscribers can create their own version by listing their interests in a database. News, and consequently advertising, can be highly specialized based on the subscriber's interests. The *Wall Street Journal Interactive* is nearly as gray as its print counterpart. No advertising appears on its front page or any subsequent section heads. What they do offer subscribers is a button on the bottom right corner of the page that says, "advertisers."

Interestingly enough, like their print counterparts, online newspaper advertising managers are involved in the creation of online banners or icons for local, but not national or international advertisers. As in the past, those national and international advertisements are created either by the corporate in-house staff or an agency that specializes in web ad design (Edwards, 1996)

These newspapers have survived major challenges from other media as well as social and political upheavals. They plan to make their web sites profitable and advertising figures heavily into those plans. Ultimately, however, it will be consumers who drive the success or failure of this new medium.

CAVEAT EMPTOR

The third issue of integrative communication is another challenge for these new media ventures. Little is known or understood about the millions of people online, yet advertisers seem to think they are a valuable market. Studies have found that electronic shopping "will not only increase but also affect mail and 800-number purchasing behavior" (RAC examines, 1990). Consumer interaction may well be the key to effective advertising on the Internet as it has been shown to be in television infomercials (Auter & Moore, 1993). In addition, a major obstacle may be overcome if the Audit Bureau of Circulation can decipher online audience use of the Web.

Although much remains unknown about advertising and the Internet, ABC bases its involvement in online auditing on the following factors:

1. Virtually all ABC member groups are actively involved in Web publishing or advertising.
2. Web audits are consistent with ABC's mission – ABC is a not-for-profit association created by the industry to audit advertiser-supported, census-based media.
3. ABC provides an industry forum for the development of measurement and reporting standards.
4. Independent audits inherently provide more accountability than does survey-based reporting.

In addition, ABC Interactive believes that like its print counterpart, it can give the Web census-based usage data as a foundation for an audit. Newspapers are anxious to see if this works to measure an online audience, as current methods are dubious. The number of web sites selling advertising has grown from none in 1994, to more than 300 by the end of 1995 (ABC, 1996). Although many of those dollars are considered to be for research and development, advertisers are beginning to demand accountability, especially because web advertising is considered the most expensive medium (Hafner & Tanaka, 1996). Most newspapers are charging by the "hit" using a base of 1,000.

Initially, *The New York Times* thought it could charge by the month, but advertisers balked at that. The *Times* has signed up five advertisers (Chemical Bank, Fidelity Investments, IBM, Maxwell House, and Toyota) in its partnership program, charging each a $150,000 annual fee. More advertisers are expected to sign up, according to the *Times*. For other advertisers, the minimum buy is $30,000 for 857,000 hits or impressions; and goes up to $120,000 for 6 million impressions. Yet, the *Times* is aware of its current limitations in the use of advertising. According to the senior vice president for sales and marketing at The New York Times Electronic Media Co., "We want 10 advertisers to use as a living laboratory. If advertising doesn't evolve beyond pointing to others' Web sites, I don't think it has much of a future" (Hafner & Tanaka, 1996).

The advertising manager of the *Wall Street Journal Electronic Edition* agrees that there are more unknown than known factors about web advertisements, noting that their research shows only 3% to 5% of those who see the icons on web pages click-on to get to the advertisers' sites. The *Wall Street Journal Interactive Edition* sells its banner ad for $20,000 a month. Nearly two dozen advertisers have signed up for Dow Jones, including Lexus, Nynex Interactive Yellow Pages, and Corestates Bank in Philadelphia (Murphy, 1996). Although the *Wall Street Journal Interactive* edition acknowledges low readership of advertising (as measured by clicking), it also claims that its demographics of online users show a very attractive audience - well educated, affluent, median age of 40 (as opposed to 50 with the print version), and their investing activity is as high or higher than those reading the print version (Murphy, 1996).

Tracking the number of "hits" was the first measure used to quantify usage. Advertisers have objected increasingly to this measure because claims of hits were not verifiable and only measured the request for information. Also with this method, each visit to a site was tallied, yielding higher numbers than may actually have viewed the information. For example, a newspaper publisher cannot claim that if an ad is seen twice by the same person, she or he counts as two potential customers. One of the newer measures is called "page views" or "page requests," which measures every hit to each file on the screen, rather than the screen as a whole. In addition, advertisers want to know the number of "impressions" - the number of times their banner is requested - that their site is accessed. Finally, what advertisers want to measure is the number of "click-throughs," or the amount of consumers who venture into the layers of information embedded in the advertisement to seek out more information. The "click-throughs" are the consumers thought to be highly motivated and interested in the product (Harrison, 1996).

CYBERDOLLARS ARE REAL AND SO IS THE COMPETITION

Advertising on the Web is expensive. Forrester Research, Inc., estimated that it costs $75 to reach 1,000 consumers, as opposed to $5.42 per thousand for television (30-second spot on a network news program) and $60.31 (full-page ad in a midsize city daily; Hafner, 1996). Given those costs, advertisers want to know who they are reaching and if their advertisements are effective.

Jupiter Communications estimates that online advertisers spent $55 million in 1995 and that figure will reach $5 billion by 2000 (Outing, 1995).

Who spent advertising dollars in the 4th quarter of 1995? (ABC, 1996)

AT&T	$567,000
Netscape	$556,000
Internet Shopping Network	$329,000
NECX Direct	$322,000
MasterCard	$278,000
American Airlines	$254,000
Microsoft	$240,000
c/net	$237,000
MCI	$231,000

Where the online advertising dollars went in 1995 (Resnick, 1996):

Netscape	$1,766,000
Lycos	$1,300,000
InfoSeek	$1,100,000
Yahoo	$1,100,000
Time Warner's Pathfinder	$ 810,000
HotWired	$ 720,000
WebCrawler	$ 600,000
ESPNet SportZone	$ 600,000
CNN	$ 594,000
c/net	$ 540,000

As these listings demonstrate, online newspapers face a critical need to solicit and post advertising on their web sites because they face competition not only from other media outlets, but from the advertisers themselves. For example, Toyota "publishes" a web site called "A Man's Life." This *zine*, as such sites are called, integrates editorial content with advertisements for its products. It is a type of soft-sell that appeals to a niche market. Advertisers have not been shy about finding out what editorial content their customers seek and then posting it to web sites. L. L. Bean, for example, retails rugged, casual clothing; their web site offers a database of the national parks, and home improvement hints can be found at Black & Decker's web site.

NEWS AND ADS: THE NEXT GENERATION

Although newspapers on the Web may not fully understand the use of advertising on their sites, they are nonetheless experimenting with new ideas. Some are even advertising on other Web sites. For example, *The Gate*, the online service of the *San Francisco Chronicle-Examiner,* advertises on Infoseek, one of the most popular search engines. Others freely admit they are experimenting on a daily basis with placement of advertising and the use of what television might call *infomercials*. The Cox newspaper chain is further experimenting with specialized information on sites hosted by its newspapers in West Palm Beach, Florida (tourist information) and Austin, Texas (college football).

Three models of generating revenue for online newspapers are developing: charge for information beyond front page, have advertisers support these pages, or the model the newspaper industry has traditionally followed of having advertisers and subscribers pay, with advertising carrying the majority of the costs (Auerbach, 1996). It remains to be seen which of these will be the most successful, yet it seems that advertising and editorial material will continue to coexist somewhere in the cyberpages of online newspapers.

REFERENCES

Audit Bureau of Circulation (1996, March 20). ABC board grants approval to officially launch trade show auditing program - tentative launch for interactive auditing service is June 1. [Online] Available: <http://www. accessabc.com>.

Auerbach, J. (1996, April 18). Premium fees the next wave for Net surfers. *Boston Globe,* p.1D.

Auter, P. J., & Moore, R. L. (1993). Buying from a friend: A content analysis of two teleshopping programs. *Journalism Quarterly, 70*(2), 425-436.

Bagdikian, B. (1990). *The media monopoly.* Boston: Beacon.

Baskette, F. K., Sissors, J. Z., & Brooks, B. S. (1992). *The art of editing.* New York: Macmillan

Brooks, B., Kennedy, G., Moen, D., and Ranly, D. (1996). *News reporting and writing,* Fifth Edition. New York: St. Martin's Press.

Cameron, G. T., & Haley, J. E. (1992). Feature advertising: policies and attitudes in print media. *Journal of Advertising , 21,* 47-55.

Covington, R. (1996, March 25). Do Internet ads sell? How can you judge? *International Herald Tribune,* p. 1D.

Duncan, T., & Caywood, C. (1996) The concept, process, and evolution of integrated marketing communication. In E. Thorson & J. Moore (Eds.), *Integrated communication.* Mahwah, NJ: Lawrence Erlbaum Associates, 13-31.

Edwards, L. (1996). Ad-webbing on the net. *Warfield's Business Record 1996, 11*(15), 1.

Emery, M., & Emery. E. (1988) *The press and America: An interpretative history of the mass media, sixth edition.* Englewood Cliffs, NJ: Prentice-Hall.

Hafner, K., & Tanaka, J. (1996, April 1). This Web's for you: Advertisers are throwing money at the Internet. Are they getting any back? *Newsweek,* 74-76.

Harrison, A. (1996) Advertising in cyber space: Where are the numbers? *Mass Tech Times Inc. 14*(7), 7.

Koon, B. (1996, January). Interview with San Jose Mercury news online editor.

Kouba, C. (1996, February). Interview with InfiNet manager.

Lacher, K. T. & Rotfeld, H. J. (1994) Newspaper policies on the potential merging of advertising and news content. *Journal of Public Policy & Marketing, 13*(2), 28.

Laurel, B. (1990). *The art of human-computer interface design.* Reading, MA: Addison-Wesley.

Leary, T. (1990). The interpersonal, interactive, interdeminsional interface. In B. Laurel (ed.) *The Art of Human-Computer Interface Design* (pp. 229-233). Reading, MA: Addison-Wesley.

Lesly, E. (1991, November). Realtors and builders demand happy news ... and often get it. *Washington Journalism Review, 20-23.*

McManus, J. (1994). *Market-driven journalism: Let the citizen beware?* Thousand Oaks, CA: Sage.

Meyer, P. (1987). *Ethical journalism.* New York: Longman.

Nua Ltd. (1998, September). [Online] Available: <http://www.nua.ie/surveys/how_many_online/index.html> and Global Internet Statistics (1998, September). [Online] Available: <http://www.euromktg.com/globstats/>, Editor and Publisher online column. <http://www.infomedia.com>.

Outing, S. (1996, May 13). Newspapers online: The latest statistics. *Editor & Publisher Web Site.* [Online] Available: *<http://www. infomedia/edpub/>*

Murphy, K. (1996). Legitimizing the new newspaper: WSJ sets pricing for Web edition. *WebInteractive.*

Peterson, I. (1996, February 25). Commitments, and questions, on electronic newspapers. *The New York Times,* p. 7D.

Resnick, R. (1996, January 29). Web ads creating millions in revenue. *The Austin American-Statesman,* p. 2C.

Sandler, D. M. & Secunda, E. (1993, May/June). Point of view: Blurred boundaries: Where does editorial end and advertising begin? *Journal of Advertising Research, 33,* 73-80.

Siebert, F., Peterson, T., & Schramm, W. L. (1956). *Four theories of the press.* Urbana: University of Illinois Press.

Singer, J. (1995, March). Interview with former prodigy manager.

Singer, S. (1991, September). Auto dealers muscle the newsroom. *Washington Journalism Review,* 24-26.

Soley, L. C., & Craig, R. L. (1992, December) Advertising pressures on newspapers: A survey. *Journal of Advertising, 21,* 1-10.

Thorson, E., & Moore, J. (1996). *Integrated communication: Synergy of persuasive voices.* Mahwah, NJ: Lawrence Erlbaum Associates.

Turow, J. (1992). *Media systems in society.* New York: Longman.

12

The Adoption of the World Wide Web by Marketers for Online Catalogs: A Diffusion Analysis

Jennifer K. Meyer

Several aspects of our environment have been altered to a certain degree as we have moved from the Industrial Age into what some are calling the Communication or Information Age (Krol & Klopfenstein, 1996). As the Industrial Revolution brought forth mass production, mass media have emerged as the critical means by which various industries market their goods. Similarly, as the Communication Age has begun to evolve, technology again is shifting the ways in which goods are marketed.

Within this revolution, several trends have emerged, including the emergence of home shopping, relationship marketing, and the development of new information and communication technologies. One technology that combines all of these trends is the World Wide Web. Over the past five years, the World Wide Web has been adopted by commercial users at a rapid pace. What will be the shopping experience of consumers in the future? Will companies adopt the Web for use as a major marketing medium?

New Age

The "Information/Communication Age, Revolution, or Society" are phrases that refer to how rapid the collection, storage, and transmission of vast amounts of data, made possible by computers, is affecting our society. With the computer processing capabilities available today, this information is a commodity that is becoming the focus of attention for companies competing in any marketplace. For example, the selling of databases that contain information about consumers is sometimes a bigger business for companies than their own core businesses. The progression into this information-based society is hastened by "the rapid convergence of communications and information technologies and the growth of integrated high capacity networks that carry communication in computer-readable digital form" (Straubhaar & LaRose, 1996).

New Marketing Paradigm

As applications of technology such as computer databases have emerged, so have new forms of marketing. Relationship marketing, one-to-one marketing, and database marketing (McKenna, 1991; Peppers & Rogers, 1993; Rapp & Collins, 1987) are three examples. Although there are differences between each, the premise remains the same: using new technology to identify, communicate, and build relationships with customers.

According to Peppers and Rogers (1993), we are undergoing a "paradigm shift" or a "technological discontinuity," where the old paradigm of mass production, media, and marketing is being replaced by a one-to-one economic system. This technological paradigm shift is mandating a new marketing paradigm, whether it is through relationship marketing, one-to-one marketing, or database marketing.

Companies are seeking ways to reach consumers efficiently and keep them coming back. There is a proliferation of media vehicles as well as products (Godin, 1995; Peppers & Rogers, 1993). Companies have been mass-producing multiple versions of product lines to try to compete by covering a new customer niche. This, in turn, has led to an increased amount of customer choice. The average grocery store in America, as an example, has gone from 10,000 items on shelves to about 25,000 items in the last decade (Godin, 1995).

With the tremendous increase in products have come the ubiquitous messages that bombard potential customers. Consumers are exposed to an average of up to 3,000 commercial messages per day (McKenna, 1991; Peppers & Rogers, 1993). With this plethora of messages, the effectiveness of each message is undermined and mass media advertising is increasingly less cost-effective (Peppers & Rogers, 1993). Additionally, with as many channels as an average household now receives and can expect to receive in the future, the concept of "mass" is limited to the number of channels on which a marketer can afford to advertise. Almost two thirds of U.S. households are cable subscribers and almost all of those households (95%) have 30 or more channels (National Cable Television Association (NCTA) Research and Policy Analysis Department, 1993). The likelihood that most companies can afford to advertise on most of these channels is minimal considering that in the last twenty years, charges for television commercials have gone up faster than the rate of inflation (Rapp & Collins, 1987).

The marketing concepts evolving from this paradigm shift recognize that customers are already deluged with information and that sending out more mass media messages is less effective. Relationship, one-to-one, and database marketing involve collecting data on their customers, whether it is from surveys on product offers or through electronic point-of-sale data at store registers. They then use their databases to identify their best customers by things such as their average purchase amount. Once these customers are identified, the marketers build relationships with those customers and distinguish their needs from customer feedback (McKenna, 1991; Peppers & Rogers, 1993; Rapp & Collins, 1987).

The Internet

Paralleling this transformation in marketing has been a revolution away from the one-to-many mass media model to a different model, as the Internet has emerged to provide interactivity (Hoffman & Novak, 1994). The portion of the Internet that is the most commercially developed is the World Wide Web (WWW).

Many marketers are proclaiming the Web as the greatest media invention since television. In fact, in early 1995, over half of the Fortune 500 companies had launched marketing programs on the World Wide Web (Jones, 1995). Some are taking full advantage of this new medium by enabling their customers to order products online; others simply are maintaining a "web presence" for public relations purposes or are still in the process of organizing for online transactions.

If a marketer's aim is to maintain a presence among actual and potential consumers, then the World Wide Web may offer an environment to do so. The number of online households worldwide will rise from 23.4 million in 1996 to 66.6 million in 2000, according to World Online Markets, a market study by Jupiter Communications (Barnako, 1996). These figures, however, have been fluctuating uncontrollably because it is difficult to estimate the numbers of web users.

Home Shopping

Another trend that has surfaced in the Communication Age is "home shopping." Because more people are shopping from their homes, the key to gaining these home consumers is the means of communication into the home available to marketers for displaying their goods. Although there are several characteristics of marketing on the World Wide Web that could make it attractive for commercial use, the Web offers a medium in which catalog companies may reach the growing numbers of "home shoppers."

Home shopping refers to the practice of consumers who make purchases by means other than physically walking into a store. In other words, home shopping occurs through channels such as mail-order catalogs, telephone, television, and the personal computer with online shopping services. Also, home shopping requires delivery of the product to the consumer. Therefore, the purchases may not always occur from the home, as some purchases may be made from the workplace, for example.

In 1993, total retail sales were $1.5 trillion (Press, 1994). Of that amount, 3.5% was catalog sales, 0.16% TV shopping sales, and 0.013% on-line shopping sales (Press, 1994). Although the numbers together and separately still represent a small percentage, the upward trend has been marked. Sroge (1991) suggested that "While the U.S. population grew about 15% in the 1980s, the number of American adults who shop by mail or phone has increased a phenomenal 59.7%.

In fact, the average consumer spends twenty minutes less per visit to shopping malls today than a decade ago (Kaufman, 1995). Online shoppers could be an increasing population because of the growth in households with personal computers equipped for an Internet connection. John Quarterman, editor of *Matrix News* and *Matrix Maps Quarterly*, noted that 13.5 million people had computers and software that can access the World Wide Web as of October 1994 (Janal, 1995). Forrester Research predicted that online shopping will grow to $4.8 billion by 1998 (Press, 1994).

Motivations

There have been various apparent motivations for the move toward home shopping. There is credit convenience and savings on sales tax if ordering out-of-state. Some people believe there to be slow service or a lack of product knowledge by in-store clerks. Others are not able to find items locally or lack the time to shop outside of the home. The most obvious motivation is the lack of time. Piirto (1994) suggested "The time constraints of middle-aged baby boomers, coupled with the increasing purchasing power of technologically savvy younger consumers, should help television and online shopping in the coming decade." Another more recently identified motivation has been a fear of crime when out shopping. In a survey done by Yankelovich Partners, it was found that "only 25% of shoppers said malls provided a safe and secure environment" (Underwood, 1994).

Not only are there customer motivations for purchasing online, but catalog marketers, the focus of this study, also have important motivations. "The problem with catalog shopping isn't the concept, it's the medium" (Koelsch, 1995). Catalog marketers have found the costs of getting their catalogs to consumers exorbitant. There was a 55% to 58% rise in paper costs from 1995 to 1996, as well as 10.3% increases in postal rates in early 1995 (Rickard & Raiston, 1995). For a company such as Land's End that mails out 191 million catalogs yearly, it could add at least $15 million to its costs of printing, producing, and mailing catalogs (Rickard & Raiston, 1995). Moreover, information provided on a WWW catalog is more current because it can be updated regularly and "an online presence is cheaper than CD-ROM catalogs, which are cheaper than print catalogs" (Press, 1994). Given these positive web attributes, why would a marketer not be anxious to go online?

The World Wide Web provides a medium where there are tremendous graphics capabilities, the elimination of printing and postal costs, ease of updating material, and most interestingly - the kind of audience it can reach. There are many similarities, for the present, between a profile of a typical catalog consumer and a typical web user. In fact, 82% of computer shoppers also buy from catalogs (Evans, 1994). Additionally, 71% of World Wide Web users buy from catalogs and of those, 68% have made purchases over the Internet (WebLink Design, 1995).

Catalog User Demographics

A distinction was made between catalog shoppers and noncatalog shoppers in a profile drawn from surveys done by Impact Resources. They found that catalog shoppers "are better educated, work in professional and managerial capacities, earn more money, and are more comfortable with modern technology and stocks and bonds" than noncatalog shoppers. It also found that more than two thirds of catalog shoppers have attended college and more than half earn between $30,000 and $99,000 annually (Braun, 1993). These profiles closely resemble those of a World Wide Web user or adopter.

In comparing the previously mentioned catalog user statistics to the following web user statistics drawn from the preliminary results of the Commerce/Nielsen Internet Demographics Survey (Hoffman & Novak, 1995), the author noted striking similarities:

- 25% of Web users have an income of $80,000 or more
- 51% are in professional or managerial capacities
- 64% have had at least four years of college

If these statistics are accurate, the World Wide Web offers an audience that is very similar to the kinds of audiences targeted by catalog marketers. In fact, they may be the same people they normally reach and could do so more cost efficiently by using the Web to distribute their offerings.

THE STUDY

With the emergence of new marketing efforts, there are also technological advancements emerging that are compatible with the goals of this marketing paradigm shift, such as the World Wide Web. Numerous publications have mentioned how the Web is a very promising innovation for catalog marketers to use as a new communication medium (Piirto, 1994; Rickard & Raiston, 1995).

Not all catalog marketers, however, have been quick to heed these proclamations. Although several catalog companies had adopted the use of online catalogs for almost one year before this study, others are in the planning stages, yet others do not have plans to adopt the Web. This makes an excellent topic of study because some are adopting the web and some are not. Researchers may learn what may encourage some organizations to adopt and others to stay clear of the innovation.

As the World Wide Web has emerged, the marketplace has recognized its potential as a marketing tool. Because its emergence has been so recent, however, marketers have little or no experience with this innovation. With its parallels to the marketing methods traditionally used by the catalog industry, the World Wide Web has obvious appeal to catalog marketers. Despite this appeal, not all catalog marketers are adopting the Web. This study seeks to investigate why. The study attempts to understand the adoption process in general and the World Wide Web in particular. In studying the adoption process, a diffusion of innovation approach was used. One aspect of the adoption process, perceived obstacles to organizational adoption, was selected for focus.

Perceived obstacles fall under the persuasion stage of diffusion of innovation. The focus is on this stage because it is the point before the decision is made. The case could be made that the decision stage is the most important and involved stage of the process as the potential adopter sorts through the positive and negative attributes of the innovation. It is the point at which relative advantage of the innovation is weighed against the perceived obstacles of the innovation.

The concept of perceived obstacles refers to those characteristics of the innovation that potential adopters could perceive as being a problem, thereby being a barrier to the innovation's adoption. They are perceived because the obstacles may not pose an actual problem, yet the potential adopters could perceive them to be problems because of past experience, media hype, or other reasons. As these obstacles have been uncovered through various media, they provide an overview of those that could possibly be perceived obstacles, or risks by those companies involved in the study.

This chapter does not suggest better ways in which catalogers can market their goods on the World Wide Web, nor does it seek out those catalogers who are having problems in devising their marketing strategies for the World Wide Web. The purpose of this chapter is to look at marketing on the World Wide Web as a communication innovation that has been, or soon may be, adopted by those who already market their products through another medium - the catalog. The Web appears especially well-suited to many of their customers. The question is not whether the Web will be used by the catalogers for marketing, but rather how particular companies have come to the decision to adopt the Web as a communication medium for reaching individuals. The study also addresses what has occurred within those organizations that have adopted the Web as a result of implementing the innovation. It also analyzes why other catalogers have not adopted the Web as a medium, as yet.

Research Questions

To address this issue, two general research questions were posed. First, what are the perceived obstacles of using the World Wide Web as a marketing tool that may keep some organizations from adopting this innovation? Second, why have some catalog marketers decided to adopt the World Wide Web for an online catalog?

Research Conducted

Diffusion of innovations was chosen as the theoretical framework in which to frame the research because it best suits the research questions as to how or why the World Wide Web is or is not adopted by certain catalog companies. The study used as its units of analysis, or potential adopters, a total of six catalog companies. Three of the chosen companies adopted the World Wide Web for an online catalog and may be considered *early adopters*. The remaining three companies may be considered *late adopters* or *non-adopters* and cannot be easily classified as either, because the commercial development of the World Wide Web is still evolving. The innovation studied will be the World Wide Web as it is used for purposes of an online catalog.

Because the commercial development of the World Wide Web is still rapidly evolving, a method was chosen that would take this into account. The case study approach was chosen as the methodology in which to study the adoption of this innovation. The six case studies reviewed here include interviews with individuals within middle-management positions. Activity on the World Wide Web was also observed, and secondary resources were employed to discover each company's level of involvement with the World Wide Web.

Six individuals, one from each of the six different catalog companies, were interviewed by telephone. Although all of the companies but two are identified by pseudonyms only, each company's characteristics are described within the study without identifying them explicitly. The companies were chosen because they had established print catalogs previous to the development of the World Wide Web. A determination of their involvement on the World Wide Web was made by observing Web activity as well as confirming with the individuals as to the extent of their involvement.

A basic outline of interview questions was used to guide the process, however each interview differed depending on the interviewee's responses. The questions were derived from the theoretical framework of diffusion of innovations and were subsequently analyzed using the same framework.

THEORETICAL FRAMEWORK AND METHODOLOGY

Theoretical Framework

A leader in the diffusion of innovations research is Rogers (1995). His book, *Diffusion of Innovation*, provides an overview of the basic elements of how an innovation is diffused into society. Rogers stated that "Diffusion is the process by which an innovation is communicated through certain channels over time among the members of a social system" (p. 5).

Diffusion theory suggests a focus on several things. It considers the communication channels employed to spread knowledge. It also examines the stages of awareness of an innovation and the criteria for any subsequent decisions on its adoption. Additionally, it looks at characteristics of potential adopters and the likely advantages of the adoption. According to W. R. Spence (1994) in his book *Innovation*, most decisions can be attributed to two major influences - the features of the innovation and the characteristics of the decision makers.

Innovation-Decision Process

One model called the Innovation-Decision Process identifies the stages of this determinative model as those of knowledge, persuasion, decision, implementation, and confirmation. Through examining these stages of adoption, some attributes in the innovation that have deterred some catalogers from adopting it are revealed. For example, in a model of the stages of the innovation-decision process, at the persuasion level, there are several characteristics that may be used as evaluative criteria for the Web.

Methodology

Case studies were chosen because they were capable of being completed with the small number of potential catalog companies used for this study. A survey would not have been sufficient because there are no two positions alike. For example, the author could not send surveys addressed to the Director of Marketing as not every company has such a position, and those that do may not have a person responsible for electronic media. Also, no two companies market the exact same products. Therefore, it was necessary to have an in-depth discussion to determine such factors. Last, no two companies are at the same stage of adoption. Web observation reveals whether or not a company is using the Web for an online catalog.

Web observation does not reveal if that company is planning to implement a Web catalog in two weeks. Case studies provide more depth in the study to reveal these issues. The organizations that were interviewed have similar characteristics. They are catalog companies that have had established print catalogs over time and before the World Wide Web was used commercially, whether or not they presently have World Wide Web sites including their catalogs for online ordering. The product offerings vary somewhat, which is important for demonstrating that not just one type of product is attractive for web catalog marketing.

RESULTS OF ADOPTERS

Department Chain. The first company studied is the only national department store with an online catalog and a print catalog. The company is identified here simply as *Department Chain*. This particular company distributes several versions of print catalogs: 3 large seasonal catalogs, 19 sales tabloids, and over 70 specialty catalogs. Annually, *Department Chain* distributes, in total, over 360 million individual catalogs.

The individual interviewed at *Department Chain* holds the position of Electronic Retailing Manager. She has been with the company for fourteen years, and her position resides within a strategic planning capacity of the catalog division in an area called New Business Development. Within this area, different new business opportunities are constantly being studied. One high priority is international expansion and the other is electronic, which is her responsibility. In general, she and an assistant work with various areas within the catalog division to implement media tests.

Summary of Case Study Findings: *Department Chain*
- Had background experimenting with new media forms (interactive television, kiosks)
- Charter members of Prodigy and CompuServe
- Began experimentation on the Web in 1994 with about 100 products
- First national department store on its own server (December, 1994)
- Their CD-ROM store already had digital assets, which made for an easy transfer to online environments
- Conducted research on customer acceptance (sample of 1,000), response was very positive
- More responsive - able to offer "late-breaking" items (products that normally would not make the print catalog deadlines)
- Highly dynamic environment - able to offer sales for one hour or even 20 minutes as opposed to six weeks or six months with a print catalog
- Reduction of printing and postal costs - as customer accepts the new formats then production savings can be passed along to the customer
- Biggest issue concern is customer acceptance, or their ease of use - equipment, hardware, and the accessibility to hardware

- Big question is "until it gets to a mass critical level of acceptance, are we really going to be able to cost-effectively offer these formats to the customer?"
- The company has only been using its toll-free number because it senses the customer is a little nervous about the security issue and it wants to make sure the customer is truly ready for online ordering before the company offers it on its site
- Volume of e-mail traffic has increased significantly - necessary to recruit and train personnel to handle traffic
- Online catalog has triggered more attention to responsiveness of inventory levels
- Online advantages to customers go beyond commerce - able to provide credit information, gift registries, and channels that allow customers to talk directly with a representative via e-mail
- New modeling techniques are necessary to forecast demand

Land's End. This store is an international direct merchant company of traditionally styled, casual clothing for men, women, and children, accessories, domestics, shoes, and soft luggage. Several of its items are positioned to be worn outdoors. *Land's End's* customers include those individuals between the ages of 35 to 64 with a median household income of $55,000. Almost 90% have college education, and more than 70% are in professional and managerial positions.

The individual interviewed holds the title of "Electronic Media Merchant." She is on a team within the marketing department whose main focus is to test out all of the upcoming new media, such as CD-ROMs, interactive television, and online services, to see what is available and if any of it makes sense for *Land's End* customers. Her main role is merchandising, but because the team is only comprised of four people, she has also been involved in some creative aspects.

Summary of Case Study Findings: *Land's End*
- Initial CD-ROM trial abandoned because of creative and navigational limitations (too many other retailers on the same CD; CDs are often associated with games and resource materials; users would still need to use the phone to place an order)
- No longer involved in interactive television but are keeping abreast of its progress
- Decided to go with an independent site for increased control, unlike the competition that had partnerships with large media companies - provided control over navigation and creative presentation

- Advantage for online is the convenience to the customer - especially advantageous to international customers. Cheaper to order online than to fax
- Biggest disadvantage is perceived security problems
- Orders are presently handled through their mail-processing department, which handles all orders - did not initially want to expand departments to handle its Web site. E-mail is handled within different departments depending on topic
- Biggest challenge is trying to keep up with the evolution of their site - must sort through such things as if it is easier to use real-time audio or video - try to keep up with the enhancements so their page looks fresh
- Another challenge is that of color. As everyone's colors show up different on their terminals, the actual colors of items may not be what the customer expects

The Sharper Image. This store is a specialty retailer of unique, innovative, and often electronic, products. The business began in 1978 by Richard Thalheimer when he placed an ad for digital stopwatches in Runner's World magazine that led to $400 in sales (Sroge, 1991). The first catalog was produced in 1979 and offered many exercise-related items, electronics, and gifts. In 1985, the catalog went monthly. The monthly catalogs are approximately 68 pages and offer between 150 and 175 products (Sroge, 1991). The catalog is mailed to about two million people every month (Sroge, 1991). The first retail store opened in 1983. The chain grew to 75 stores by 1990 (Barrier 1991), and had 74 stores in 1995. The company went public in April, 1987. The characteristics of customers are that they are college-educated, professional males whose average household income exceeds $76,000. In fact, 65% of their customers are men (Morgenson, 1992).

The individual interviewed holds the title of "Director of Marketing." He is responsible for the strategic planning of all advertising campaigns. It is his job to figure out who gets mailed which catalog, when they get it, how often they receive it, and what kind of sales promotions are in each. He does this using the company's databases that have several million customers on file, and which are constantly updated. The director is responsible for all of the sales forecasting for financial purposes. He is also in charge of the development of the electronic catalog on the World Wide Web and a CD-ROM catalog. Additionally, his responsibilities include acquiring new customers.

Summary of Case Study Findings: *The Sharper Image*
- Has historically been involved in various forms of electronic media
- July of 1995 - *The Sharper Image* put its own catalog on the World Wide Web

- Electronic cataloging is a hot topic in the direct mail industry because of the paper and postage cost increases
- Not everyone has a computer and not everyone is willing to purchase in that manner
- Everybody agrees that this is definitely a wave of the future, but right now the are just too many problems with it for it to be really viable at least for the next two to three years
- Takes too long to download information if you do not have a state-of-the-art computer
- Another problem is one of fraud, which can be tied in with security
- Disagrees with the position that the Web will replace the catalog as a method of purchase. People buying over the Web do not tend to buy as often or as much as those who buy from the print catalog
- It is almost like a new market as opposed to a replacement for the catalog they were so quick to adopt because they tend to get approached rather steadily by everyone with a new technology because everyone thinks they should be there
- *The Sharper Image* sells high-tech items mostly for men - it is believed that most of the Web buyers are also men "who are willing to spend a few bucks on some new gadgets"
- It was a natural progression from their work with *2 Market* on their CD-ROM catalog, and later *2 Market's* decision to go online
- Trying to attempt new technology by dividing labor among existing staff
- By having their catalog online, they have discovered that it has actually created more work in fraudulent orders. These orders usually come from children who are making phony orders with phony credit card numbers. They get about three or four times the amount of fraudulent orders over the Web than they do through the usual catalog
- They are seeing a higher percentage of orders coming from overseas compared with their print catalog
- They tend to put items online that are lower-priced and easily shipped. They have found the Web to be a very price-sensitive market

RESULTS OF LATE OR NON-ADOPTERS

The late or nonadopter category consists of three catalog companies that had not fully adopted the World Wide Web for online catalogs at this study's inception. One of the companies has only gone online with one of its subsidiaries. Another was in the planning stages to develop an online catalog. The third company does not have plans to go online.

Upscale Items. This term is the pseudonym chosen for this company because it well represents its type of merchandise. The company is focused on the high-end segment of the specialty retailing marketplace serving affluent customers and is known for its high fashion merchandise. The first store opened in 1907. There are now 28 stores and a mail-order business, which is comprised of several different companies. *Upscale Items* offers extravagant brand names such as *Adolfo, Armani, Bill Blass, Chanel, Hermes, Paloma Picasso, Valentino,* and *Ungaro* among others. The catalogs have been distributed annually since 1939. The mail order business, however, was not in place as a major operation until the 1950s (Sroge & Highum, 1987). The mail order operations had revenues of $247.9 million in 1995. A total of 84 catalogs were mailed during 1995 with an average circulation of 1.2 million households per book. *Upscale Item's* main target group is a female in her fifties who is fairly conservative and traditional. In fact, 60% of their customers are upscale women.

The title of the individual interviewed is "Vice President of Creative Services and Advertising." Under that position, she and her team are responsible for turning the merchandise into a catalog. Her department consists of about eighty people. They decide what the catalogs will look like, they take the pictures, do the color separations, and printing, and then send them into the mail stream. She is also in charge of public relations.

Summary of Case Study Findings: *Upscale Items*
- located in a popular cybermall
- At this site, consumers may go into a personal shopper section that runs across all of the catalogs or they may go into individual catalogs to browse
- The consumers are able to buy items by calling a special toll-free number because Time Warner is still working on an encryption coding system it feels will give its consumers the best protection against credit card fraud
- Feels that all of their companies are very female-dominated, and they do not believe their target matches a typical web user
- The target audience of *Upscale Items* is a fairly conservative and traditional woman who is very fashion-conscious
- Decided not to continue with the CD-ROM catalog because everything in the CD-ROM catalog had to be stable for four to six months, which was not an improvement on their print version. Even though they had decent results, they had a lower than normal average order
- Believes it is evolving to the point where sites need to be more dynamic
- Believes it will not reach any critical mass, but might be an extra source of revenue

- Believes customers not ready yet for electronic shopping and will not be ready until marketers learn to provide added value information

Vintage Clothing. This business began in 1988 when the owner discovered a popularity for a duster coat he had purchased in Wyoming. He bought an advertisement in *The New Yorker* magazine and ended up selling 500 of the coats rather quickly (Sporkin & Shaw, 1990). At that time, he decided to publish a catalog and the first one went out in late 1988 or early 1989. The company has grown to approximately 300 employees now, and there are three stores in addition to the catalog operation (Sporkin & Shaw, 1990). The merchandise they sell is upscale, unique men's and women's clothing that they have given the name "vintage-inspired." They are called "vintage-inspired" because much of the clothing is based on historical designs or styling. The catalog is known for its watercolor-painted images as opposed to photographs and its copy that conjures up images of precious finds from faraway lands. In 1990, the business was said to have made $20 million (Sporkin & Shaw, 1990).

The individual interviewed holds the title of "Marketing Analyst." His position has to do with anything related to new sales growth. He tries to discover how to mail the catalog to new groups of people, new countries, or a new sales medium like the Internet. There are four people within his department.

Summary of Case Study Findings: *Vintage Clothing*
- Not on the Web at the time of the interview but was planning for a site
- There is definitely a lot of talk about the World Wide Web in the catalog industry because of the increases in paper and postage costs
- Plan to give service provider a percentage of sales as payment for creating their web site. *Vintage Clothing* has no upfront risk
- The most attractive feature of having an online catalog is being able to reach a new market. It is believed they will be able to reach a whole new customer instead of overlap customers. It is also believed that the Web catalog will reach a younger group of well-educated people
- Feels there will be a reluctance of people to use their credit cards online, but does not view the security issue as a major constraint

Women's Resortwear. This business is a privately held mail-order company that sells swim and resortwear. The company was established in 1980 and acquired in 1982 by its parent company, which began in 1952 as a terry cloth apparel manufacturing partnership (Sroge & Highum, 1987). The primary merchandise lines are positioned at the affordable end of the upscale market. As of 1987, the catalogs from this division were mailed to more than four million households each year. As of that same year, there were approximately 70,000 active buyers on file with an average order of $75. Also in 1987, *Women's*

Resortwear's revenues were estimated at $5.7 million (Sroge & Highum, 1987). The target audience is women between 35 and 65 with a combined household income of over $100,000.

The title of the individual interviewed is "Production Manager." Her position includes the responsibility of making sure all internal deadlines are met. She is an assistant to the President and assists her in viewing color on the book for printing and color separations. Basically, she is delegated projects by the President on just about everything to do with the catalog.

Summary of Case Study Findings: *Women's Resortwear*
- Have no experience with the Web
- Believes catalogs are becoming more popular because people do not want to deal with the malls and if they can shop 24 hours a day, then it is a great vehicle
- Feels *Women's Resortwear* specifically should not have an online catalog because its traditional audience is older than the young audience believed to be on the Web. It does not believe its frequent users are on the Internet
- Do not want their catalog to go out to people who are not going to buy. Because the catalog has a lot of scantily clad girls in bathing suits, fear men who only want to view their swimsuit models will be viewing their catalog without buying
- Perceives the most attractive thing to catalog companies about an online catalog is that customers would like shopping through the Web because it is in the privacy of their own home, it is interactive, and you can flip through screens as easily as you could flip through printed pages
- Assigns a low priority to adopting the Web with the economy and the retail industry being bad lately, the company's goal this year is just to sell merchandise. *Women's Resortwear* does not want to try to sell through a new medium because its most recent difficulties have been selling through the same medium in which it has sold items for fifteen years
- Lack of knowledge and the economy are stated reasons for not adopting the Web. She stated, "I feel like it would be hard at this point, given the current economy to venture out into something that we're pretty clueless about"

CONCLUSION

This study is believed to be the first study that traces the innovation-decision process of catalog companies adopting the World Wide Web for online versions of their catalogs. The thesis draws on the innovation decision process model and the premises established by Everett Rogers (1995) in his book *Diffusion of Innovations*.

Perceived Obstacles of Marketing on the World Wide Web

To answer the first research question about perceived obstacles in the adoption of the World Wide Web, secondary resources were utilized in addition to the case studies to gather characteristics that have been publicly proclaimed by some to be obstacles of marketing on the World Wide Web. Throughout the study, however, additional characteristics were uncovered in the qualitative research conducted. Some of the obstacles discussed in the literature review were not mentioned at all by the respondents, such as global market concerns and limited rural access. In fact, additional perceived obstacles were discovered that had not been found through the literature review, which are discussed later.

The case studies of both the adopters and the non adopters or late adopters aided in answering this research question. Even though the adopters' existing perceived obstacles did not prevent their adoption, they were helpful in learning what obstacles catalog companies are considering. A study of those perceived obstacles may reveal those obstacles that perhaps may not be perceived as being serious enough to halt adoption.

The perceived obstacles mentioned most often were those of security, resources, and customer acceptance. Out of the three adopters, one named security as its top concern and another as the second of its concerns relating to consumer acceptance. In fact, none of the catalog marketers themselves are concerned with the security of credit card transactions. They do believe consumers are skeptical of the security and will, therefore, cause a reluctance of consumers to adopt these methods. Two respondents from the non adopters or late adopter categories cited security as the main perceived obstacle in saying they believe there is a problem with consumer acceptance because of the security issue. Therefore, security was found to be the most important perceived obstacle.

Only *The Sharper Image* and *Women's Resortwear* did not mention the security issue as being a perceived obstacle. *The Sharper Image* along with *Department Chain* believed the largest perceived obstacle to be resources. They both felt that before their adoption, the companies were concerned about splitting the additional labor required for the web catalog among their existing staff. They both mentioned that because the Web is considered to be an important venture, they want to give it 100%. By this they meant that they would like to keep their web pages updated more often, offer new promotions, and generally try to generate more sales from the site. Doing so would be difficult given that they had not expanded any of their staff to accommodate the new medium. They said that this is true anytime a company makes a new business decision (innovation) and is not particularly a problem of the Web itself.

Women's Resortwear was different than all of the companies, as they did not mention any of the three most mentioned perceived obstacles of security, resources, or consumer acceptance. *Women's Resortwear* believed its biggest obstacle to be that its target market is one it feels cannot be reached via this new medium. This is because *Women's Resortwear's* target audience consists of older females, while the typical web audience is considered to be male. This relates to the demographic drawbacks discussed earlier.

In talking with the individuals from the adopter category, some additional challenges that those organizations have faced in implementing their online catalogs were discovered. These challenges could come to be obstacles to late adopters if they become aware of them from their communication with early or current adopters. Interestingly, these challenges all varied among the different companies. *Department Chain* was more focused on what they could do to provide more to their customers, such as customer service and responding to customers through e-mail. *Land's End* was concerned about the specific challenges the web site presents, such as keeping up with the evolution of the site and the fact that color is different on various computer monitors. Finally, *The Sharper Image* finds that their biggest challenge is getting customers to make larger purchases from the site.

The individuals from the adopter category also provided insight into what they would perceive as the largest concerns if they were adopting a web catalog today. *Department Chain* believes that resources would still be a major issue, as well as the issue of having to develop new modeling techniques for forecasting demand. *Land's End* also maintains that resources would be a major concern, along with security. They also now consider the difficulty of being found among all of the Internet traffic to be an obstacle. *The Sharper Image* believes that its biggest concern today, knowing what they do now, would be dealing with Web providers amicably and dealing with the larger number of fraudulent orders.

Reasons for Adopting a World Wide Web Catalog

In answering the second research question as to why catalog marketers have decided to adopt the World Wide Web, a general focus was on the adopter category. The nonadopter or late adopter category, however, was also used in extracting respondents' views on perceived advantages of the Web. Half of the study participants said that the biggest advantage of the Web is that it adds convenience to the customer.

Two of those that had this response were from the adopter category, while the third was from *Women's Resortwear*, which has no plans to develop a web catalog. The convenience for the customer ranged from *Department Chain's* response that there is an amazing turnaround time for merchandise offerings to *Land's End's* mention of added value for international customers. Another reason included the need to explore a new area by *The Sharper Image*, which represents a need for status as they carry high-tech merchandise.

Finally *Upscale Items*, which has responded skeptically to the use of the Web for full-scale use, described that the only advantage is that the Web provides an alternative channel of distribution, showing its belief that the Web may offer a supplement to a print catalog, but never a replacement.

Although security of credit card transactions was considered a concern by two of the adopting companies, *Department Chain* and *Land's End*, it obviously did not impede them from adopting. Their biggest concern with this perceived obstacle is that it is perceived by the consumers to be unsafe, so they took that into consideration in the implementation of their web sites. *Department Chain* was only taking telephone orders when they first began their site, and *Land's End* communicated to their customers that their order form was downloadable and encrypted. No concerns of privacy were ever voiced by any of the companies from either category.

In answering this research question, it was felt that change agents were a significant factor in adoption. All three of the adopters studied had been previously involved in using or trying new media such as CD-ROM or interactive television. *Department Chain* was involved in *Shopping 2000* through *ContentWare*, who also maintained the company's CD-ROM store. Both *Land's End* and *The Sharper Image* participated in CD-ROM catalogs with *2 Market*, which made a deal with *America Online*. Although *Land's End* decided to go ahead with its own site, *The Sharper Image* participated in *2 Market's* agreement to go on *America Online*. After that trial with the Internet, *The Sharper Image* decided to have its own web site. The decisions to go out with their own site were due to an issue of control. After trying the Web with a provider, the companies wanted to acquire control of their own content.

Change agents also seem to be playing a part in encouraging those who have not yet fully adopted, such as *Vintage Clothing* and *Upscale Items*. *Vintage Clothing*, although a late adopter, was ultimately persuaded to adopt a web catalog through a service provider that agreed to take on the risk for the company. This aided in their adoption as the company has not previously been involved in other new media. *Upscale Items*, which is still in the trial stages with a catalog subsidiary, had previously been involved in new media trials. It was involved with *Catalog 1*, a service provided through *Spiegel* and *Time Warner*. The *Dream Shop* site in which *Upscale Items* is trying their Web catalog, is also provided by *Time Warner*.

Consistencies Among Categories

The companies within the adopter category can be considered to still be within the implementation stage of their adoption. This is because their web sites have not really become a regular part of their business, compared to their print catalogs. Although, they believe they are fully implementing the online catalogs, they still have not reached the volume of products offered, nor the number of consumers reached, compared to their regular business. Within the late or nonadopter category, *Women's Resortwear* is the only company within the knowledge stage of adoption. *Vintage Clothing* and *Upscale Items* are somewhere between the persuasion stage and the decision stage as they have made a decision to adopt a catalog, yet their opinions of it are not yet declared. *Vintage Clothing* may not be convinced, but feel they have nothing to lose with the arrangement with their service provider. *Upscale Items*, by analogy, only has "one foot in the water." They are not risking their main catalog with the innovation to date.

All of the adopters have had previous experience with new media. This shows their potential interest in at least trying out the Web. The adopters all were established before the 1980s showing the stability of being in business for so long. Two of the companies in the adopter category have approach or exceeded a billion dollars in sales. These companies also have high distribution of their print catalogs, ranging from 31 million to 360 million catalogs distributed annually.

With the exception of *Upscale Items*, the companies in the late adopter or nonadopter category have the opposite characteristics in common. They were established during the 1980s. They have sales figures in the low millions and have a lower distribution of their print catalogs. Finally, they have had no prior experience with new media.

The exceptions in each of the categories include *The Sharper Image* in the adopter category and *Upscale Items* in the late adopter or nonadopter category. *The Sharper Image* was established closer to the 1980s and has lower sales and distribution figures. *Upscale Items* was established very early, has relatively high revenues, and although is not distributed to as many people as *Land's End* or *Department Chain,* has a distribution figure of 1.2 million. They have also had trials in new media.

The differences in these two exceptions provide logical reasons for their adoption status. *The Sharper Image* seems to be related to those companies fitting in the late adopter or nonadopter category, however, there is a significant difference. *The Sharper Image* carries products that are targeted toward the audience that is supposed to be prevalent on the World Wide Web. *The Sharper Image* carries technical novelty items that are geared toward a male audience and therefore they may have had a status motivation for adoption.

Upscale Items represents a different company in the late adopter or nonadopter category as they have adopted, but only with one of their subsidiaries. This company is comprised of a rather conservative audience and is very concerned about the security issue.   Also, because of their target audience, the company does not believe it can reach a significant portion of consumers to provide a large enough profit stream. They seemed to be mainly concerned with the risk of upsetting customers if something were to go awry with the security of credit card transactions.

From the discussion of perceived obstacles earlier, the only subjects not mentioned by any of the participants were those of limited rural access and privacy. This is probably due to the fact that limited rural access may only be seen as a concern of consumers at this point, as the catalog companies have not completely integrated their online catalogs into their normal business routines. Privacy may not be seen as a concern of catalog marketers because they are accustomed to the subject from their print catalog business.

There are some consistencies among those companies that have decided to adopt the Web for an online catalog and those who have not yet done so. Any noted exceptions may be attributed to certain factors - either the target audience of the organization, the products they offer, or the amount of risk they perceive exists, which has to do with the company's size or what opportunities service providers have offered them.

REFERENCES

Barnako, F. (1996, November 19). Closing bell. *Internet Daily*, 15.

Barrier, M. (1991, November). How Richard Thalheimer is trying to sharpen an out-of-date image. *Nation's Business,16*, 18.

Braun, H. D. (1993, March). The catalog shopper of the '90s. *Direct Marketing*, 15-18.

Evans, C. R. (1994). *Marketing channels: Infomercial and the future of televised marketing.* Englewood Cliffs, NJ: Prentice Hall.

Godin, S. (1995). *Emarketing: Reaping profits on the information highway.* New York: Perigree Books.

Hoffman, D. L. & Novak, T. P. (1994, March). Commercializing the Information Superhighway: Are we in for a smooth ride? *Project 2000: Research Program on Marketing in Computer-Mediated Environments.* [Online] Avaliable: <http://www 2000.ogsm.vanderbilt.edu/smooth.ride. html>.

Hoffman, D. L. & Novak, T. P. (1995, October 30). Measuring the Internet: Preliminary results of the Commerce/Nielsen Internet Demographics Survey. *Project 2000: Research Program on Marketing in Computer-Mediated Environments.* From <http://www2000.ogsm.> [Online] Available: <vanderbilt.edu/novak/CN.prelim. results.oct30.html>.

Janal, D. S., (1995b). author of *Online Marketing Handbook.* Interview by author, 18 December, Bowling Green, Ohio. Telephone Interview.

Jones, T. (1995). *Marketing guide to the Internet: The executive guide to marketing on the new Internet.* [Online] Available: <http://www.industry. net/guide. html>.

Kaufman, L. (1995, September 11). That's entertainment: Shopping malls are borrowing ideas from theme parks to survive. *Newsweek, 132*: p. 72.

Koelsch, F. (1995). *The infomedia revolution: How it is changing our world and your life.* Whitby, Ontario, Canada: McGraw-Hill Ryerson.

Krol, E. & Klopfenstein, B. (1996). *The Whole Internet User's Guide and Catalog: Academic edition.* Cambridge, Massachussetts: O'Reilly and Associates, Inc., Preface.

McKenna, R. (1991). *Relationship marketing: Successful strategies for the age of the customer.* Reading, MA: Addison-Wesley.

Morgenson, G. (1992, October 26). The Sharper Image's sharper image. *Forbes, Vol 157*: p. 212, 216.

NCTA Research and Policy Analysis Department. (1993). Twenty-first century television. Washington, DC, National Cable Television Association. Quoted in Joseph Straubhaar and Robert LaRose. 1996. *Communications Media in the Information Society.* Belmont, CA: Wadsworth.

Peppers, D., & Rogers, M. (1993). *The one-to-one future: Building relationships one customer at a time.* New York: Doubleday.

Piirto, R. (1994, September). Catalogs with byte. *American Demographics, 16*(9), p. 6.

Press, L. (1994, November). Commercialization of the Internet. *Communications of the ACM*, New York: Association for Computing Machinery (ACM), 17-21.

Rapp, S., & Collins, T. (1987). *Maximarketing: The new direction in advertising, promotion, and marketing strategy.* New York: McGraw-Hill.

Rickard, L., & Raiston, J. (1995, July 10). Catalogers order changes to beat costs. *Advertising Age*, p. 1, 10.

Rogers, E. (1995). *Diffusion of innovations (4th ed).* New York: The Free Press.

Spence, W. R. (1994). *Innovation.* London: Chapman & Hall.

Sporkin, E., & Shaw, B. (1990, September). Suburban cowboy John Peterman rides the long coattails of his dude-ish duster to catalog success. *People Weekly, 42*, 127-8.

Sroge, M., & Highum, B. (1987). *Inside the leading mail order houses* (3rd ed). Lincolnwood, IL: NTC Business Books.

Sroge, M. (1991). *The United States mail order industry.* Homewood, IL: Business One Irwin.

Straubhaar, J., & LaRose, R. (1996). *Communications media in the information society.* Belmont, CA: Wadsworth Publishing.

Underwood, E. (1994, January 17). Mall busters, like crime, a boon for home shopping. *Brandweek, 38*: p. 18, 20.

WebLink Design Services. (1995). WWW Demographics (From Hermes WWW Users Survey 1995). [Online] Available: <http://www.serix.com/ weblink/demogr. html>.

13

Advertising in an Interactive Environment: A Research Agenda

Eloise Coupey
Virginia Polytechnic Institute & State University

The use of interactive technology, such as the World Wide Web, provides advertisers with a new medium for transmitting their message about various products and services. Much attention has been paid - primarily in the popular press - to the potential of this medium for marketers and for consumers. There is, however, a dearth of research to provide information about how consumers will use the medium and the effect of this medium on consumer knowledge and choice. The objective of this chapter is to present an agenda for research that can address the issues of whether and how the medium affects consumption-related decisions.

The research agenda incorporates an information processing perspective with characteristics of interactive media. This perspective is used because it provides a general description of the mental processes carried out by consumers in the course of making consumption-related decisions.

Three areas of information processing serve as the focus for describing the research agenda: information search, decision making, and memory. These areas were selected because of their importance in consumption-related actions (Bettman, 1979). The research attention accorded these areas with respect to traditional media provides a benchmark for assessing the effects of interactive media on consumers' behaviors within each area. Insights from a program of research designed to ascertain the nature and scope of the information processing in interactive environments are needed to enable marketers to effectively tailor information displays.

In this chapter, several issues related to the development of a systematic program of research are considered. These issues include whether the Internet really does constitute a new medium with characteristics that distinguish it from traditional venues for advertising, and the appropriate scope and goals of a research agenda.

IS THE INTERNET REALLY DIFFERENT?

The potential for redundancies in research efforts can be reduced by recognizing the similarities between interactive media and traditional media. The unique features of the media can provide a focus for researchers to extend or to create theory, methodologies, and the discovery of new phenomena (e.g., net surfing). Thus, prior to launching a research program, consumer and marketing researchers need to determine whether the Internet is truly unique. Such an assessment will influence the form of the research agenda, such as whether the focus should be on the use of extant theory to explain behavior or on the development of new theory and conceptual foundations.

Newness and Scientific Revolution

Newness in knowledge has historically been described as occurring at a point where available theoretical and methodological traditions are not sufficient to explain a phenomenon (Kuhn, 1962). When these traditions are no longer adequate, having been overwhelmed by an accumulation of anomalies, the paradigm they define may be replaced by a new approach, thereby constituting a revolution in thought and practice. The introduction and acceptance of behaviorism is an example of a revolution in thought, method, and the problems appropriate to study (Brinberg & McGrath, 1985). The form of behaviorism espoused by Watson (1930) and others differed from other extant explanations of behavior in three ways: the role of past experience as a cause of behavior; the instrumentality of the external environment as a cause of behavior; and the focus on overt behavior rather than on internal, psychological states. These differences, which constituted a major shift in conceptual thought, provoked concomitant changes in the methods used to assess behavior, and in the approach to a wide range of substantive problems (e.g., language acquisition, learning). Thus, Watsonian behaviorism exemplifies the ideas of scientific revolution and discovery elucidated by Kuhn (1962).

Once a paradigm is accepted, research conducted within the paradigm to explain phenomena is described as normal science (Kuhn, 1962), which is characterized by consensus acceptance of methods and theories, directed toward filling gaps in knowledge (Barnes, 1982). Lakatos (1970) extended the goal of normal science to suggest that the cumulative effect of such science is to delegitimize a previously accepted paradigm. In other words, a revolution in scientific thought does not occur simply when an alternative explanation for a phenomenon is presented but only when the tenets of the alternative explanation effectively refute the preceding explanations. This view is reflective of a generalized notion of falsifiability (Popper, 1968).

To develop a research agenda, we must first determine whether types of interactive media, such as the World Wide Web, constitute a situation in which extant theories and methods cannot be used to predict or explain behaviors of consumers (or marketers) who use the medium. If forms of interactive media necessitate new theoretical and methodological approaches to examining consumer behavior, then the substantive component - the medium itself - may indicate a paradigm shift. The need to develop new sets of theories and methods suggests a research agenda quite different from an agenda appropriate for extending extant theories and methods to a new domain.

The World Wide Web is an environment in which consumers and marketers can communicate more rapidly. Traditional barriers of time and distance are minimized by the marketer's ability to create databases of product information, and by the consumer's ability to selectively obtain information (Cronin, 1994). The Web, and more generally the Internet, has been the focus of many marketers interested in taking advantage of interactive media to inform consumers about their products and services and, in many cases, to sell products and services online. Thus, the medium may serve many functions including advertising, communications, merchandising, and distribution (Klein, 1995).

The Web differs from traditional outlets for advertisements, such as television, print, and radio, in three fundamental ways. First, the interactive technology can combine the modalities of television, print, and radio into a single presentation of video, text, and sound. This combination of modalities may have a unique effect on information search, choice, and memory. For example, if consumers are typically exposed to advertisements in a print media (e.g., some prescription drugs), then use of an interactive medium that combines video and print components may cause cognitive interference and reduce the quality of consumers' decisions about and memory for the information contained in the advertisement. Second, the advertiser can allow the consumer to tailor the advertisement to his or her particular needs and preferences by allowing various point-and-click options in the advertisement. Third, the range and depth of information is much greater with interactive technology than with traditional media per unit cost (i.e., the consumer's time and effort), as is the ability of the consumer to specify desired characteristics as the basis for information that will be included in the constructed display (e.g., products under a cutoff price). Consumers can acquire information about products and services from multiple sources and restructure the information to facilitate decision making. Each of these differences may affect how much and what type of information consumers acquire, the strategies with which they integrate the information to make a choice, and the amount and structure of information retained in memory for subsequent purchases.

A question as yet unanswered, and largely unaddressed by consumer researchers, is whether the key differences between interactive and traditional media are limited to the substantive issues (i.e., the medium itself), or whether they reflect technological changes in an applied setting that can be exploited to push the limits of extant theories and methods for explaining aspects of information processing.

In sum, Internet networks such as the World Wide Web may establish new and more efficient forms of communication between people, including consumers and marketers. Clearly the Internet is not limited to conveying information about goods and services, but may also include communication that affects people's perceptions of their position in a rapidly changing global community (e.g., cultural values, norms). The networks that comprise the Internet may constitute a form of cultural revolution. However, the applications of the Internet from a marketing perspective do not necessarily imply a scientific revolution.

In the remainder of this chapter, a traditional information processing perspective (e.g., Bettman, 1979) is used to consider how interactive media may influence consumers' use of information in a nontraditional, electronic environment. The explanatory power of existing theories within the information processing paradigm suggests that calls for new conceptual foundations may not be warranted. In addition, methods for assessing information processing, such as response latencies, recognition and recall measures, and process tracing approaches, can be used to examine characteristics of information processing in the new media. The ability to extend these approaches suggests that although interactive media may seem revolutionary in terms of the increased immediacy and accessibility of information for consumers, electronic media such as the Web do not necessitate a wholesale reformulation of theory and method.

DEVELOPING A FRAMEWORK FOR RESEARCH

An initial step in developing a research framework is to identify the groups of individuals who are intended to benefit from the research. For advertising in interactive media, three groups play major roles: people who develop the technologies that make the interactive medium possible; people who provide or receive information from the medium (i.e., marketers and consumers) and people who regulate the information environment (i.e., policy makers); and people who extrapolate theory to explain and predict behavior in the new, interactive environment (i.e., academic researchers).

Each of these interest groups faces an idiosyncratic set of problems. For example, marketers and consumers face dilemmas created by the ability to provide or access vast amounts of information (Cook & Coupey, 1995). For technology developers, the interactive nature of the medium raises concerns about how to construct the environment to manage the influx of information and the strategies for retrieving it (e.g., browser software).

The framework described next incorporates each of these groups and suggests possible linkages between each group in terms of shared interests. The philosophy underlying the research agenda is that greater research benefits overall can be obtained when the accumulated knowledge that guides the behavior in one group can be used to inform the research/behavior of another group.

To illustrate this principle, consider the concept of information overload. A marketer concerned about the possibility that consumers who visit his web site may be overwhelmed by the sheer amount of available information can use insights from theory-driven research on the effects of quality (versus quantity) of information (Keller & Staelin, 1987, 1989) to guide the construction of the site in terms of the type and amount of information he includes.

In a similar vein, the development of technology designed to facilitate the progress of a consumer across a number of web sites can be guided by an understanding of how people select from among a repertoire of decision heuristics (cf., Payne, Bettman, & Johnson, 1988, 1993), trading-off effort to manage the information load and decision quality.

The second step in developing the research agenda is to organize the interest groups and their goals into a framework that recognizes the characteristic differences between the groups and emphasizes the linkages between their concerns. Such a framework can then be used to guide the development of a systematic program of research. The research agenda proposed in this chapter is guided by the Validity Network Schema (VNS), developed by Brinberg and McGrath (1985).

The VNS describes the stages and components of the research process and various research orientations. In this approach, research is composed of three domains: substantive, conceptual, and methodological. The substantive domain contains the phenomena or applied problems of interest. The conceptual domain contains the ideas or theories that can be used to explain the phenomena. The methodological domain contains the measures and designs used in a research project. Figure 13.1 contains the framework and three orientations toward research, each reflected by a domain. The relations between the domains reflect various styles of research. For example, developing insights into the fundamental characteristics of information overload by examining information acquisition from various interactive formats would reflect a theoretical path to knowledge that emphasizes the link between the conceptual and substantive domains. In contrast, an experimental path is one in which a researcher focuses on the conceptual model and then selects a measure and design to operationalize and test that model, emphasizing the conceptual-methodological link. Applied research to develop software that facilitates information search on the Web would emphasize the link between the methodological and substantive domains.

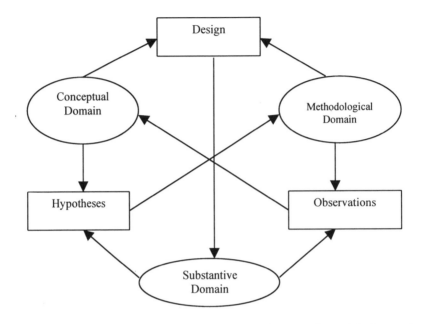

Fig. 13.1: The validity network schema. Adapted from *Validity and the Research Process*, Brinberg & McGrath, Sage Publications, 1985.

Brinberg and McGrath (1985) argued that within each domain, research can be characterized by the search for patterns or relations among elements in some type of embedding systems. These components - elements, relations and embedding systems - are different in each domain.   For instance, in the methodological domain, the element might be a measure for assessing some aspect of behavior, such as using a count of information acquisitions to assess information load. The relation is the technique that will enable the researcher to ascertain whether a pattern exists between two elements, such as number of acquisitions and time to make a decision.   Relations in the methodological domain are often designs, such as an ANOVA design. The embedding system is the larger context in which the relations are examined, such as lab experiment or field study.

The VNS can be used to provide coherence to a program of research that addresses the three interest groups for interactive marketing. Marketers, consumers, and policymakers can be characterized as possessing goals that are largely applied in nature, and that are thus commensurate with aspects of the substantive domain. In contrast, academic researchers who seek to extend or to develop and assess theories about information use in interactive environments reflect a theoretical orientation that emphasizes characteristics of the conceptual domain.   People responsible for the technological advances, which make possible the current interactive environments and which also enable effective use of these environments (e.g., by consumers), reflect a methodological orientation.

Within each of the domains that reflect interest groups, the elements, relations, and embedding systems can be specified to further organize the research agenda. In the substantive domain, for example, the enduring characteristics of an individual (e.g., a consumer) that he or she brings to any particular context are elements. The consumer's behavior, such as acquiring information within a web site, is a relation when it is combined with an enduring characteristic of the individual (e.g., need for cognition). The interactive medium in which the patterns of behavior exhibited by the consumer are observed is the embedding system. Examples of elements, relations, and embedding systems for the three domains are included in Table 13.1.

TABLE 13.1
Applying the Validity Network Schema:
Sample Elements, Relations and Embedding Systems in the Three Interest Groups

	Consumers, Marketers, & Policy Makers (Substantive)	Academic Researchers (Conceptual)	Technology Developers (Methodological)
Element	Individual characteristics (e.g., personality traits, expertise)	Heuristics, familiarity	Information acquisitions
Relation	Amount of information obtained in a web site	Heuristics x familiarity: effects on information use	Experimental design (e.g., Amount of Information x time pressure)
Embedding System	Interactive media	Effort/accuracy framework	Process tracing

Using the VNS as a framework within which to integrate the concerns of the main interest groups in the use of interactive information environments suggests an agenda for research in which each of the three groups provides a different, yet related, set of questions: what do we not know about the effects of interactive environments on information use? (substantive); what would we study to find answers? (conceptual); and how would we do it? (methodological). In the following section, these questions are addressed, building on the idea of elements, relations, and embedding systems, and recognizing links between the three interest groups, to define a systematic agenda for research.

TOWARD AN INTEGRATIVE RESEARCH AGENDA

This agenda for research is based on an effort/accuracy view of consumer choice (e.g., Christensen-Szalanski, 1978), which characterizes consumers as having limited cognitive resources used to trade-off decision quality against the costs of processing information. The tradeoffs consumers make of effort and accuracy may influence all aspects of information processing: how much information they seek, what type they acquire, how they use it to make a choice, and what is retained in memory.

There has been extensive research on information use in decision making, in psychology (e.g., Newell & Simon, 1972; Payne, Bettman, & Johnson, 1993), in economics (Wilde, 1980), and in marketing (Bettman & Kakkar, 1977; Coupey, 1992, 1994). Most of the research on information processing for consumer choice has, however, been conducted in static settings; respondents are presented with a display of information and asked to make a choice.

Advertising in interactive formats needs not, and often does not, follow such a constrained or well-structured format. Interactive shopping services, such as the computer-based services of CompuServe and America Online, provide information about available goods and services in a variety of formats. The consumer often determines the amount and organization of information that will be used in making purchase decisions. Coupey (1994) noted that consumers are flexible in the way they construct information displays, and that they are influenced by the initial form of the information and by their display-relevant knowledge.

Creating easy-to-use information displays may increase the influence of interactive advertisements on consumers' attitudes and behaviors. Little research has been conducted to examine display construction. Because consumers may often construct displays in interactive media, research is needed to determine the strategies consumers use to construct information displays and the factors that tend to evoke particular decision strategies. This agenda for research can be used to address questions relevant for understanding consumers' processing of advertising in interactive formats, such as constructing displays. Sample questions include the following: how do consumers use displayed information? what are the effects of various interactive displays on consumer decision making (e.g., choice quality and choice satisfaction/confidence)? and, what effect do past choices using interactive information displays have on subsequent decision making?

The primary focus of research within the proposed agenda is on the linkages between the different domains. For the purpose of understanding the effects of interactive media on consumer decision making and memory, the emphasis in this framework is on the substantive and conceptual domains. The substantive domain delimits the questions of interest to marketers, consumers, and policymakers, while the conceptual domain contains the theories and concepts that can be applied in problem-specific settings (e.g., information acquisition in a web site) from the substantive domain. In this particular agenda, the methodological domain serves primarily as a source of tools for executing the research based on the other two domains.

In the proposed agenda, as in most other research endeavors, one domain takes precedence and dictates the nature and form of the suggested research. For example, if the goal is to answer the question of what information will be accessed from a web site, the substantive domain is central, and the conceptual or methodological domain is secondary, serving as a means to an end by providing explanatory theories or tools for data collection and analysis.

Organizing the Agenda

The element, relation, and embedding system levels within each domain of the VNS suggest a general approach for organizing the research that can be conducted on the use of information presented on interactive media such as the World Wide Web. Information use on the Web can be distinguished by whether it is examined by researchers or marketers within a particular site or across multiple sites. Within-site strategies for information acquisition and decision making, and the resulting effect on the information that is encoded into long-term memory, may be very different from the behaviors consumers exhibit in across-site information use. A within-site consideration of behavior reflects the element level of the VNS. Across-site consideration of behavior, which subsumes interactions between the formats of different sites and consumers' reactions to them, exemplifies the relation level of the framework.

The difference between the two levels can be illustrated with the analogy of a consumer who examines one catalog looking for a particular item or learning about the array of products offered by the marketer, compared with the behavior of another consumer who pores over catalogs from several different marketers. Differences in the amount and depth of information processing may occur given constraints on processing capacity and on motivation (Payne, Bettman, & Johnson, 1988). For example, a consumer who expects to look at information from only one source may be willing to invest far more cognitive effort in acquiring, evaluating, and learning the information available from that source than a consumer who anticipates the need to examine several sources of information. Multiple sources may also influence the content of information in memory, depending on the sequence of sources examined, and the accessibility of information, as through primacy and recency effects (Lynch & Srull, 1982).

In addition, retroactive interference may affect subsequent information acquisition and use.

One objective of current research is to ascertain whether and how information use in interactive media differs from information use in traditional media. By incorporating the level of the embedding system in the substantive domain into the proposed research agenda, this objective can be directly and systematically addressed. With single and multiple sites as the element and relation levels, the embedding system is the type of interactive medium, such as the Web. For purposes of comparison, these levels could be contrasted relative to, for example, levels consisting of single and multiple catalogs, nested within the embedding system of print media.

To summarize the preceding discussion, one approach to designing research that explains consumption-related behaviors in interactive media is to use the substantive domain as a starting point. For interactive media such as the Web, within-site information processing behaviors reflect the element level, while across-site behaviors reflect the relation level. The form of the medium itself comprises the embedding system. Although research to assess the newness of interactive media can be conducted by manipulating the context defined by the embedding system, research intended to elucidate the information processing behaviors of consumers in interactive media can be completed at either the within-site level (element) or the across-site level (relation). Examples of each type of research, and the position of each example within the broader research agenda, are described in the following section.

Planning Research by Link and by Level

Once the framework for the agenda is established, the next step is to lay out the components of each domain and the links between domains that would constitute viable areas of research. Because it would be impractical and probably impossible to indicate *all* of the areas of potential focus, the agenda is guided by a set of questions. These questions reflect the goal of providing insights into the effect of interactive media on consumer information processing. To this end, the questions reflect concerns in the substantive domain. Sample issues for each question are presented to demonstrate the utility of the framework in the development of the research agenda. The questions used to illustrate the agenda reflect the aspects of information processing delimited earlier and are constrained to apply to the Web. They are: What information will consumers acquire in an interactive medium such as the Web? How will consumers use information from an interactive web source to make decisions? and what will be the effects of information use in interactive web environments on subsequent decision making? Each of these questions is addressed using the framework and levels to organize the possible types of research into a coherent agenda.

What Information Will Consumers Acquire on the Web? To answer this question, a researcher (e.g., academic or marketer) must first determine whether the focus of the research is within-site or across-site. Then, the researcher selects a secondary domain (i.e., conceptual or methodological). The links between these two domains direct the nature of the research effort. If the research is to provide an answer for a particular web site, then the methodological domain may be the more appropriate secondary domain for this applied research. If the researcher wants to provide insights about information acquisition that may generalize to a number of different products or situations, then the conceptual domain is more appropriate.

Once the domains are specified, the researcher specifies the components of each domain at the element, relation, and embedding system levels. For example, to examine information acquisition from a web site, in the conceptual domain the elements are constructs. A subset of these constructs might include motivation, framing effects, and familiarity (as with a product category). The relations serve as the hypotheses that guide the researcher's expectations about the behaviors that might reasonably be expected. These hypotheses can reflect interactions between constructs. For example, Coupey, Irwin, & Payne (1996) demonstrated that product category familiarity interacts with the task (e.g., judgment or choice) to influence the type and amount of information consumers acquire in order to construct a preference. In this example, the effect of interactive media on the acquisition of information (as to construct a preference) can be assessed by manipulating differences at the level of the embedding system (e.g., interactive media and print media).

Note that the links between domains confer benefits to the interest groups associated with each domain. Marketers and policy makers benefit from the selection of the conceptual domain as the secondary domain because it provides direction for systematic analysis of individual-level acquisition behavior in the interactive medium. Academics benefit from the link because the substantive domain provides a new venue for assessing the robustness of a theory.

Suppose that the substantive interest was across-site information acquisition behavior. In the conceptual domain, the constructs might include task effects and restructuring, the process of constructing an information display for decision making (Coupey, 1994). From the academic's perspective, using extant theory on display construction to guide research on across-site information use may suggest the examination of particular formats within and across web sites. From the marketer's perspective, understanding characteristic patterns of display construction by consumers may enable marketers to predict the final form of the constructed displays, including a determination of which competing vendors might be represented and the form of the final representation of options that will be used by the consumer.

In each of the preceding examples, the link has been between the substantive and conceptual domains. It should be noted that the methodological domain, though not of primary interest, is still a necessary part of the agenda. In each example, the methodological domain contains the sets of techniques that are appropriately used to test hypotheses that result from the specification of the relation level. For instance, to examine information acquisition across sites by a number of consumers, the measure at the element level might be a count of the times a web site was accessed for each site of interest. Web utilities such as AccessWatch (Maher, 1996) provide data about the number of times a site was accessed in a defined time period and track the identity of hosts who accessed the site. A similar technique uses a browser that tracks the sites visited by a set of consumers (Mandese, 1995). These types of data can be used to test hypotheses at the relation level, such as predictions about the interaction effect of a particular within-site format and time pressure on information acquisition. The embedding system level in this example is a general process tracing orientation.

A research agenda based on the specification of levels and links between interest groups and their related domains enables researchers to design research that capitalizes on complementary approaches in the methodological domain. Although the Web may contain vast amounts of information, what is desirable for a particular research endeavor may not be available. For example, Hoffman and Novak (1995) noted the difficulty associated with attempts to obtain data across web sites. Experiments that create simulated web environments can make use of extant methods and technology to measure information acquisition, for example, as is possible with Mouselab (Johnson, Payne, Schkade, & Bettman, 1989).

How Will Consumers Use Information From the Web to Make Decisions? Of particular interest to marketers is how consumers will use the information they acquire from the Web, integrating it to arrive at a decision, such as a judgment about the relative desirability of a product or brand. The interactive environment may influence both the quality of decision making and the consumer's satisfaction with both the process and the result of the decision. The issue of how interactive environments will affect evaluative processing may be addressed on both the within-site and across-site levels. For either level, within the substantive domain the consumer and his or her characteristics constitute the element level. The interaction determined by the consumer's individual knowledge level and other elements of the situation (e.g., site characteristics, product category) comprises the relation level. This interaction and its effect on information use can be explained in greater detail by relying on theory from the conceptual domain, thus enabling marketers to tailor interactive environments.

In the conceptual domain, the element level constructs of interest might include familiarity (as with the attributes of the presented brand), heuristics (as for making a choice), decision quality, and satisfaction. Hypotheses based on the interaction of these constructs would define the relation level, enabling the marketer or researcher to develop predictions about how the format of an information display will affect decision making. For example, research on how people weight attributes in making a decision (e.g., Slovic & MacPhillamy, 1974) can be coupled with research on familiarity effects on choice processes (e.g., Bettman & Park, 1980) to develop predictions about information use in an interactive environment, as within a web site. To illustrate, a large body of research on information use in decision making has provided convergent evidence that consumers who are familiar with a particular choice domain tend to be more efficient in their information search and use (e.g., Johnson & Russo, 1984). Extending these conclusions to interactive environments suggests that consumers who have greater familiarity with the product category may tend to spend less time in a site, be more selective in the attribute information that guides the decision, and experience greater satisfaction with the decision process than consumers who are less familiar with the product category.

Research in decision making can also be used to develop an understanding of consumers' information use across web sites. The same element and relation levels considered for within-site effects - familiarity and heuristics - can be extended to multiple sites. In addition, embedding these levels within a general effort/accuracy framework can suggest areas for research in interactive environments. For instance, interactive media such as the Web may exacerbate the relationship between information use and satisfaction by accentuating the link between familiarity and information accessibility. Lewis (1996) noted that in interactive media, compared with traditional media, the consumer must take a more active role in dictating which information will be used. To build the base of knowledge about available products or vendors, the consumer must type a keyword into a search engine (e.g., Yahoo! or WebCrawler). As a result, the starting point for the search influences the structure and sequence of the decision. although the effects of decision structuring have been examined in more traditional media (e.g., Coupey, 1994; Kahneman & Tversky, 1979; Ranyard, 1989), the extensibility of the observed processes and their effects should be evaluated with respect to the idiosyncrasies of an interactive environment.

What Will Be the Effects of Information use in Interactive Web Environments on Subsequent Decision Making? Consumers who acquire and use information from interactive environments may store in memory aspects of the experience, such as knowledge obtained about products or inferences about a company. The content and structure of this stored information may guide the acquisition and use of information in subsequent decisions. The effects of retrieved information on behavior can be observed both within and across web sites. Some of the conceptual constructs that comprise the element level include processing capacity, order effects, context effects, categorization, and familiarity. As with the previous areas of substantive interest, the relation level in the conceptual domain consists of the linkages between constructs. The embedding system is an information processing paradigm.

To illustrate the use of the framework to define an area for research on memory effects and interactive media, the constructs of processing capacity and categorization can be used to consider within-site information effects on memory, and memory effects on within-site information use. Given constraints on processing capacity (Miller, 1956), consumers may attempt to search information presented in a site based on guidance from information in long-term memory. For example, consumers often form categories to structure and store vast amounts of product-related information (Coupey & Nakamoto, 1988; Sujan, 1985). The content and structure of these categories may then guide subsequent acquisition, use, and storage in memory of presented information (Coupey & Jung, 1996; Sujan & Bettman, 1989). In an interactive environment, the information consumers choose to encode in memory may be determined by the match between consumers' categories and the form of the presented information (e.g., the available attribute information), as well as the ease with which information can be obtained.

Memory factors may also influence information use across sites in interactive environments. Researchers have demonstrated that consumers' information processing tends to be guided by the format in which information is presented. For example, receiving information in a brand-by-brand format tends to result in brand-based evaluation (Bettman & Kakkar, 1977) and brand-based storage in memory (Biehal & Chakravarti, 1982). These findings lend support to the principle of concreteness (Slovic, 1972), which characterizes people as cognitive misers who tend to process information "as is," rather than exerting the effort to change it. Contrary to this view, Coupey (1994) suggested that the tendency to concreteness may be moderated by people's ability to effect changes. For instance, providing consumers with the opportunity to make notes, effectively generating an "external memory," results in substantial changes to the information display used to make a decision, and in the strategies used to make decisions. Internet browsers, such as Netscape, enable consumers to create external memories by using "bookmarks" to tag sites of particular interest. These external memories may influence not only consumer decision making across sites, but also the content and structure of site information in memory. For example, the decreased costs to acquire information when an external memory can be readily generated and easily reviewed may affect the amount and depth of processing consumers allocate to information within and across sites. Because the depth of processing can affect the encoding and subsequent accessibility of information (Craik & Tulving, 1975), the amount of information available for subsequent decision making may be reduced by the use of external memory facilitated by the interactive technology.

On a more general level, the role of memory can be considered across modalities, such as broadcast, print, and interactive media, thus defining research at the embedding system level. For example, the context in which information is initially processed may affect the storage of information and serve as a cue for retrieval (Tulving & Thomson, 1973). This "encoding specificity principle" can be extended to encompass the idea that the context in which information is initially learned affects the encoding and subsequent accessibility of the information (Smith, Glenberg, & Bjork, 1978). If information is stored with respect to context, then marketers should consider the implications of the type of modality in which they present information for the way information will be encoded, and of the sequence of modalities to which consumers may be exposed. For instance, learning information from a radio ad may interfere with the type of learning for the same brand or product that occurs within an interactive environment.

Research approaches to three questions about consumers' use of information in interactive environments provide an illustrative overview of the research agenda, and of the manner in which areas of research can be defined. Although these questions reflect a substantive focus, the framework used to develop the agenda is flexible. Alternative approaches for developing knowledge of behavior in interactive media can be specified by shifting the selection of primary and secondary domains, and by focusing on different elements and relations within each domain.

THE AGENDA REPRISED

The World Wide Web may be viewed as revolutionary from the perspective of consumers in that the substantive domain differs from traditional media, and because these differences may influence the ways in which consumers acquire, use, and remember information from interactive environments. However, for researchers who attempt to explain and predict the nature of the changes in behavior, and thus suggest reasonable actions for marketers and advertisers, interactive media do not necessarily constitute a revolution that warrants the wholesale overthrow of previous theories and methods.

The determination of whether the Internet is truly new in terms of scientific revolution is important because it directs the development of any agenda for research. We suggest that many extant theories and methods can be extended to interactive media to explain and predict consumption-related phenomena in the new media. We propose an agenda for research that uses an information processing perspective, with its associated theories and methods, as a starting-point for a systematic program of research on the effects of interactive media.

The agenda proposed in this chapter incorporates the goals and interests of three groups: practitioners (e.g., marketers, consumers, policymakers), academic researchers, and technology developers. The premise used to guide specification of the agenda was that by recognizing the core differences between the groups, a framework could be developed which emphasized the linkages between groups, thus resulting in an agenda with mutually beneficial research endeavors. This agenda not only provides direction for research, but reduces the potential for redundancy in research efforts by delimiting the characteristic concerns and abilities of each interest group.

Recognizing Other Linkages

The interest groups around which the agenda was developed reflect the substantive (practitioners), conceptual (academics) and methodological (technology developers) domains (Brinberg & McGrath, 1985). Although the focus in this chapter was centered largely on the linkages between the substantive issues dictated by the desire to explain behavior in interactive media, other linkages form an important part of the research agenda. For example, the link between the conceptual and methodological domains subsumes research directed toward the development of technology/software to facilitate consumers' use of interactive media (e.g., browsers and search engines). In addition, theories of information use are abetted by the ability to collect detailed data with which to test theories. For example, Canter, Rivers, and Storrs (1985) developed a set of indices for describing information acquisition from interactive databases. Determination and verification of the indices would be difficult, if not impossible, in the absence of the appropriate technology.

The link between the substantive and methodological domains has also resulted in research that benefits all three interest groups. For example, researchers interested in human-computer interaction (Nickerson, 1969) combine theory and technology in an applied setting to determine what constitutes an effective user interface (i.e., a computer screen layout and a set of potential actions; cf, Hix & Hartson, 1993).

CONCLUSIONS

As the number of people with access to the Internet continues to grow, the economic opportunities for marketers also increase, making the Internet a highly desirable venue for providing information about companies, goods, and services. Despite the intuitive appeal of the Internet to marketers, relatively little is yet known about how consumers will make use of the Internet. A comprehensive agenda for research can organize the attempts to understand, explain, and predict behavior in a complex and rapidly changing environment.

REFERENCES

Barnes, B. (1982). *T. S. Kuhn and social science.* New York: Columbia University Press.

Bettman, J. R. (1979). *An information processing theory of consumer choice.* Reading, MA: Addison-Wesley.

Bettman, J. R., & Kakkar, P. (1977). Effects of information presentation format on consumer information acquisition strategies. *Journal of Consumer Research, 3,* 233-240.

Bettman, J. R., & Park, C. W. (1980). Effects of prior knowledge and experience and phase of the choice process on consumer decision processes: A protocol analysis. *Journal of Consumer Research, 7,* 234-248.

Biehal, G. J., & Chakravarti, D. (1982). Information presentation format and learning goals as determinants of consumers' memory retrieval and choice processes. *Journal of Consumer Research, 8,* 431-441.

Brinberg, D., & McGrath, J. E. (1985). *Validity and the research process.* Newbury Park, CA: Sage.

Canter, D., Rivers, R. & Storrs, G. (1985). Characterizing user navigation through complex data structures. *Behaviour and Information Technology, 4,* 93-102.

Christensen-Szalanski, J. (1978). A mechanism for decision strategy selection and some implications. *Organizational Behavior and Human Performance, 22,* 307-323.

Cook, D. L., & Coupey, E. (1998). Consumer Behavior and Unresolved regulatory issues in electronic marketing. *Journal of Business Research,* 231-328.

Coupey, E. (1992). Restructuring: A process for constructing representations for choice. In V. L. Crittenden (Ed.), *Developments in Marketing Science, Vol. XV* (pp. 27-32). Coral Gables, FL: Academy of Marketing Science.

Coupey, E. (1994). Restructuring: Constructive processing of information displays in consumer choice. *Journal of Consumer Research, 21,* 83-99.

Coupey, E., Irwin, J. R., & Payne, J. W. (1998). Product category familiarity and preference expression. *Journal of Consumer Research, 24,* 459-468.

Coupey, E., & Jung, K. (1996). Forming and updating product category perceptions: The influence of task goals and attribute discrepancy. *Psychology and Marketing.* 695-713.

Coupey, E., & Nakamoto, K. (1988). Learning context and the development of product category perceptions. In M. Houston (Ed.), *Advances in Consumer Research, Vol. 15* (77-82). Provo, UT: Association for Consumer Research.

Craik, F. I. M., & Tulving, E. (1975). Depth of processing and the retention of words in episodic memory. *Journal of Experimental Psychology: General, 104,* 268-294.

Cronin, M. J. (1994). *Doing business on the Internet: How the electronic highway is transforming American companies.* New York: Van Nostrand Reinhold.

Hix, D., & Hartson, H. R. (1993). *User interface development: Ensuring usability through product and process.* New York: John Wiley & Sons.

Hoffman, D., & Novak, T. P. (1995). Marketing in hypermedia computer-mediated environments: Conceptual foundations. Working paper, Owen Graduate School of Management, Vanderbilt University. [Online] Available: <http://www2000.ogsm.vanderbilt.edu>.

Johnson, E. J., Payne, J. W., Schkade, D. A., & Bettman, J. R. (1989). Monitoring information processing and decisions: The Mouselab system. Unpublished manuscript, Duke University, Center for Decision Studies, Durham, NC.

Johnson, E. J., & Russo, J. E. (1984). Product familiarity and learning new Information. *Journal of Consumer Research, 11*, 542-50.

Kahneman, D., & Tversky, A. (1979). Prospect theory: An analysis of decision under risk. *Econometrica, 47*, 263-291.

Keller, K. L., & Staelin, R. (1987). Effects of quality and quantity of information on decision effectiveness. *Journal of Consumer Research, 14*, 200-213.

Keller, K. L., & Staelin, R. (1989). Assessing biases in measuring decision effectiveness and information overload. *Journal of Consumer Research, 15*, 510-512.

Klein, L. (1995). Evaluating the potential of interactive media through a new lens: Search versus experience goods. In R.R. Dholakia and D. Fortin (Eds.), *COTIM-95 Conference on Telecommunications and Information Marketing.* Kingston, RI: University of Rhode Island.

Kuhn, T. S. (1962). *The structure of scientific revolutions.* Chicago: University of Chicago Press.

Lakatos, I. (1970). Falsification and the methodology of scientific research programmes. In I. Lakatos & A. Musgrave (Eds.), *Criticism and the growth of knowledge.* Cambridge: Cambridge University Press, 3-93.

Lewis, H. G. (1996). Copywriting for interactive media: New rules for the new medium. In E. Forrest and R. Mizerski (Eds), *Interactive marketing: The future present.* Chicago: NTC Business Books.

Lynch, J. G., Jr., & Srull, T. K. (1982). Memory and attentional factors in consumer choice: Concepts and research methods. *Journal of Consumer Research, 9*, 18-37.

Maher, D. (1996). *AccessWatch, v. 1.32*, [Online] Available: <http://www. accesswatch. com>.

Mandese, J. (1995, March 20). "Clickstreams" in cyberspace. *Advertising Age*, 18.

Miller, G. A. (1956). The magical number seven, plus or minus two: Some limits on our capacity for processing information. *Psychology Review, 63*, 81-97.

Newell, A., & Simon, H. A. (1972). *Human problem solving.* Englewood Cliffs, NJ: Prentice-Hall.

Nickerson, R. S. (1969). Man-computer interaction: A challenge for human factors research. *Ergonomics, 12*, 501.

Payne, J. W., Bettman, J. R., & Johnson, E. J. (1988). Adaptive strategy selection in decision making. *Journal of Experimental Psychology: Learning, Memory, and Cognition, 14*, 534-552.

Payne, J. W., Bettman, J. R., & Johnson, E. J. (1993). *The adaptive decision maker.* Cambridge: Cambridge University Press.

Ranyard, R. (1989). Structuring and evaluating simple monetary risks. In H. Montgomery and O. Svenson (Eds.), *Process and structure in human decision making*, New York: Wiley, 112-128.

Popper, K. R. (1968). *The logic of scientific discovery.* New York: Harper & Row.

Slovic, P. (1972). From Shakespeare to Simon: Speculations and some evidence about man's ability to process information. *Oregon Research Institute Bulletin, 12*(3), 1-29.

Slovic, P., & MacPhillamy, D. (1974). Dimensional commensurability and cue utilization in comparative judgment. *Organization Behavior and Human Performance, 11*, 179-194.

Smith, S. M., Glenberg, A. & Bjork, R. A. (1978). Environmental context and human memory. *Memory & Cognition, 6*, 342-353.

Sujan, M. (1985). Consumer knowledge: Effects on evaluation strategies mediating consumer judgments. *Journal of Consumer Research, 12*, 16-31.

Sujan, M., & Bettman, J. R. (1989, November). The effects of brand positioning strategies on consumers' brand and category perceptions. *Journal of Marketing Research*, 454-467.

Tulving, E., & Thomson, D. M. (1973). Encoding specificity and retrieval processes in episodic memory. *Psychological Review, 80*, 352-373.

Watson, J. B. (1930). *Behaviorism*. Chicago: University of Chicago Press.

Wilde, L. L. (1980). The Economics of Consumer Information Acquisition, *Journal of Business, 53*, s143-s165.

Part 3

Public Policy Issues

14

Cyber-Cookies: How Much Should the Public Swallow?

Sandra Davidson
University of Missouri

"Would you like a cookie?" If the question involves cyberspace, perhaps the answer should be, "It depends. What kind do you have?" Of course, the possibilities do not include chocolate chip or Oreos. Cookies were originally called "magic cookies," named after the tokens with mystical powers that are a part of role-playing games (Wildstrom, 1996).

A cookie is a crumb of software stored in the computer of a visitor to a web site (to see what a typical "cookie" looks like, see Berg, 1996). The web site provides the cookie, and the visitor's web browser installs the cookie on the visitor's hard drive. The cookie permits the web-site operator to track the movements of the visitor on the operator's web site (Schwartz, 1996; Woody, 1996). Another analogy is that the cookie "brands" the user's computer with profile information (Angwin, 1997; Bell et al., 1997; Berg, 1996; Shaw, 1997;). Netscape and Microsoft browsers allow cookies ("Interactive technologies," 1997). America Online does not (Hide your cookies," 1997; Kilshimer, 1997). Netscape and Microsoft, however, do limit the number of cookies on a hard drive, kicking the oldest out first or kicking them out by the expiration dates they contain (Glass, 1996).

Cookies come in two flavors - persistent and session. *Persistent* cookies remain in a visitor's hard drive after a session of visiting a web site is over, versus *session* cookies that end with the session (Kyber, 1997).

The view that cookies are only beneficial and benign is half-baked, as is the view that they are inherently evil. Not all cookies are created equal. Some could be beneficial, and some could be toxic.

One commentator categorizes cookies as "the good, the bad, and the ugly" (Hertzoff, 1996). The *good* cookie allows the web site operator to customize the web site for the visitor's convenience. The *bad*, according to the commentator, permits the web site operator to track the visitor's movements, collecting data to use for marketing and for sharing with other marketers. The *ugly* would be a cookie that plants a virus in the visitor's machine. Also ugly are bugs in programs that give talented hackers an opportunity to read cookies. A 15-year-old hacker created a "cookie muncher," allowing him to steal information from thousands of cookies (Hawking, 1996; Taft, 1996). Apparently a flaw in Netscape Navigator 3.01 could give web-site operators access to the hard drives of their web site users who browse with that version of Navigator (Mannix & Thomas, 1997; Trager, 1997) and who also use Windows (Coile, 1997). It is also possible to transmit computer viruses through email (Cannell, 1998, Crabb, 1998). Finally, "identity thieves" can have a field day lurking on the Net (Kenworthy & Lang, 1998).

Clearly, cookies have aroused a lot of public concern, and media pundits have rushed to educate and to amuse, with titles such as "Can Cookies Crumble Your Browser?" ("much ado," 1996) and "Internet `Cookies' Raise a Batch of Privacy Concerns" (*Los Angeles Times* 1996).

Yet, privacy is a serious matter. Cookies could gather a lot of personal information about web site visitors. Some web sites require a visitor to fill out a registration form before visiting the web site (Two firms seek," 1996).[1] The web site operator can then store this voluntarily provided information in a cookie, implant the cookie in the visitor's computer, and then access the information anytime the visitor revisits the web site (Bransten, 1996). This practice can be either positive or negative, of course, depending on the use of the information. Another aspect to consider is whether receipt of the cookie was voluntary or unknowing.

Cookies have many positive aspects. For instance, they can make ordering products over the Internet easier because the buyer who has already received the appropriate cookie from the web site seller will not have to re-enter information such as the buyer's mailing address (Presswire, 1996).

Cookies can also be used to store name and password so that a visitor does not have to type in that information every time he or she visits a site requiring visitors to register. For example, *The New York Times* web site <http://www.nytimes.com> requires registration, which is then stored in a cookie (Berg, 1997). In this way, cookies help the Internet provide "instant access" to

---

[1] "Universal registration" is something a San Francisco-based Internet Profiles Corporation would like to see. Under its "I/CODE" system, users would register only once, filling out a form containing personal, identifiable information (name, street and e-mail address as well as anonymous demographic information (gender, age, education, employment, income). Then the user would receive a password, an "I/CODE," to use whenever visiting a web site that is an I/CODE member. Internet Profile Corporation even offered prizes for persons who registered for an I/CODE. The prize campaign, launched in March, 1996, included a $10,000 vacation as a grand prize. For more information on I/CODE, see <http://icode.ipro.com/>.

information (McKim, 1997). Likewise, a visit to the Microsoft Network's homepage <http://www.msn.com> results in a customized web page on the next visit to that site (Komando, 1997).

Cookies can also store the last date and time of a visit to a web site in order to customize the page so that the visitor sees what happened since his or her last visit; the online magazine (e-zine) *Spiv*, at <http://www.spiv.com>, uses cookies for that purpose (Standage, 1996). In addition, cookies permit online shoppers to pay at the end of their shopping sprees instead of having to pay for items one at a time. Cookies store the information about what the shopper wants to buy, thus acting as a cybershopping cart (Kilsheimer, 1997).

Cookies can also allow the web site operator to improve the web site by tracking what interests visitors (Bransten, 1996). The Internet marketing community calls information gained from tracking web site user's movements "clickstream data" (Erickson, 1996)." Software from NetGravity, Inc., tags web site visitors with ID numbers. Its software permits a corporation to read information on the corporation's cookie, such as how many times the visitor has visited, what he or she clicked, and how long he or she has lingered. NetGravity also permits target advertising: A web server pulls the visitor's registration number, then sends details to AdServer, which will then choose the ad to present to the user (Moeller, 1997 ; "Netgravity," 1996).

On the other hand, this sort of technology can be unsettling. One commentator draws an analogy between Internet shopping and shopping at a supermarket (Komando, 1997). What if a shopper visited a supermarket, and a computer kept track of the shopper's movements down the aisle and what items land in the shopper's cart? Then, the next time the shopper goes to the supermarket, he or she discovers that there is only one aisle, and it contains only the items the shopper wanted the first time. This shopping could be efficient - but unsettling. A downside to cookies is the Orwellian notion of "Big Brother" watching one's movements. For example, if one visits the web site of a car manufacturer and lingers over a particular model, the web site operator knows. Imagine such information being pooled, along with information on political matters or maybe visits to racier sites. In short, the trail of cookie crumbs could provide more information about a person than that person might want shared.

Or, depending on one's viewpoint, the trail could lead to more efficient marketing techniques. DoubleClick, Inc., a New York-based Internet advertising broker, has set up a web-site network for its clients (Moukheiber, 1996). A visitor who first visits one of these networked web sites receives a cookie with a DoubleClick ID number. DoubleClick's database then stores information about the visitor's journeys to web sites of its other clients. A web site server notifies DoubleClick, which delivers the ad to the user's screen within 25 milliseconds or less ("It is 15 milliseconds," 1997; McChesney 1996). DoubleClick's president, Kevin O'Connor, emphasizes that the cookie files mean that web site visitors see ads that appeal to their tastes and do not have to keep seeing the same ad, which can lead to "banner burn out" (Foster, 1996; McChesney, 1996). Banner selection apparently is the only use DoubleClick has been making of its profiles (Shaw, 1997). It claims to have profiles on 10 million people who visit web sites (Komando, 1997). Focalink is another online advertising agency that uses cookies to track users of its clients' ads (Angwin, 1997; Bell et al., 1997).

Saying that nothing nefarious is going on over the Internet and that profiles are being amassed only under ID numbers assigned by companies (not names, addresses of any sort, or social security numbers) still does not allay all fears. If a potential for nefarious purposes exists, and if the technology permits it, should users trust that no evildoers will decide to do evil?

A survey by a Boston Consulting Group showed that 86% of persons polled wanted to control the use of demographic information about them; 81% agreed that sites have no right to resell such information without consent; and 70% said their primary reason for not registering at web sites was a concern for privacy (Clark, 1997; Kyber, 1997; Mannix & Thomas, 1997).[2]

Perhaps it is part of the independent spirit that helped create the Internet in the first place and that helps attract web site visitors to the Internet that also compels many of these visitors to want to have matters under their own control. Many do not want to trust something so precious as personal privacy to the goodwill of others over whom they do not exert control. Whatever the driving forces, the "toss your cookies" movement seems to have developed a great deal of momentum - enough so that the industry cannot ignore it. Or, perhaps it is more accurate to say that web site visitors, instead of wanting to toss their cookies, do not want companies force feeding them cookies. Many want to determine what cookies end up on their plates. In that sense, this cookie-controlling movement is a "pro-choice" movement.

Self-Help Is Certainly a Possibility

An individual may determine the presence on his or her hard drive of surreptitiously received cookies and from what web sites they came by simply searching for and then opening a file named "cookie" (Berg, 1996; Bransten, 1996). Netscape Navigator 3.0 and Microsoft's Internet Explorer 3.0 permit users to decide whether to accept a cookie (Hertzoff, 1996). However, a window warning of cookies can become annoying to some users (Gellene, 1997; Cyber, 1997; PR Newswire, 1996). Navigator 4.0 offers filtering that lets users automatically reject all cookies (Bell et al., 1997).

---

[2] Of the more than 70% who fear invasion of privacy, some gave false information instead of no information.

A "proxy" server also protects privacy. For instance, the service of "Anonominity.com" lets users simply make their http requests through the service instead of directly (Catchings & Van Name 1996). Another intermediary is "NetAngels" ("Online spying," 1996).

IEClean software for users of Microsoft Internet Explorer (1996) and NSClean for Netscape users are available for purchase at <http://www.axxis. com/altus/products.html> (For demo downloads of either IEClean or NSClean, visit <http://www.wizvax.net/kevinmca/>). They also permit users of Microsoft Internet Explorer and Netscape to employ an alias instead of their user Ids (IEclean," 1996b; "Internet security & privacy," 1997; ("NSclean," 1996a). NSClean will purge cookies, its advertisements say. PrivNet aims to prevent cookies or unwanted ads (spam) from ever getting to one's computer (Berg, 1996; Woody, 1996).

CookieMaster, a ZDNET software product, is available free at <http://www.hotfiles.com>. As the executive editor of ZDNET Software Library, Preston Gralla, says, "Some cookies you will want, others you'll want to delete." The software provides users "choice" (Abate, 1997; "Internet security," 1997). Over 60,000 people had downloaded this software by mid December 1996 ("Much ado about cookies," 1996).

Pretty Good Privacy, Inc., has created PGPcookie.cutter, available at <http:/www.pgp.com> (Bell et al., 1997; Internet access, 1996).

In June, 1997, Luckman Interactive, Inc., announced a free utility called "Luckman's Anonymous Cookie for Internet Privacy," which can be down-loaded at <http://www.luckman.com>. It disables cookies and allows Internet browsing with anonymity (Hide Your Cookies, 1997). One can also erase one's electronic footprints left by web browsing (Clearing one's tracks, 1998; Nelson, 1998; Crabb, 1998, McChesney & Werthheimer, 1997). Of course, as soon as any list of self-help products is made, it is out-of-date.

Some persons object to having to bother with purging or rejecting cookies. Certainly, a lot of web site visitors are not aware that they should be concerned about cookies. Some do not even know cookies exist because cookies can be given to web site visitors without the visitors' knowledge. The secrecy of cookies is particularly bothersome to some cyberspace users.

Cookies can also raise legal questions. Cookies invade privacy, some Netizens believe - an intrusion into seclusion which occurs when a person or a device physically intrudes on another's space.[3] After all, it is the visitor's computer that is being invaded. Invasion of privacy, in the sense of intruding

---

[3] The Restatement (Second) of Torts, a legal treatise that is highly influential with courts, says: "One who intentionally intrudes, physically, or otherwise, upon the solitude or seclusion of another or his [or her] private affairs or concerns, is subject to liability to the other for invasion of his [or her] privacy, if the intrusion would be highly offensive to a reasonable person." Restatement (Second) of Torts 652B (1976).

into seclusion, is closely related to trespass. Further, the visitor's computer is being used for a purpose to which the unknowing receiver of a cookie has not consented. Using another's property without the property owner's consent, generally, is called "conversion," which is an illegal act. Conversion is a form of stealing.[4] Arguably, a little bit of space on the visitor's computer is being stolen by the cookie provider. Also, in some cases, information might be stolen. If the information is private, and if the private information is shared with others, an invasion of privacy, in the sense of giving publicity to private facts, might occur.[5] Regardless of whether the infringement on privacy is severe enough to warrant legal sanctions, a perceived invasion of privacy can violate a sense of ethics and fair play.

The urge to fight back and protect what is one's own - one's own privacy, one's own computer equipment - has been kindled for some individuals and for some groups that are championing what they perceive to be a wrong committed against them individually and collectively by some purveyors of cookies.

The Center for Democracy and Technology has a privacy site on the Web at <http://www.13x.com/cgi-bin/cdt/snoop.pl> which allows visitors to the web site to see how easily cookie technology allows a web site operator to gain information. If a visitor merely clicks onto the site, it will display information about the visitor, such as the computer model and perhaps the visitor's work place and e-mail address (McChesney, 1996; Schwartz, 1996).

Also, persons interested in examining the privacy policies of some major Internet providers may access the Center for Democracy and Technology's information at <http://www.cdt/privacy/contents.html> (Hawking, 1996). Commonly, browser software lets a web-site operator know basic information about the web site visitor's hardware and software because the operator needs to knows in order to enable the web page to appear on the visitor's screen (Moukheiber, 1996). Normally, cookie information does not include a visitor's e-mail address (McChesney, 1996). However, if a web site visitor is using

---

[4] Although conversion can be a criminal offense, it can also be a tort, a civil wrong for which a private individual can seek damages. The Restatement (Second) of Torts says: "Conversion is an intentional exercise of dominion or control over a chattel, which so seriously interferes with the right of another to control it that the actor may justly be required to pay the other the full value of the chattel." Restatement (Second) of Torts 222A(1).

[5] The Restatement (Second) of Torts says: One who gives publicity to a matter concerning the private life of another is subject to liability to the other for invasion of his privacy, if the matter publicized is of a kind that (a) would be highly offensive to a reasonable person, and (b) is not of legitimate concern to the public. Restatement (Second) of Torts 652D.

JavaScript, it can add information to cookies, such as the visitor's e-mail address (Glass, 1996). And sometimes, what seems innocuous at first may develop into something a little more troublesome. For example, under NetCount's HeadCount, when the user first encounters a web site provided by a Netcount member, the user is asked to provide his or her street and zip code. Then NetCount tags the user only by average demographic information based on "cluster data" (Jaffee, 1996; "Two firms," 1996). But NetCount has developed technology to capture the user's name, e-mail address, and other information (Messmer, 1996).[6]

Consent is always an important legal issue. A survey by the Electronic Privacy Information Center in Washington found that only 17 out of 100 popular web sites disclose to their users their policies on privacy; 49 requested personal information; 23 used "cookies" (Clark 1997).

Note that some government agencies now have web sites, but these agencies have no choice but to disclose if they are releasing personal information about individuals. Under the federal Privacy Act, passed in 1974, federal agencies may not release personal information to third parties without the *written* permission of the person whose information will be released (Gellman, 1996).[7] Further, Congress amended the Act in 1988 and 1989, adding the Computer Matching and Privacy Protection Act, which generally forbids federal agencies from comparing their databases with databases of other federal agencies or with private data bases.

Some organizations, such as the Direct Marketing Association (DMA), are pressing for voluntary moves to help allay public fears about cookie technology. The DMA urges its members to disclose their cookie practices; its web site contains its policy, which could be used as a model (Bransten, 1996).

Another group, the Internet Engineering Task Force, has formulated voluntary rules requiring that Web software include cookie warnings and that users have control over their cookie trails (Angwin, 1997). Browsers would have a default setting to reject cookies under these proposed standards (Kyber, 1997), which are available at <http://portal.research.bell-labs.com/dmk/cookie. html>

---

[6] The information that NetCount will be able to access is X.509 certificate information. For more on x.509 certificates, see "CAs: How Valuable Are They?" Network, 8(6), April, 1997, p. 45. ("CA" stands for "certificate authorities." The certificates are designed to protect information. As the article says, "For many, the acceptance and implementation of systems based on the International Telecommunication Union (ICU) x.509 certificate standards offers the promise of secure transmission across the Net." Id.

[7] 5 USC ' 552(b). The Privacy Act does permit release of information without consent if the information is exempt from this Privacy Act. The primary exemption is the federal Freedom of Information Act. If information is public under the federal Freedom of Information Act, third parties may generally gain access to it. 5 U.S.C. 552(b).

(Bell et al., 1997). The rejection default is opposed by the online industry's largest group, the Association of Online Professionals (Kyber, 1997).

In June 1997, Netscape led a group of 40 companies proposing an Open Profiling Standard. Under Open Profiling Standards, a form filled out by a user would provide information (name, residential, and e-mail address and personal information such as age, marital status and hobbies) available to Open Profiling Standard web sites. Approximately 60 companies have supported the Open Profiling Standard (Kyber, 1997). On June 11, 1997, Microsoft Corporation announced that it, too, would join the plan (Gellene & Miller, 1997; "Micro Mass," 1997; *MIN's New Media Report*, 1997; "One-to-one," 1997). But even if the World Wide Web Consortium (W3C) adopts the standard, cookies will remain, according to industry analysts ("Hide your cookies," 1997; Kyber, 1997; "Microsoft endorses," 1997).

The Electronic Frontier Foundation, a San Francisco organization that advocates privacy, is not necessarily against all cookies, but wants "informed consent" (Abate, 1997). The Electronic Frontier Foundation, along with some other organizations, has formed "eTrust," an organization to rate the privacy policies of various web businesses and to license logos for their web sites to use. Three different logos will be available (for a price): for sites that collect no data on users; for sites that collect data only for their own use; and for sites that share or sell the data they collect with third parties (Bransten, 1996; Wildstrom, 1996). These trustmarks - no exchange, "1 to 1 exchange," and "3rd party exchange" - have received support of America Online and at least 45 other companies that have agreed to a pilot program (Kyber, 1997).

The government also is considering regulation of cookies. On June 10, 1997, the Federal Trade Commission began hearings that investigate into cookie technology. Reportedly, however, the FTC would prefer that the online industry devise a solution that includes ethical standards as well as technological safeguards (Gellene, 1997; Mannix & Thomas, 1997).[8]

Regulatory legislation is another possibility. Representative Bruce Vento, a Democrat from Minnesota, introduced legislation entitled the "Consumer Internet Privacy Protection Act of 1997" on January 7, 1997 (for other attempts at legislation concerning privacy, see Alster, 1996). A copy of the proposed legislation is attached as an appendix to this chapter.

Given all of the hassles, then, why keep cookies? Besides the convenience of cookies, there is the dough. Online shoppers must remember that cookies act as a shopping cart. Because of their cookie's memory, shoppers only have to

---

[8] At the FTC workshop, eight of the major credit reference services announced that they had entered an agreement to try to prevent misuse of the information found at the top of credit reports, such as name address, and Social Security number. Information from the body of credit reports, for example, concerning loans and credit-card accounts, is protected under the Fair Credit Reporting Act.

pay at the end of their spree. Online shopping, of course, has become big business. And even when users do not place an order through the Internet, many make their purchasing decisions because of online advertising. In 1996, $200 million was spent on online advertising. Estimates of the amount to be spent on online advertising in the year 2000 are as high as $3 billion to $6 billion, although some other analysts are skeptical that the figures will be so high (Gellene, 1997; Messmer, 1996).

Regardless of the exact dollar figures, Internet advertising revenue will remain a potent factor in the advertising industry. For the foreseeable future, if advertisers are to "milk" the Internet for what it is worth, they will also have to pass the "cookies." This milk-and-cookies attitude, however, is not incompatible with a pro-choice attitude for web site visitors, who should have the freedom to "just say no!" Educating Netizens on the benefits as well as the potential down side to cookies is an important part of informed choice, which should perhaps be the goal for all advertising.

REFERENCES

Abate, T. (1997, December 20). Web site cookies track what we view; Small program hides out on our hard drives. *The San Francisco Examiner*, p. C2.

Alster, N. (1996). Big brother Is watching in world of cyberspace. *Investor's Business Daily*, Oct. 16, p. A8.

Angwin, J. (1997, June 15). Toss your cookies back at Web: Electronic data files used to track visitors can be refused, curbed. *Rocky Mountain News*, p. 12g.

Bell, J., Castagna, R., Ginsburg, L., Johnson, A. H., Morgan, C., Ruley, J. D., Silverman, P., & Yacono, J. J. (1997, July 1). Rev up the Web - the world's best techniques, tips and free software. *Windows Magazine*.

Berg, A. (1996, July 8). Cookies nibble at your disk drive. *LAN Times*, 85.

Berg, A. (1997, January 17). *op. cit.*; NPR, Talk of the Nation Science Friday, Transcript # 97011702-211, available on Lexis/Nexis computerized database service.

Bransten, L. (1996, October 28). Cookies leave a bitter taste: Invasive data collection is widespread. *Financial Times* (London edition 1), p. 15.

MicroMass embraces open profiling standard as part of strategy to give users control over privacy of personal information., (1997, June 12). *Business Wire*.

Cannell, M. (1998, October 19). Computer viruses; how computers get sick and how to cure them, *Science World*, 55(4), 18.

Catchings, B. & Van Name, M. (1996, July 29). Web security and the cookie controversy. *PC Week*, 13(30), p. 6.

Clark, D. (1997, July 3). Worries about privacy rain on net commerce parade. *American Banker*, 14.

Crabb, D. (1998, August 13). How to protect yourself from predators on Net, Chicago Sun-Times, 28.

Clearing one's tracks – From cybrslob to cyberchondriac, (1998, August 27). Businessworld (Philippines).

Coile, Z. (1997, June 13) "How Internet Users Can Protect Themselves," *The San Francisco Examiner*, p. A-20 (interview with Jake Kirchner, editor of *PC Magazine*).

Erickson, J. (1996, June 30). Are those who go online to send junk mail out of line?; Growth of unsolicited direct mail on Internet raises questions of privacy. *Star Tribune*, p. 3D.

Foster, E. (1996, July 22). The gripe line: Can mixing cooking with online marketing be a recipe for heartburn? *InfoWorld*, p. 54.

Gellene, D. (1997, June 9). The cutting edge; Net marketers propose online privacy reform; cyberspace: The industry is hoping to fend off federal regulations to protect and to give more control to consumers. *Los Angeles Times*, p.Dl.

Gellene, D. & Miller, G. (1997, June 12). Microsoft, Netscape pair up on net privacy; cyberspace: Plan would give consumers more control over information collected on them. *Los Angeles Times*, p. D3.

Gellman, R. (1996, May 27). Action for privacy can force cookies to crumble. *Government Computer News*, *15*(11), p. 35.

Glass, B. (1996, July 15). Help desk: Cookies won't spoil your diet but might hurt Web security. *InfoWorld*, p. 54.

Hawking, R. (1996a, May 14). Cookie Threat May Be Broken But Crumbs of Concern Linger. *The San Diego Union-Tribune*, p. 3.

Hawking, R. (1996b, August 13). Junk e-mail problem growing but solutions may be on way. *The San Diego Union-Tribune,* p. 3.

Hertzoff, I. (1996, November 25). Cookies are not always a treat for Web users. *Network World*, p. 38.

Hide your cookies. (1997, June 24) *Canada Newswire*,

IEClean gives surfers privacy (1996b, December 16). *PR Newswire*.

Interactive technologies aid market research. (1997, May 20) *Interactive PR*, *2*(10).

Interactive Week (1996). Oct. 7,1996, [Online] Available: <http://www/zdnet.com/intweek/print/961007/nettools/ doc4.html>. Cited in Marketing News (1997, February 17). Much ado about cookies. *Marketing News*, Section: Interactive Marketing

Internet access: Pretty Good Privacy, Inc. introduces PGPcookie.cutter for private and anonymous Web browsing. (1996, December 16). *Business Wire*.

Internet security & privacy--IEClean gives surfers privacy. (1997, January 1).*Internet Content Report*, *1*(19).

It is 15 milliseconds, according to Judith Messina, New media's hot play: DoubleClick infusion largest ever in city, (1997, June 16). *Crain's New York Business* .

Jaffee, L. (1996, April 8). Software lets Web advertisers track results. *National Mortgage News*, p. 15.

Kenworthy, K. & Lang, N. A. (1998, December 1). How safe is the Net? *Windows Magazine*, *9*(12), 144.

Kilsheimer, J. (1997, June 19). Net issues -- Tossing your cookies takes some deft switching. *The Seattle Times*, p. C2.

Komando, K. (1997, June 9). No milk needed with these cookies. *Los Angeles Times*, p. D5.

Kyber, P. (1997, June 5). Unwitting 90's Hansels and Gretels leave behind computer cookie trail. *The Richmond Times Dispatch*, p. D-15.

The Los Angeles Times, Dec. 23, 1996, [Online] Available: <http://www. latimes.com/>. Cited in (1997, February 17) Much ado about cookies. *Marketing News*, Section: Interactive Marketing.

Mannix, M., & Thomas, S. (1997, June 23). Exposed online. *U.S. News & World Report*, p. 59.

McChesney, J. (1996, July 14). Cookie tracks net user's visits to Web sites, *All Things Considered* NPR. Radio broadcast., available on LEXIS/NEXIS.

McChesney, J & Werthheimer, L. (1997, May 27). Netscape leads push for web privacy standards. *All Things Considered*, Transcript #97042716-212 (available on LEXIS/NEXIS).

McKim, R. (1997, January 13). Web sites need easier access; Make it simpler for your customer to return. *Web Marketing News*, p. 18.

Messmer, E. (1996, October 21). New wave of 'net marketing invades consumer privacy; Expect the next to be collecting your e-mail address and personal data off X.509 Digital   Certificates. *Network World*, *13*(43), p. 42.

Microsoft endorses W3C's HTML 4.0; Announces support in Microsoft Internet Explorer 4.0, (1997, July 8). *PR Newswire*.

MIN's New Media Report. (1997, June 9). Major online publisher shows support for personalization/privacy standard. *3*(18).

Moeller, M. (1997, June 17). NetGravity AdServer pulls its weight in targeted ads. *PC Week*, *13*(24), p. 39.

Moukheiber, Z. (1996, November 4). DoubleClick is watching you. *Forbes*, *158*(11), p. 342.

Nelson, M. (1998, October 8). Net Nanny takes security beyond passwords, *Infoworld Daily News*.

NetGravity tames the Web cookie monster (1996, June 19). *Newsbyters*.

Net Nanny takes security beyond passwords, 'First of its Kind' keystroke dynamics security technology, at Fall Internet World (1998, October 8). *Business Wire*.

NSClean foils cybersnoops, enhances privacy (1996a, December 16). *PR Newswire*.

One-to-one Powerhouse BroadVision, Inc. endorses two key online privacy and security initiatives; BroadVision joins electronic frontier foundation's TRUSTe Initiative and supports OPS industry profiling standard for electronic commerce privacy. (1997, June 24). *Newswire*

Online spying (1996, November). *PC Computing*, *9*(11), 358.

Schwartz, J. (1996, June 24). Trail of crumbs leads right to the cyber-cookie jar. *The Washington Post*. p. F19.

Shaw, H. B. III (1997, June 22). You don't need to accept cookies from strange sites. *The Capital*, Available on LEXIS/NEXIS.

Standage, T. (1996, July 30). Connected: Leaving a trail of crumbs many Web sites rely on cookies. *The Daily Telegraph*, p. 7.

Taft, D. K. (1996, April 29). Netscape's Navigator--Teenager responsible for hacking out bugs in popular Netscape browser. *Computer Reseller News,* p. 1;

Taking orders over the Web now easier than ever (1996, October 15). *Presswire*.

Trager, L. (1997, June 13). Netscape flaw lets snoops see files; Web site operators can view browsers' hard drives. *The San Francisco Examiner*, p. A1.

Two firms seek to register all Web users and deliver demographics to Websites, advertisers (1996, March 11). *Interactive PR.*

Wildstrom,S. H. (1996, December 16). Privacy and the `cookie' monster. *Business Week*, n. 3506, p. 22.

Woody, T. (1996, November 11). Net gain; A cure for "net nausea"; Toss your cookies. *Texas Lawyer*, p. 32, available on LEXIS/NEXIS.

APPENDIX

Consumer Internet Privacy Protection Act of 1997

105TH CONGRESS; 1ST SESSION
IN THE HOUSE OF REPRESENTATIVES
AS INTRODUCED IN THE HOUSE

H. R. 98

1997 H.R. 98; 105 H.R. 98

SYNOPSIS:
A BILL To regulate the use by interactive computer services of personally identifiable information provided by subscribers to such services.

DATE OF INTRODUCTION: JANUARY 7, 1997

DATE OF VERSION: JANUARY 14, 1997 -- VERSION: 1

SPONSOR(S):
Mr. VENTO INTRODUCED THE FOLLOWING BILL; WHICH WAS REFERRED TO THE COMMITTEE ON COMMERCE

TEXT:
Be it enacted by the Senate and House of Representatives of the United States of America in Congress assembled,

SECTION 1.   SHORT TITLE.
This Act may be cited as the "Consumer Internet Privacy Protection Act of 1997."

SECTION 2. REGULATION OF USE BY AN INTERACTIVE COMPUTER SERVICE OF A SUBSCRIBER'S PERSONALLY IDENTIFIABLE INFORMATION.
(a) DISCLOSURE OF PERSONALLY IDENTIFIABLE INFORMATION WITHOUT CONSENT PROHIBITED.-
(1) IN GENERAL.-AN INTERACTIVE COMPUTER SERVICE SHALL NOT DISCLOSE TO A THIRD PARTY ANY PERSONALLY IDENTIFIABLE INFORMATION PROVIDED BY A SUBSCRIBER TO SUCH SERVICE WITHOUT THE SUBSCRIBER'S PRIOR INFORMED WRITTEN CONSENT.
(2) REVOCATION OF CONSENT.-SUCH SERVICE SHALL PERMIT A SUBSCRIBER TO REVOKE THE CONSENT GRANTED UNDER PARAGRAPH (1)

AT ANY TIME, AND UPON SUCH REVOCATION, SUCH SERVICE SHALL CEASE DISCLOSING SUCH INFORMATION TO A THIRD PARTY.

(b) KNOWING DISCLOSURE OF FALSIFIED PERSONALLY IDENTIFIABLE INFORMATION PROHIBITED.-AN INTERACTIVE COMPUTER SERVICE OR AN EMPLOYEE OF SUCH SERVICE SHALL NOT KNOWINGLY DISCLOSE TO A THIRD PARTY ANY PERSONALLY IDENTIFIABLE INFORMATION PROVIDED BY A SUBSCRIBER TO SUCH SERVICE THAT SUCH SERVICE, OR SUCH EMPLOYEE, HAS KNOWINGLY FALSIFIED.

(c) SUBSCRIBER ACCESS TO PERSONALLY IDENTIFIABLE INFOR-MATION.-

(1) IN GENERAL.-AT A SUBSCRIBER'S REQUEST, AN INTERACTIVE COMPUTER SERVICE SHALL-

(A) PROVIDE THE SUBSCRIBER'S PERSONALLY IDENTIFIABLE INFORMATION MAINTAINED BY THE SERVICE TO THE SUBSCRIBER;

(B) PERMIT THE SUBSCRIBER TO VERIFY SUCH INFORMATION MAINTAINED BY THE SERVICE; AND

(C)PERMIT THE SUBSCRIBER TO CORRECT ANY ERROR IN SUCH INFORMATION.

(2) ACCESS TO IDENTITY OF RECIPIENTS OF INFORMATION - AT A SUBSCRIBER'S REQUEST, THE SERVICE SHALL PROVIDE TO THE SUBSCRIBER THE IDENTITY OF THE THIRD PARTY RECIPIENTS OF THE SUBSCRIBER'S PERSONALLY IDENTIFIABLE INFORMATION.

(3) FEE.- THE SERVICE SHALL NOT CHARGE A FEE TO THE SUBSCRIBER FOR MAKING AVAILABLE THE INFORMATION UNDER THIS SUBSECTION.

SECTION 3. ENFORCEMENT AND RELIEF.

(a) FEDERAL TRADE COMMISSION.-THE FEDERAL TRADE COMMISSION SHALL HAVE THE AUTHORITY TO EXAMINE AND INVESTIGATE AN INTERACTIVE COMPUTER SERVICE TO DETERMINE WHETHER SUCH SERVICE HAS BEEN OR IS ENGAGED IN ANY ACT OR PRACTICE PROHIBITED BY THIS ACT.

(b) RELIEF.-

(1) CEASE AND DESIST ORDER.-IF THE FEDERAL TRADE COM-MISSION DETERMINES AN INTERACTIVE COMPUTER SERVICE HAS BEEN OR IS ENGAGED IN ANY ACT OR PRACTICE PROHIBITED BY THIS ACT, THE COMMISSION MAY ISSUE A CEASE AND DESIST ORDER AS IF SUCH SERVICE WERE IN VIOLATION OF SECTION 5 OF THE FEDERAL TRADE COMMISSION ACT.

(2) CIVIL ACTION.-A SUBSCRIBER AGGRIEVED BY A VIOLATION OF SECTION 2 MAY IN A CIVIL ACTION OBTAIN APPROPRIATE RELIEF.

SECTION 4. DEFINITIONS.

As used in this Act-

(1) the term "interactive computer service" means any information service that provides computer access to multiple users via modem to the Internet;

(2) the term "Internet" means the international computer network of both Federal and non-Federal interoperable packet switched data networks;

(3) the term "personally identifiable information" has the meaning given such term in section 631 of the Communications Act of 1934 (47 U.S.C. 551);

(4) the term "informed written consent" means a statement-

(A) in writing and freely signed by a subscriber;

(B) consenting to the disclosures such service will make of the information provided; and

(C) describing the rights of the subscriber under this Act; and

(5) the term "third party" means, with respect to the disclosure of personally identifiable information provided by a subscriber to an interactive computer service, a person or other entity other than-

(A) such service;

(B) an employee of such service; or that subscriber to such service.

15

From Spam to Stern: Advertising Law and the Internet

Sandra Davidson
University of Missouri

> "Spam. Spam. Spam. Spam. Spam. Spam. Spam." A response to an inquiry about what's on the menu in *Monty Python's Flying Circus.*

"Spam," of course, is a term for junk e-mail. The proper term is "unsolicited commercial e-mail" (UCE; Loundy, 1997), but "spam" is the term that seems to have caught on. Hormel, the manufacturer of the canned meat, has asked the junk-mail giant, Cyberpromotions, to quit using the term Spam, which Hormel has trademarked, but to no avail (Hopkins et al., 1997). Will a law suit follow?

The Internet provides enterprising advertisers with a multiplicity of opportunities for creative advertising - and for running afoul of the law. How to advertise creatively without breaking the law is the subject of this chapter.

PRINCIPLE 1: "Old" law of advertising still applies to the new medium of the Internet.

Despite opinions to the contrary, the Internet is not a brave new frontier where all new law must be created out of whole cloth to meet the new challenges of this new medium. Quite the opposite, courts have said time and time again that when a new medium pops up, they will simply apply old law to it (*Sony Corp. v. Universal City Studios*, 464 U.S. 417: 1984).

The concept of new media, of course, is not itself new. At one time, for example, broadcast was a new medium. Yet, courts did not have to throw out old law and start anew. What the courts did have to do is this: Decide which of the preexisting "pigeonholes" into which to shove broadcasting.

233

For instance, it was inevitable that broadcasting would lead to broadcast defamation, but defamation had two branches: libel and slander. Libel was printed words, and libel was considered more serious than slander, which was spoken words of limited reach. Libel, because of the nature of the printed word and its ability to be disseminated broadly, could potentially cause more damage to the reputation of the defamed individual than slander because the spoken word evaporated with the breath that carried it, leaving only rumormongers to spread the erroneous information. The question presented to jurists, then, was whether to pigeonhole broadcast defamation with libel or with slander. Although the spoken nature of broadcast words would seem to favor the slander pigeonhole, the ability to tape record and therefore replay the exact words favored the libel pigeonhole. Further, the damage capabilities of broadcast defamation more closely resembled those of libel. It simply made no sense to say the damage of a coast-to-coast spoken broadcast was less than the damage of a written article in a small newspaper. Broadcast defamation, therefore, became a part of libel (for example, *Farmers Education & Cooperative Union, North Dakota Div. v. WDAY, Inc.*, 360 U.S. 525, 537, 544-45: 1959).

The Federal Trade Commission rules over almost all advertising[1] with all the powers and abilities to penalize conferred upon that administrative body by the United States Congress: "The Commission is hereby empowered and directed to prevent persons, partnerships, or corporations. . . from using unfair methods of competition in or affecting commerce and unfair or deceptive acts or practices in or affecting commerce (15 U.S.C. ? 45)."

The Lanham Act (15 U.S.C. ? 1051, *et seq.)*, a federal law, prohibits:

> *false designation* of origin, false or misleading description of fact, *or false or misleading representation of fact,* which -
>
> (A) is *likely to cause confusion*, or to cause mistake, or to deceive as to the affiliation, connection, or association of such person with another person, or *as to the origin*, sponsorship, or approval of his or her goods, services, or commercial activities by another person, *or*
>
> (B) in commercial advertising or promotion, *misrepresents* the nature, characteristics, qualities, or geographic origin of his or her or another person's *goods, services, or commercial activities....* (15 U.S.C. ? 1125(a)(1) (emphasis added).

---

[1] The Federal Trade Improvements Act, however, did restrict the FTC's power over "children's advertising." 15 U.S.C. ' 57a. (The FCC regulates children's television advertising, which is limited to "10.5 minutes per hour on weekends and not more than 12 minutes per hour on weekdays. 47 U.S.C. '303a.). Also, the FCC Improvements Act restricted the FTC's power to regulate the funeral industry. P.L. 96-252 ' 19, 94 Stat. 391 (May 28, 1980).

The act permits plaintiffs to seek injunctions as well as monetary damages (15 U.S.C. ? 1125c). Every state's attorney general can also police the Internet for deceptive trade practices. In short, the attitude that "it's a jungle out there" in the Internet is problematic: The Internet is not a jungle in the sense of being a totally wild and unfettered (cyber) place with no laws to restrain it. It may give persons more opportunity to hide while breaking established law, but once perpetrators are caught, they cannot slip through the legal net by claiming their activity occurred on the Internet so "regular" law does not apply. It does. In short, every admonition on what not to do in order to avoid legal problems when advertising applies to the Internet.

To use a kitchen (if not kitchy) analogy, advertising on the Internet rather than in newspapers or in magazines or over the radio and TV airwaves is like serving the same meal but on a different type of platter. Whether one serves spaghetti on porcelain, everyday stoneware, a plastic or paper plate, or a metal tray, it is still spaghetti. The medium on which it is served does not change the fact that it is spaghetti. Think of murder: No matter how "high tech" the weapon, murder is still murder.

PRINCIPLE II: Commercial Speech, Including Internet Advertising, Receives First Amendment Protection

In 1976, the Supreme Court extended constitutional protection to purely commercial advertisement. In *Virginia State Board of Pharmacy v. Virginia Citizens Council, Inc (*425 U.S. 748: 1976), the Court struck down a Virginia statute. This statute prohibited advertising prices of prescription drugs. The Court said that information on drug prices was of value to the public. For instance, the cost of tetracycline could range from $1.20 to $9.00. Pharmacists did not want the ban lifted. The Court emphasized the public interest in receiving such information. "[C]onsumer's interest . . . in the free flow of commercial information may be as keen, if not keener by far, than his [or her] interest in the day's most urgent political debate" (425 U.S. 763: 1976). In short, commercial speech is protected by the First Amendment. "What is at issue is whether a state may completely suppress the dissemination of concededly truthful information about entirely lawful activity. . . . [W]e conclude that the answer. . . is in the negative." (425 U.S. 748: 1976).

In 1980, in *Central Hudson Gas & Electric Corp. v. Public Service Commission* (447 U.S. 557: 1980), the Supreme Court struck down a New York regulation that barred all advertising promoting the use of electricity by electric utilities. The overly broad regulation even prohibited promotion of energy-saving uses of electricity. Insofar as the regulation suppressed speech that did not impair the state interest in promoting conservation of energy, the regulation violated the First Amendment. The Supreme Court said that for commercial speech to receive First Amendment protection, it must meet a four-part test of whether: the ad is legal; the ad is not misleading; the regulation advances a substantial governmental interest; and, the regulation is "not more extensive than necessary" (i.e., the regulation is narrowly tailored) (447 U.S. 566: 1980).

The Supreme Court seems to be "watering down" the narrow-tailoring requirement, instead requiring only a "reasonable fit" between the regulation and the interest the regulation protects. For example, the Supreme Court in 1986 upheld Puerto Rico's legislation that says "no gambling room shall be permitted to advertise its facilities to the public of Puerto Rico." The Court, applying the *Central Hudson* test, decided Puerto Rico's legislature was "not unreasonable" in deciding "excessive casino gambling" by Puerto Ricans "would produce serious harmful effects" (Posadas de Puerto Rico Associates v. Tourism Co. of Puerto Rico, 478 U.S. 328, 341: 1986). And in 1989, the Supreme Court upheld regulations at the State University of New York that prohibited commercial activities in dormitories - in this instance, a Tupperware party. The Court said:

> Although *Central Hudson* and other decisions have occasionally contained statements suggesting that government restriction on commercial speech must constitute the least restrictive means of achieving the governmental interests asserted, those decisions have never required that the restriction be absolutely the least severe that will achieve the desired end. Rather, the decisions require only a reasonable "fit" between the government's ends and the means chosen to accomplish those ends.[2]

PRINCIPLE III: First Amendment Protection Does Not Extend to "Deceptive" Advertising

Although nonmisleading ads for legal activities receive protection, the converse is that misleading ads or ads for illegal activities are unprotected. Like obscenity, misleading ads have no redeeming social value, so they receive no First Amendment protection.

If a state has the power to outlaw prostitution or the sale of marijuana, the reasoning goes, then the state should have the power to outlaw ads for these illegal services or commodities. Because of the relative anonymity that medium provides, ads for "escort" services and "personal massages" have proliferated on the Internet. Of course, just because an activity flourishes does not mean it is a legal activity.

Deceptive advertising provides more serious questions for analysis than do ads for illegal transactions. One of the more difficult questions is this: What constitutes a "deceptive" ad? One that has the "tendency" to deceive its target

[2] Board of Trustees of S.U.N.Y. v. Fox, 492 U.S. 469, 470: 1989 (syllabus, citing pp. 475-481). On "reasonable fit," see also 44 Liquormart, Inc. v. Rhode Island, 116 S. Ct. 1495: 1996; Rubin v. Secretary of Treasury, 514 U.S. 476: 1995.

audience. It has this tendency if it contains any false or misleading statements that are material (15 U.S.C. ? 55a 1), i.e., that might affect a consumer's decision to buy a product. Omissions (half-truths) can be deceptive, and statements that are literally true may be deceptive if they leave a misleading impression. For example, Old Gold cigarettes claimed that an independent study found Old Gold lowest in tar and nicotine. That is true. The study also said the difference was infinitesimal and thus negligible (P. Lorillard Co. v. Federal Trade Commission, 186 F.2d 52: 4th Cir. 1950).

The FTC will allow *puffery*, which is exaggeration of subjective claims for the taste, feel, appearance, and smell or a product. The FTC believes that consumers do not take such claims seriously anyway. (Would anyone really think that bathroom tissue is softer than a "white cloud"?) The FTC also allows "mock-ups" but does not allow deceptive mock-ups. As an example, the FTC issued a cease-and-desist order against an ad for Rapid Shave aerosol shaving cream. Rapid Shave could even soften coarse sandpaper, the ad said, and Rapid Shave appeared to immediately allow the shaving of sandpaper. Actually, it took 80 minutes for sandpaper to get soft enough to shave, and the mock-up was sand on plexiglas, not sandpaper. The Supreme Court upheld the FTC's cease-and-desist order. The Court said, "It is a material deceptive practice to convey to television viewers the false impression that they are seeing an actual test, experiment or demonstration which proves a product claim when they are not because of the undisclosed use of mock-ups" (Federal Trade Commission v. Colgate-Palmolive Co., 380 U.S. 374, 374: 1965).

The FTC can hold administrative hearings and issue "cease and desist" orders to advertisers. If the advertisers do not comply, the FTC can levy civil fines of up to $10,000 a day for each offense.[3] The FTC can also get an injunction from a federal district court to stop false advertisements (15 U.S.C. 53). Congress gave the FTC this power in 1973 (see the Lanham act of 1982).

The FTC uses publicity, as well, issuing news releases on complaints and orders. Corrective advertising is a potent weapon in the FTC arsenal. The FTC can demand that companies make "affirmative disclosures" about their earlier ads that were deceptive. For instance, in May 1997, the FTC attacked the R.J. Reynolds Tobacco Company for its "Joe Camel" ads that appeal to children. This precipitated speculation in the media that the FTC might require corrective advertising (e.g., Neergaard,1997). The FTC was poised to seek a cease-and-desist order against Joe from an administrative law judge when R.J. Reynolds filed suit in North Carolina to block the FTC. Then, on July 10, 1997, the tobacco company voluntarily pulled Joe Camel (Levin, 1997; Media business, 1997; Nowell, 1997), which precipitated publication of tongue-in-cheek

---

[3] See 15 USC ' 45(b) on cease and desist orders. For fines, see ' 45(k)(1). This statute also gives citizens the right to appeal FTC action to a United States circuit court of appeals. See ' 45(d).

obituaries in some newspapers (e.g., "Joe Camel, the suave dromedary who excelled at billiards, played the saxophone and tirelessly promoted R. J. Reynolds Tobacco Co.'s Camel cigarettes from behind dark glasses, died Thursday at his home in North Carolina. He was 9-years-old."; Hassell & Thompson, 1997).

Despite its power, the FTC obviously can use all the help it can get. States' attorneys general also regulate deceptive trade practices.

PRINCIPLE IV: Libel Law Applies to Internet Advertising

Perhaps the greatest communications law case of all time, *New York Times Co. v. Sullivan* (376 U.S. 254: 1964), involved a paid political ad taken out by a civil-rights group. Of course, that ad was not suggesting a commercial transaction. But the Court made a broad statement: "...we hold that if the allegedly libelous statements would otherwise be constitutionally protected..., they do not forfeit that protection because they were published in the form of a paid advertisement" (376 U.S. 266: 1964). So all the protections of libel occur within paid advertisements, but the down side is that all the liability pertains as well. The Court values libel protection because it values people's reputations.. As Justice Stewart said, "The right of a man [or woman] to the protection of his [or her] own reputation from unjustified invasion and wrongful hurt reflects no more than our basic concept of the essential dignity and worth of every human being" (Rosenblatt v. Baer, 383 U.S. 75, 92: J. Stewart, concurring).

Not only individuals but also small groups (generally 25 or fewer persons) and corporations can be libeled. A corporation is a legal entity - a "person" under the law for some purposes. A comparative ad that contains an untrue statement that damages the business reputation of a corporation could be libelous. The plaintiff would have to prove five elements to win:

1. The statement is *defamatory*, meaning it is false and that it is harmful to reputation.
2. The statement was *published or broadcast*. If a third person hears or reads the statement, that is enough. Posting a statement on the Internet constitutes publication.
3. The statement *identifies* the plaintiff. The identification does not have to be by name.
4. The statement caused injury to the plaintiff. Damage to reputation and emotional distress are compensable injuries, as are money losses, say, from lost sales.
5. The defendant acted with fault.[4]

---

[4] "Fault" is an important element in libel cases. The United States Supreme Court overturned strict liability, a doctrine that said that if a defendant published or broadcast defamatory words, that defendant could be liable no matter how careful that defendant

Clearly, individuals who libel others, no matter how, including in advertisements and over the Internet, can be held liable for libel. The Internet thus raises the interesting question of whether an online service provider (such as America Online or Prodigy) can likewise be held liable for the libelous messages of their users.

In 1991, CompuServe won a libel suit in a New York federal trial court (Cubby, Inc. v. CompuServe, 776 F. Supp. 135: S.D.N.Y. 1991). CompuServe had made a contract with another company to provide a daily newsletter about journalism for CompuServe subscribers. That second company had used yet a third company to provide the newsletter. CompuServe made no attempts to review the newsletter's contents (Cubby, Inc. v. CompuServe, 776 F. Supp. 137: S.D.N.Y. 1991).

The court called CompuServe "high technology" and a part of the "information industry revolution," but the court applied old law. Because CompuServe did not try to exercise any editorial control over the newsletter, the court let CompuServe off the hook for libel. In effect, the court shoved CompuServe into a safe pigeonhole - that of libraries or news vendors or bookstores that are unaware of the libel their books or newspapers might contain. No library can be held responsible if a book that the librarian has not reviewed contains libel. CompuServe, the court said, was providing an "electronic, for-profit library contents" (Cubby, Inc. v. CompuServe, 776 F. Supp. 140: S.D.N.Y. 1991).

In 1995, Prodigy found itself in a different pigeonhole - that of a publisher. Prodigy controlled the content of its computer bulletin boards in order to promote itself as family oriented. It used an "automatic software screening program" to look for forbidden words, and its editorial staff bounced allegedly offensive notes. Unfortunately for Prodigy, no list of software-generated words could screen for libel. Prodigy sealed its own fate. The New York state trial court said that by holding itself out as exercising editorial control, Prodigy was

---

had been. In New York Times v. Sullivan, 376 U.S. 254: 1964, the Court ruled that public officials must prove actual malice - that a statement was made with "knowledge that it was false or with reckless disregard of whether it was false or not." Id. at 279. The Court later held that public figures must also prove actual malice. See Curtis Publishing Co. v. Butts, 388 U.S. 130: 1967 (decided together with Associated Press v. Walker).

But in Gertz v. Robert Welch, Inc., 418 U.S. 323: 1974, the Court decided that the Constitution does not require that private individuals prove actual malice in order to win a libel case, although states may require actual malice if they wish. The Court said, "We hold that, so long as they do not impose liability without fault, the States may define for themselves the appropriate standard of liability for a publisher or broadcaster of defamatory falsehood injurious to a private individual." Id. at 347. But in order to collect punitive damages, the Court ruled, even private individuals must prove actual malice. Punitive damages are "private fines" that should only be levied by juries "to punish reprehensible conduct." Id. at 349-350.

"expressly differentiating itself from its competition and expressly likening itself to a newspaper." In short, the court shoved Prodigy into the pigeonhole of a newspaper, which could be found liable for libel (Stratton Oakmont, Inc. v. Prodigy Services, Co., 1995 N.Y. Misc. LEXIS 229: 1995).

In 1996, the United States Congress decided to protect online service providers such a Prodigy. Attempts to filter obscene or otherwise objectionable material will not result in the online service provider being deemed a publisher (see the attached appendix).

PRINCIPLE V: Negligence Law Applies to Internet Advertising.

Asleep at the wheel.   Sooner or later almost everybody experiences that phenomenon.   The person did not *mean* to cause a problem but failed to be careful enough. The result? Unintentional harm caused by negligence.

The key to liability in negligence cases is "foreseeability." If an individual engages in conduct that could foreseeably create harm, and if that harm occurs, the individual may be held liable for negligence. Foreseeability refers to what a "reasonably prudent person" would "reasonably" foresee under similar circumstances (Gallick v. Baltimore & Ohio Railroad Co., 372 U.S. 108, 118: quoting instructions to the jury). "Ordinary care" is the standard one must meet in order to avoid liability circumstances (Gallick v. Baltimore & Ohio Railroad Co., 372 U.S. at n.6; Inman v. Baltimore & Ohio Railroad Co., 361 U.S. 138, 146 n. 2: 1959). "Negligence" is a concept that can apply to almost any human activity.   Drivers can be negligent, causing accidents that reasonably prudent drivers would avoid by using ordinary care.   So can builders by, say, cutting corners and thereby creating dangerous conditions.   And now, so can advertisers, as the following case demonstrates (for more extended coverage of negligence, see Davidson, 1977).

Soldier of Fortune magazine, which caters to lovers of weaponry and war, lost a major legal battle. In January 1993 in *Braun v. Soldier of Fortune* (Braun v. Soldier of Fortune Magazine, Inc., 968 F.2d 1110 (11th Cir. 1992), *cert. denied*, 113 S. Ct. 1028: 1993), the Supreme Court let stand an award of $4,375,000 to brothers Michael and Ian Braun for the murder of their father.

The magazine had printed this ad: "GUN FOR HIRE: 37-year-old professional mercenary desires jobs. Vietnam veteran. Discrete [sic] and very private.   Bodyguard, courier and other special skills.   All jobs considered." Michael Savage, the man from Knoxville, Tennessee, who placed the ad, received a call from Richard Braun's business partner. On August 26, 1985, Savage and two other men waited in ambush in Atlanta, Georgia, as Braun and his 16-year-old son Michael drove down the driveway of their home. Using a MAC 11 automatic pistol, the hit-squad wounded the son and pumped fatal bullets into the father.

During the ensuing wrongful-death trial against *Soldier of Fortune*, the sons maintained that the magazine had been negligent in publishing the ad. The jury agreed (Braun v. *Soldier of Fortune* Magazine, Inc., 968 F.2d 1110 (11th Cir. 1992), *cert. denied*, 113 S. Ct. 1113: 1993). The Eleventh Circuit Court of Appeals approved of the trial court's instruction to the jury that the magazine could be found liable if "on its face" "the ad in question contains a clearly identifiable unreasonable risk, that the offer in the ad is one to commit a serious violent crime, including murder" *(*Braun v. *Soldier of Fortune* Magazine, Inc., 968 F.2d 1110 (11th Cir. 1992), *cert. denied*, 113 S. Ct. 1114-15, 1118-19: 1993).[5]

Likewise, an Internet ad offering an assassin's services obviously could lead to murder - and to legal liability under negligence law. Words that forseeably lead to the flowing of blood can also lead to the flowing of money via a damage award.

PRINCIPLE VI: Privacy Law Concerning Appropriation of Name, Likeness, or Voice Applies to Internet Advertising

Plaintiffs can receive awards for appropriation of their names or likenesses or voices or identities - commercial exploitation, a trespass upon the pocketbook of the famous. The "right of publicity" is another term for appropriation.[6]

Name. For instance, in 1980, Johnny Carson recovered for appropriation of his name. Carson sued because a portable toilet being marketed as "Here's Johnny" - "The World's Foremost Commodian." The Sixth Circuit Court of Appeals said there was an even clearer appropriation of Johnny Carson's persona than if his full proper name had been used. (Note: The full name need not be used for a successful suit.)

Likeness. Mohammed Ali won an injunction against *Playgirl* magazine (*Ali v. Playgirl, Inc.*, 447 F. Supp.: 1978). On its cover, *Playgirl* used an illustration

---

[5] On the positive side for advertisers, the court of appeals said:
[W]hile Defendants owe a duty of reasonable care to the public, the magazine publisher does not have a duty to investigate every ad it publishes. Defendants owe no duty to the Plaintiffs for publishing an ad if the ad's language on its face would not convey to the reader that it created an unreasonable risk that the advertiser was available to commit such violent crimes as murder.

[6] Carson v. Here's Johnny Portable Toilets, Inc., 698 F.2d 831, 834 (6th Cir. 1983). "Appropriation" or the "right of publicity" is one of the four forms of invasion of privacy enunciated by William Prosser. Id. (citing W. Prosser, Privacy, 48 Cal. L. Rev. 383, 389: 1960).

of Ali sitting naked in the corner of a boxing ring. The doggerel in the text did not mention Ali by name but did refer to "The Greatest," which Ali called himself. The injunctio forbade any further distribution of the *Playgirl* featuring Ali's image. (Note: A drawing is sufficient for a suit, and a name does not have to be used.)

Voice. "The Divine Miss M," Bette Midler, won the right to sue in a case involving appropriation of her voice in broadcast ads for Ford Motor Company (*Midler v. Ford Motor Co.*, 849 F.2d: 9th Cir. 1988). The imitation Midler was singing "Do You Want to Dance" in a manner so convincing that even her friends thought Bette was hawking cars. The court said, "We hold . . . that when a distinctive voice of a professional singer is widely known and is deliberately imitated in order to sell a product, the sellers have appropriated what is not theirs."[7] (Note: A convincing "sound alike" is enough for a successful suit.)

Identity. Vanna White won the right to sue for appropriation of her identity. A series of ads for Samsung Electronics set an item from popular culture and a Samsung product together in the 21st century to show the product would still be used. An ad for Samsung VCRs showed a robot wearing an evening gown, blonde wig and large jewelry standing beside what was clearly a "Wheel of Fortune" board (1992 U.S. App. LEXIS 19253, *1-*2). The caption said: "Longest-running game show, 2012 A.D." Although the Ninth Circuit Court of Appeals stated flatly that the "robot . . . was not White's `likeness,'" the court concluded that she could sue for appropriation of her "celebrity identity."[8]

As the Vanna White case shows, the tort of appropriation is expanding through case law. It is also expanding through statutes. As an example, Indiana has a broad statute that protects "use of a personality's name, voice, signature, photograph, image, likeness, distinctive appearance, gestures, or mannerisms. . .." (Burns Ind. Code Ann. 32-13-1-1: c).

---

[7] The case was remanded for trial. Id. at 463-464. Midler won a $400,000 jury award. St. Louis Post-Dispatch, Nov. 1, 1989, at 4A, col. 1.
For misappropriation of voice and for false endorsement under the Lanham Act, gravelly voiced singer Tom Waits won a total of $2.6 million in damages and attorneys fees against Frito-Lay. A voice-alike imitated Waits in a radio commercial for Doritos. Tom Waits v. Frito-Lay, Inc., 23 U.S.P.Q.2d 1721: 1992.

[8] The court said, "The law protects the celebrity's sole right to exploit this [celebrity identity] value whether the celebrity has achieved her fame out of rare ability, dumb luck, or a combination thereof." Id. at *12-*13. Judge Alarcon wrote a blistering dissent. White won $403,000. (Barnett, 1994)

Defenses. The First Amendment can protect authors who want to mention famous people in their works.[9] Newsworthy uses, of course, receive protection; otherwise reporting of news would come to a halt. Consent, which may require money, is also a protection--so long as the consent is broad enough to cover the use.

Warning 1. Using the names or images of dead people used to be safe (*See* Guglielmi v. Spelling-Goldberg Productions, 603 P.2d 454, 455: Cal. In Bank 1979 - involving Rudolf Valentino; Lugosi v. Universal Pictures, 25 Cal. 3d 813, 603 P.2d 425: 1979 - involving Bela Lugosi as Dracula). But the trend is for courts to treat the right of publicity as a property right - something that is inheritable. Elvis Presley has made more law in this area than anyone else (See, e.g., Estate of Presley v. Russen, 513 F. Supp. 1339: D.N.J. 1981). Many states now have statutes that protect the right of publicity after death. For example, California protects the right of publicity for 50 years after a celebrity's death (Cal. Civ. Code ? 990).

Warning 2. Disclaimers are not enough. As an example, comedian Woody Allen got an injunction against a clothing store, Men's Fashion World, that was using a Woody Allen look-alike in an ad.[10] The caption said, "Men's Fashion

---

[9] ABC aired a film, Legend of Valentino: A Romantic Fiction. Guglielmi v. Spelling-Goldberg Productions, 603 P.2d 454, 455 (Cal. In Bank 1979) (Rudolf Valentino's real name was Rudolpho Guglielmi.) In denying the appropriation suit, the Supreme Court of California said, "No author should be forced into creating mythological worlds or characters wholly divorced from reality. The right of publicity derived from public prominence does not confer a shield to ward off caricature, parody and satire. Rather, prominence invites creative comment. Surely, the range of free expression would be meaningfully reduced if prominent persons in the present and recent past were forbidden topics for the imaginations of authors of fiction." Id. at 460. The Court then gives the example of cartoonist Gary Trudeau and his "Doonesbury" strip, which satirizes famous people. Id. at n.12. Although few courts have considered the question, the court said, consistently "the right of publicity has not been held to outweigh the value of free expression." Id. at 461-462.

See also, Rogers v. Grimaldi, 695 F. Supp 112 (S.D.N.Y. 1988), aff'd., 875 F.2d 994 (2d Cir. 1989), Ginger Rogers sued MGM/UA over its release of the film "Ginger and Fred," created and produced by Federico Fellini. Rogers lost. 875 F.2d at 997-1005. The film is about two fictional dancers who imitated Rogers and Fred Astaire in their cabaret act. Id. at 996-997.

[10] Allen v. Men's World Outlet, Inc., 679 F. Supp. (S.D.N.Y. 1988). See also an earlier case involving the same Woody Allen look-alike, Phil Boroff, Allen v. National Video, Inc., 610 F. Supp. 612 (S.D.N.Y. 1985). Allen used the Lanham Act, 15 U.S.C. Sec. 1125(a).

World made me a sex symbol." Even though the ad had a disclaimer which said that the man pictured was a celebrity look-alike (679 F. Supp. at 362, 367), a New York federal trial court thought consumers could be confused over whether Woody Allen endorsed the fashions from Men's Fashion World.

PRINCIPLE VII: An Exception to Appropriation Law Exists for Some Advertisements: "Incidental Use"

Radio shock-jock Howard Stern lost to Delphi Internet Services Corporation (626 N.Y.S.2d: 1995). Delphi used a photo of Stern in leather pants that showed his bare buttocks to advertise Delphi's bulletin board about Stern's candidacy for governor of New York. The ad asked whether Stern should be elected, and then it proclaimed:

> You've seen him. You've been exposed to his Private Parts. . .
> Maybe it's time to tell the world exactly what you think. . . So
> whether you think Howard-the-Aspiring-Governor should be
> crowned King of the Empire State, or just greased up and sent face-
> first down a water slide, don't put a cork in it. Sit down, jack in, and
> be heard.

Responsible for $1.7 million in fines for indecency against Infinity Broadcasting, Inc., Howard Stern did not complain about his backside being displayed. His complaint was that Delphi appropriated his name and likeness (Ballard & Riverz-Sanchez, 1996).

Appropriation law has an exception called "incidental use." The exception applies to news vendors such as newspapers or broadcasters that may use a person's name or photo in ads if they have already used the material for a news purpose (626 N.Y.S.2d at 697-698). Delphi had first used Stern's name and likeness in an Internet bulletin-board discussing Stern's gubernatorial race. Because of this permissible use, the Court decided that Delphi could also use Stern's name and photo in its ad. The court said it would give Delphi the "same protection" that it would give "a more traditional news disseminator engaged in the advertisement of a newsworthy product" (626 N.Y.S.2d at 698). Delphi was promoting political speech, which is at the core of speech protected by the First Amendment. Of course, courts want to encourage political discourse. The United States Supreme Court, for example, speaks of "a profound national commitment to the principle that debate on public issues should be uninhibited, robust, and wide-open. . ." (*New York Times Co. v. Sullivan*, 376 U.S. 254, 270: 1964).

PRINCIPLE VIII: Privacy in the Form of Intrusion Into Seclusion Could Be a Problem with "Cookie" Technology

Putting a device where it should not be, such as putting a "cookie" to track a web-site user's movements in the user's computer without consent, raises concerns about invasion of privacy. So does a web-site operator's requiring information from kids before they can visit web sites. For extended coverage of this topic, see chap. 14, "CyberCookies: How Much Should the Public Swallow?"

PRINCIPLE IX: Copyright Law Applies to the Internet

Copyright law is old! The United States Constitution, Article I, Section 8, proclaims: "The Congress shall have power . . . to promote the Progress of Science and useful Arts by securing for limited Times to Authors and Inventors the exclusive Right to their respective Writings and Discoveries." The notion of copyright protection developed before the invention of radio and television, but copyright applies to broadcasts. Likewise, copyright law applies to the Internet. It applies to "literary works; musical works; dramatic works; pantomimes and choreographic works; pictorial, graphic, and sculptural works; motion pictures and other audiovisual works; sound recordings; and architectural works." The works must be in "fixed" form, but virtually any fixed form, including digital form, is sufficient. In fact, the copyright statutes anticipate new media: "Copyright protection subsists . . . in original works of authorship fixed in any tangible medium of expression, now known or later developed, from which they can be perceived, reproduced, or otherwise communicated, either directly or with the aid of a machine of device@ (17 U.S.C. ? 102a).

The following provide a check list of sorts for avoiding infringement on other persons' or corporations' copyrights. If using a work that is not one's own original work, ask these questions:

    1. Is it in the Public Domain? All publications of the United States government are in the public domain. Copyright law expressly states that "protection . . . is not available for any work of the United States Government" (17 U.S.C. ? 105). Thus, many useful materials, such as government maps, are available for use. Public records in general are available for public use. For example, court cases and the material they contain are public records.

    Old works likewise may be used without fear. Any work that went into the public domain before January 1, 1978, must remain in the public domain (Act of Oct. 19, 1976, Pub. L. No. 94-553, ?103, 90 Stat. 2599). Copyright lasts for the duration of the life of the copyright owner plus 50 years. If the author is a corporation or anonymous, 75 years (17 U.S.C. ? 302). Although one must be careful, however, of using recent recordings or translations of works. For example, although the notes of Beethoven's *Eroica* would receive no copyright protection, a recording of *Eroica* by the St. Louis Symphony Orchestra could have copyright protection. In short, the tune is free for anyone to use, but a particular rendition of it by recording artists is not.

   2. *Is it an Idea or Fact and Thus not Copyrightable?* Facts and ideas cannot be copyrighted.[11] Only *expression* of ideas and facts may be copyrighted - the manner and style of communicating (e.g., word choice and order). Any author may write about any subject. As an example, no author could copyright the idea "the butler did it." But the author could receive protection when that idea has received expression--when the author has developed the butler into a distinct character, say, who wears a Fedora, walks with a limp, and likes a specific type of liqueur.

   Copyright protection used to be extended to valuable lists that had taken a lot of effort to prepare. But this "sweat of the brow" doctrine is dead. In 1991, the Supreme Court refused to extend copyright protection to the white pages of a company's telephone directory. The Court said that "originality . . . remains the touchstone of copyright protection in directories and other fact-based works" (Feist Publications v. Rural Telephone Service, 499 U.S.: 1990). Flatly, the Court declared: "Rural's selection of listings could not be more obvious: It publishes the most basic information - name, town, and telephone number - about each person who applies to it for telephone service. This . . . lacks the modicum of creativity necessary to transform mere selection into copyrightable expression."

   Whatever is not protected by copyright is available to anyone.

   3. *Is it Copyrighted but the Use of it is "Fair Use"?* Courts first carved out the doctrine of "fair use," which was then incorporated by Congress into the Copyright Act of 1976: "Fair use is a privilege in others than the owner of a copyright to use the copyrighted material in a reasonable manner without his [or her] consent, notwithstanding the monopoly granted to the owner . . ."(*Rosemont Enterprises, Inc. v. Random House Inc.*, 366 F.2d 303, 306: 2d Cir. 1966).

   Unfortunately, the test for determining whether use is a "fair use" remains fuzzy. Although no clear line can be drawn between a "fair use" and infringement, the Copyright Act provides four "factors" to consider: (1) "the purpose . . . of the use" (for profit?) (for educational purposes?) (2) "the nature of the copyrighted work"; (3) the amount used in relation to the whole work (one line from a short poem might violate "fair use"); and (4) "the effect of the use

---

[11] The statute says: "In no case does copyright protection for an original work of authorship extend to any idea, procedure, process, system, method of operation, concept, principle, or discovery, regardless of the form in which it is described, explained, illustrated, or embodied in such work." 17 U.S.C. ' 102(b).

upon the potential market for or value of the copyrighted work" (17 U.S.C. ? 107).

Although the test is fuzzy, the basic gist of it is fairly clear: If a person has used so much of an original work that the use has undercut the market for the original work, then the use probably is not fair.

Of course, particularly in these days of digital photography and computer manipulations, one cannot only *use* another's work but can also *transform* it. If a work has been so totally transformed that the original cannot even be recognized, then one does not have to worry about a copyright violation. The problem is that a jury might end up deciding whether a copyrighted work has been so transformed or whether a copyright violation has occurred. Like obscenity, transformation may lie in the eye of the beholder.

4. Is the Use in a Parody That Has Transformed the Original? The Supreme Court recognizes that in order to create a parody of a work, enough of the original must be used in order for the audience to recognize the original work. In 1994, the Court decided that 2 Live Crew's "Pretty Woman" parody of Roy Orbison's song "Oh, Pretty Woman" could be a fair use (*Campbell v. Acuff-Rose Music, Inc.*, 510 U.S.: 1994). The Court appended the lyrics of Orbison's and 2 Live Crew's versions to the case so readers could compare the lyrics. Although Orbison sang only of "Pretty Woman," the 2 Live Crew version slid from "Pretty Woman" to "Big Hairy Woman" to "Bald-Headed Woman" to "Two-Timin' Woman." Clearly, a person wanting to hear Orbison's "Oh, Pretty Woman" would not find 2 Live Crew's parody an adequate substitute!

The Court apparently likes transformative works. It said that "the goal of copyright, to promote science and the arts, is generally furthered by the creation of transformative works" and that "the more transformative the new work, the less will be the significance of other factors, like commercialism, that may weigh against a finding of fair use." In short, the more a parody transforms a work, the less one has to worry about fair use.

In part, the Court may be favorably predisposed to parodies because parodies are so often used for political commentary and, of course, the Court wants to promote political speech instead of chilling it. The Court did not allow Jerry Falwell to recover for a ridiculous parody of a Campari Liqueur ad in *Hustler* magazine; the "first time" parody was of Falwell with his mother in an outhouse (See *Hustler* Magazine v. Falwell, 108 S. Ct. 876, 878: 1988). As for other examples of songs being used in satire, "Maria" became transformed into "Scalia" (who is a Supreme Court justice), and "I Feel Pretty" became transformed into satire about President Bill Clinton's infamous hair cut in a plane on a Los Angeles runway.

5. Is There Consent for the Use of the Copyrighted Work? Consent must be broad enough to cover the use.

Consent may be broad or narrow.   Under the broadest consent, an individual would give unlimited use of his or her copyrighted work to another individual. This is not the usual situation. More typical is a consent for limited use. Perhaps an author will give consent to an individual to use certain passages from his or her work in a particular new book; the consent is only good for use of that author's words in the designated new book. Likewise, if a photographer gave consent for one picture to be used in a specific magazine, the consent is specifically limited. Here common sense is important: if permission is granted for use of A (words, pictures) in B (a book or magazine), then use of anything other than A in any place other than B is *verboten*. A new agreement would have to be reached for consent to expand.

6. If a person has only answered "no" to the five questions above, the remaining question is, "Does that person have a good lawyer"? In short, that person is at risk of being sued for copyright infringement.

One must not assume that just because a work is posted on the Internet it is therefore in the public domain. The questions listed above still pertain. Persons who post copyrighted material on the Internet may also subject the operators of their bulletin board systems and their Internet access providers to liability. If the BBS operator or the access providers knows a subscriber is infringing on a copyright, then liability for "contributory" copyright infringement is a possibility (See   Religious Technology Center v. Netcom On-Line   Communication Services, Inc., 907 F. Supp. 1361 (1995) and Sega Enterprises Ltd. v. MAPHIA, 857 F. Supp. 679 (N.D. Cal. 1994). The operator and provider might even be found liable for direct copyright infringement, although this possibility is less likely. A federal trial court in Florida, in a case involving a BBS containing *Playboy* pictures, found direct liability because the BBS *distributed* and *displayed* the pictures uploaded by the subscriber. The court declared that "unauthorized display and distribution of . . . copyrighted material is copyright infringement . . ." (Playboy Enterprises, Inc. v. Frena, 839 F. Supp. 1552, 1559: M.D. Fla. 1993). The court's reasoning is based on the fact that copyright is a cluster of five different rights - the rights to reproduce, adapt, distribute, perform, and display (17 U.S.C. ? 106). A subscriber might reproduce and adapt a work, and a BBS system operator and an online access provider might distribute and display a copyrighted work. All have violated copyright law, under this reasoning, even though only the subscriber knew that the infringing work had been posted on the BBS. The Florida trial court held the BBS operator and the online access provider strictly liable. The court said, "It does not matter that [the defendant] may have been unaware of the copyright infringement. Intent to infringe is not needed to find copyright infringement . . . [T]hus even an innocent infringer is liable for infringement . . ." (839 F. Supp. at 1552).

However, as the court points out, "innocent infringement" is relevant when the court assesses damages. The statutory award for innocent infringement can be as little as $200.[12] Another possibility, however, is that the plaintiff will elect to collect actual damages, which might be substantially higher.[13] Even higher might be the attorney fees that a successful plaintiff could receive (See Basic Books v. Kinko's Graphics Corp., 21 U.S.P.Q.2d 1639: S.D.N.Y. 1991. In a case involving *Kinko's*, damages amounted to $510,000, but attorney fees were $1,365,000. On the $510,000 figure, see Basic Books v. Kinko's Graphics Corp., 758 F. Supp. 1522, 1526: S.D.N.Y. 1991).

Note that if copyright infringement occurs before the copyright owner has registered his or her work, then the copyright owner cannot ask a judge for statutory damages. Instead, the copyright owner can only receive payment for actual damages, which he or she must prove. Perhaps even more important, if infringement occurs before registration, the copyright owner will have lost the opportunity to collect for his or her attorney fees (17 U.S.C. ? 412).

PRINCIPLE X: Trademark Law (Which Includes Trade Names) Applies to the Internet

Federal trademark law prohibits "imitation of a registered mark in connection with the sale, offering for sale, distribution, or advertising of any goods or services" when "such use is likely to cause confusion, or to cause mistake, or to deceive" (15 U.S.C. ?1114(1)(a)). Many companies spend a great deal of money advertising their products, of course, but they cannot benefit fully from their advertising if consumers are confused or tricked and thus buy other companies' products. Avoiding confusion is a major reason to protect trademarks. But even when there is no possibility of confusion (say, because corporations are making totally dissimilar products), protection of trademarks is important to avoid "dilution" of the trademarks. The statutory definition of dilution is the "lessening of the capacity of a famous mark to identify and distinguish goods or services, regardless of the presence or absence of : (1) competition between the owner of the famous mark and other parties, or (2) likelihood of confusion, mistake, or deception" (15 U.S.C.? 1127).

When innocent infringement occurs and causes dilution, an injunction is the only remedy (15 U.S.C. ? 1125(c)(2) - ". . . the owner of the famous mark

---

[12] 17 USC ' 504(c)(2). On the other hand, "...the court in its discretion may increase the award of statutory damages to a sum of not more than $100,000." Id.

[13] Copyright law says that "the copyright owner is entitled to recover the actual damages suffered by him or her as a result of the infringement, and any profits of the infringer that are attributable to the infringement and are not taken into account in computing the actual damages." 17 USC. ' 504(b).

shall be entitled only to injunctive relief . . ."). Trademark law says that "[t]he owner of a famous mark shall be entitled, ... upon such terms as the court deems reasonable, to an *injunction* against another person's commercial use in commerce of a *mark or trade name*, if such use begins after the mark has become famous and causes dilution of the distinctive quality of the mark..." (15 U.S.C. ?1125(c)(1)(emphasis added). Note that the statute talks in terms of "a mark or trade name." Trademark includes trade name. *Black's Law Dictionary* defines the difference between the two in this manner: "A `trade name' is a descriptive of a manufacturer or dealer and applies to business and its goodwill, where `trademark' is applicable only to vendable commodities" (Black's Law Dictionary, 1990).

Willful infringement, as opposed to innocent infringement, can lead to hefty damage awards.[14] The owners of a registered trademark may generally recover any profits the willful violator received; damages the owner sustained; and the costs of suing (which means the court costs, such as filing fees). In these willful infringement cases, the court has broad discretionary power to award the amount of money it deems "just," which in some cases could be less than the profits. But, on the other hand, the court may even award *treble* damages. And "in exceptional cases," the court may award attorney fees to whichever side wins.[15] Sometimes attorney fees greatly exceed damage awards (See *supra* note 91 and accompanying text on the attorney fees in the Kinko's case).

In cases of *counterfeit* trademarks, treble damages is the rule - "unless the court finds extenuating circumstances." If no circumstances exist to soften the violation, the judge must award the plaintiffs either (1) three times the amount of profits the counterfeiter made or (2) three times the amount of damages the plaintiff sustained - "whichever is greater." In addition, the judge must award "reasonable attorney's fees" to the plaintiff and may award prejudgment interest (15 U.S.C. ?1117(b)).

In cases involving counterfeit marks, instead of asking for treble profits or treble damages, a plaintiff can elect to have the judge award "statutory damages" - the amount the judge considers "just" and that fits within the statutory

---

[14] Owners of trademarks "shall not be entitled to recover profits or damages unless the acts have been committed with knowledge that such imitation is intended to be used to cause confusion, or to cause mistake, or to deceive." 15 U.S.C. ' 1114(1)(b).

[15] The statutory language says: In assessing damages the court may enter judgment, according to the circumstances of the case, for any sum above the amount found as actual damages, not exceeding three times such amount. If the court shall find that the amount of the recovery based on profits is either inadequate or excessive the court may in its discretion enter judgment for such sum as the court shall find to be just, according to the circumstances of the case. . . . The court in exceptional cases may award reasonable attorney fees to the prevailing party. 15 U.S.C. ' 1117: 1997.

guidelines. In the case of inadvertent use of the counterfeit mark, these guidelines call for a judgment amount of "not less than $500 or more than $100,000 per counterfeit mark per type of goods or services sold, offered for sale, or distributed . . ." But in cases of "willful" use of a counterfeit mark, the guidelines call for a judgment amount of up to $1,000,000 (15 U.S.C. ?1117(c)).

A plaintiff can also ask the court for seizure of goods that bear counterfeit marks and seizure of the means for making those marks (17 U.S.C.? 1116(d)). Of course, a plaintiff can also seek an injunction against the defendant who is using the counterfeit marks (17 U.S.C. ?1116(a)).

Trademark law also protects "a newspaper, magazine or other similar periodical" or "an electronic communication" carrying ads that infringe. An injunction can only apply to "future issues." Further, an injunction is not available if it would "delay" the normal delivery of the newspaper, magazine, or electronic communication (15 USC ? 1114 (2) (B), (C)).

As in copyright law, parody can be a successful defense to a charge of trademark infringement. One such parody case, *Jordache Enterprises, Inc. v. Hogg Wyld, Ltd.*(828 F.2d 1482: 10th Cir. 1987), involved a small New Mexico enterprise, Hogg Wyld, Limited, which later changed its name to Oink, Inc. Two women ran the home-based operation that made jeans for larger women. They considered several names for their jeans, including "Calvin Swine" and "Vidal Sowsoon," but then settled on the name "Lardashe." Jeans manufacturer Jordache filed suit for trade name infringement under the Lanham Act's prohibition of an unauthorized use of a trademark in a manner which "is likely to cause confusion" (15 U.S.C. Sec. 1141(1)(a)). The Tenth Circuit Court of Appeals decided the name Lardashe was meant to amuse, not to confuse: "An intent to parody is not an intent to confuse the public" (828 F.2d at 1486).

In another parody case, the Second Circuit Court of Appeals decided that Spa'am, the Muppet character in Jim Henson's movie *Muppet Treasure Island* would not dilute the trademark of SPAM, Hormel's canned meat. The court opined:

> Although the name "Spa'am" is mentioned only once in the entire movie, Henson hopes to poke a little fun at Hormel's famous luncheon meat by associating its processed, gelatinous block with a humorously wild beast.

However, the executives at Hormel are not amused. They worry that sales of SPAM will drop off if it is linked with "evil in porcine form." . . . Spa'am, however, is not the boarish Beelzebub that Hormel seems to fear (Hormel Foods Corporation v. Jim Henson Productions, Inc., 73 F.3d 497, 500 (2d Cir. 1996)).

Likewise, a lampooning poster of a smiling, pregnant Girl Scout, captioned "BE PREPARED," withstood a trademark infringement suit.[16] Yet, some parodies have lost in cases involving trademark infringement. A 1997 case involved both copyright and trademark infringement. The Ninth Circuit Court of Appeals upheld an injunction against "The Cat NOT in the Hat!" by Dr. Juice, a parody of Dr. Seuss's "A Cat in the Hat." The parody was a poetic rendition of the alleged O. J. Simpson double murder (Dr. Seuss Enterprises, L.P. v. Penguins Books USA, Inc., 109 F.3d 1394 (9th Cir. 1997)).

Courts were also not amused with: "Michelob Oily," believing it could be confused with "Michelob" dry (Anheuser-Busch, Inc. v. Balducci Publications, 814 F. Supp. 791 (1993)); a "Mutant of Omaha" caption, under an emaciated Indian's head with a feather bonnet, on T-shirts and cups (Mutual of Omaha Ins. Co. v. Novak, 836 F.2d 397 (8th Cir. 1987)); a "Genital Electric" monogram on underwear (bags (General Electric Co. v. Alumpa Coal Co., 205 U.S.P.Q. 1036 (D. Mass. 1979)); or "Gucchi Goo" diaper.

The Internet has provided a fertile ground for trademark suits. The year 1966 saw a lot of court traffic involving the Lanham Act:

- Comedy III Productions, Inc., has the exclusive right to exploit the trademark and images of the "Three Stooges," a New York federal trial court ruled. Comedy III discovered a web site offering shirts with images of the Three Stooges. The interloping defendants violated a preliminary court order to stop exploiting the Three Stooges name. According to the court, the interloper added to its web site that "The Three Stooges merchandise was unavailable `right now' and 'at this time.'" The court

---

[16]   Girl Scouts of the U.S.A. v. Personality Posters Mfg. Co., 304 F. Supp. 1228 (S.D.N.Y. 1969).

In another case, a federal trial court in Illinois found no threat of confusion or dilution in a Coors advertisement spoofing Eveready's pink "Energizer Bunny." Eveready Battery Co., Inc. v. Adolph Coors Co., 765 F. Supp. 440 (N.D. Ill. 1991).

In a federal trial court in the state of Washington, an environmental group prevailed over the Forest Service. The First Amendment, according to the court, protected the group's use of Smokey Bear wielding a chainsaw in a political advertisement. Lighthawk, the Environmental Air Force, v. Robertson, 812 F. Supp. 1095 (W.D. Wa. 1993) (Robertson was Chief of the U.S. Forest Service).

See also, e.g., Cliff's Notes v. Bantam Doubleday Dell Publishing Group, Inc., 886 F.2d 490 (2d Cir. 1989) (a spoof on Cliff's Notes); L.L. Bean, Inc. v. Drake Publishers, Inc., 811 F.2d 26, 27 (1st Cir. 1987) (a High Society magazine article, "L.L. Beam's Back-To-School-Sex-Catalog).

Playboy Enterprises, Inc. v. Universal Tel-A-Talk, Inc., 1998 U.S. Dist. LEXIS 17282 (E.D. Pa. 1009) (injunction, statutory damages and attorney fees granted against defendant for trademark infringement and related violations brought under the Lanham Act).

slapped the defendants with a permanent injunction and a citation for contempt of court (Comedy III Productions, Inc. v. Class Publications, Inc., 1996 U.S. Dist. LEXIS 5710 (S.D. N.Y. 1996)).

- A federal trial court in Missouri ruled that "www.cybergold.com" could be confused with <www.goldmail.com> (Maritz v. Cybergold, Inc., 947 F. Supp. 1338 (E.D. Mo. 1996)).

- A federal trial court in California ruled that "SUNDANCE," a thermal transfer label printer, could be confused with Sun Microsystems's computer products, which all use the name "Sun" (such as SUNSERVICE, SUNDIALS, SUNERGY, and SUNBUTTONS).   The court enjoined SUNDANCE from using that name on its web page or any other place in connection with computer devices (Sun Microsystems, Inc. v. Astro-Med, Inc., 39 U.S.P.Q.2d 1144 (N.D. Cal. 1996)).

Courts seem particularly reluctant to side with defendants who are not only diluting a trade name but arguably tarnishing it as well with some sex and sleaze.

"Adults `R' Us" could be confused with or dilute or tarnish the trade name "Toys `R' Us," according to the federal trial court in California that granted a preliminary injunction (Toys "R" Us v. Akkaoui, 40 U.S.P.Q.2d 1836 (N.D. Cal. 1996)). In *Playboy Enterprises, Inc. v. Chuckleberry Publishing, Inc.* (39 U.S.P.Q.2d (S.D.N.Y. 1996)), *Playboy* prevailed when a company displayed a "Playmen" Internet site in two versions: (1) "Playmen Lite," which was available free and offered only "moderately explicit images," according to the New York federal trial court which heard the case, and (2) "Playmen Pro," which required a paid subscription. The court slapped an injunction against the Playmen Internet Service, which Playmen violated. The court then hit Playmen with contempt of court (Playboy Enterprises, Inc. v. Chuckleberry Pub., 939 F. Supp. 1032 (S.D.N.Y. 1976)).

Likewise, in *Hasbro, Inc. v. Internet Entertainment Group (*40 U.S.P.Q.2d 1479 (S.D. Wa. 1976)), a federal trial court in the state of Washington had no sympathy for what it called a "sexually explicit" Internet site - "CANDYLAND," available at the time at <candyland.com>. The Internet site diluted Hasbro's "CANDY LAND" mark, the court concluded, ruling that the "public interest" favored a preliminary injunction.

The Internet has also provided a new way to engage in the old mischief of trade name confusion. For mischief or for money, some folks have purposefully registered domain-site names, using trade names belonging to others.   For instance, in an effort to extract money, a man registered Panavision's trade name as a domain name. Panavision International took him to court and won on the grounds of dilution (*Panavision International v. Toeppen*, 945 F. Supp. 1296 (C.D. Cal. 1996)). In another example, Princeton Review, which is a company that helps prepare college students to take standardized tests such as the MCAT,

LSAT, and GRE, registered the domain name of "kaplan.com." (Kaplan is Princeton Review's rival.) Registration of domain names is done through Network Solutions, Inc., which does so under contract with Internet organizations (Donatiello, 1997; Stern, 1996). An arbitration panel ruled in Kaplan's favor, and Princeton yielded. Sprint likewise engaged in domain-name mischief with "mci.com" (Firms fight, 1996).

In short, trademark and trade name cases comprise one of the hottest areas in law related to the Internet.

PRINCIPLE XI: There is no First Amendment right to distribute advertisements over Internet services

The problem of promoters disseminating unsolicited advertisements, especially obscene ones, is nothing new.

In 1970, Congress passed laws to regulate the junk mailing of "sexually oriented advertisements." Anyone doing such mailings must include his or her name or address on the envelope. Anyone who is receiving these unsolicited ads and who has a person under 19 in his or her household can fill out a form at a Post Office to have his or her name removed from the sender's mailing list (39 USC ?3101). If the sender refuses to comply, the U.S. Postal Service can request that the United States Attorney General file a civil suit against the sender.[17]

The advent of the telephone gave advertisers a new avenue on which to ply their trade--and an increased opportunity to disturb their target advertisers. Not even the dinner hours are held sacred by the most relentless telephone solicitors. But federal regulation does make illegal such calling before 8 a.m. and after 9 p.m. ("Telemarketing - Pesky pests," 1993). In short, the telephone solicitors are somewhat restrained now, but certainly not out of business. The "Telemarketing and Consumer Fraud and Abuse Prevention Act," passed by Congress, gave the Federal Trade Commission broad parameters in which to control telemarketers. The Act speaks of the FTC's power to "prescribe rules prohibiting deceptive telemarketing acts or practices and other abusive telemarketing acts or practices" (15 U.S.C. ?6102). It also gives the state attorneys general and private individuals the power to bring civil actions in federal courts against telemarketers (15 U.S.C. 6103 B6104). Private individuals, however, must have suffered damages of at least $50,000. Criminal penalties also apply (18 U.S.C. 2326 (five years generally; 10 years for persons targeting the elderly)), as does restitution (18 U.S.C. 2327). Federal law also prohibits "automatic" telephone dialing, automatic FAXing, and use of an "artificial or prerecorded voice," and

---

[17] 39 U.S.C.'3011. If the mail is obscene or if mail fraud is involved, then the power of the federal criminal justice system can be employed to halt the activity, with fines and imprisonment. On mail fraud, see 18 U.S.C. ' 1341 (five years imprisonment; $1,000,000 and 30 years if banks are defrauded). On obscenity, see 18 U.S.C. '1465 et. seq and 18 U.S.C. ' 1737 (five years for first offense; ten years for subsequent offenses).

private individuals may seek fines and injunctions in their state courts if this law is violated.

Congress granted the FTC broad powers for rule-making to control telemarketers, but the FTC has not employed all the permissible (but not required) means. For example, a national database of "telephone numbers of residential subscribers who object to receiving telephone solicitations" has not been instituted reportedly because of prohibitive costs (National Public Radio, "Telemarketing - Pesky Pests or Way of Life?" *op. cit)*. Congress also suggested "industry-based or company-specific `do not call' systems" or "special markings of area white page directories" to let telemarketers know persons did not wish to receive telephone solicitations. The purpose is protection of "privacy rights."

The Internet has added a new layer to the "junk" mail and unsolicited telephone call phenomenon - "spam," more formally known as "unsolicited commercial e-mail." A whining cafe patron in Monty Python's "Flying Circus" pretty well summarized prevailing views on this dubious form of advertising: "I don't like Spam!" Some Internet advertisers do like spam, which raises the question: Is there a legal right to "spam"? No.

In November 1996, a federal trial court in Pennsylvania ruled that Cyber Promotions, Inc., did not have a constitutional right under the First Amendment to send unsolicited e-mail (spam) to America Online subscribers (Cyber Promotions, Inc. v. America Online, Inc., 1996 U.S. Dist. LEXIS 16237 (E.D. Pa. 1996)). The court simply rejected Cyber Promotions argument that America Online is a "public forum."` To sum up the case simply, "The `Spam King' . . . got canned" ("Judge: Firm has," 1996; Hilzenrath, 1996).

The biggest complaint of America Online's subscribers at that time had been junk e-mail (Dean, 1996). About 20% America Online's e-mail was junk (Lesser, 1997; Mannix & Thomas, 1997), or, in numbers, 3 million pieces of junk mail per day for its 8 million readers (Mannes, 1997). Because subscribers have to pay for online time, they could end up paying for the time to skim and discard the unwanted e-mail. Some commentators describe this situation as the equivalent of telemarketers' calling people collect (Dean, 1996). Some e-mail can be quite enticing, say, "CALL ME PLEASE" when the subscriber does not know what the message is about (Mannes, 1997). Some are more obviously junk: "Prevent Fat Absorption . . .," "GET OUT OF DEBT. . .," "MEET SOMEONE SPECIAL . . ." (Erickson, 1996).

There can be a connection between spam and Internet cookies. When a person visits a web site, the web-site operator can give the web-site user a "cookie," which can gather information useful to advertisers. (See Chapter 14 on cookie technology). The information gathered can lead to a barrage of spam. Signing up for free e-mail accounts which require one to fill out lengthy registration forms can also lead to spam because the information could be sold to advertisers (Cooper, 1996).

For self-help, Microsoft's "Outlook" includes a shield. Also, the IC Group, at <www.icgroup.com>, has programs that allow users to block e-mail from addresses that have already sent junk mail or that include certain phrases, such as "You Have Won One Million Dollars!"

Three bills introduced into Congress would attempt to control junk e-mail. Legislation already exists to control unwanted faxes (Wildstrom, 1996: See *supra* note 134 and accompanying text. But this legislation does not apply to junk e-mail). One bill, introduced by Rep. Chris Smith, a Republican from New Jersey, would extend the FAX legislation to include e-mail. A bill introduced by Sen. Frank Murkowski, Republican-Alaska, would require unsolicited, commercial e-mail to be labeled as such (Kleiner, 1997; Mannes, 1997). In addition, the bill would require e-mail senders to delete from their e-mail lists within 48 hours, the names of persons requesting removal (Stapleton, 1997). A bill introduced by Sen. Bob Torricelli, a Democrat from New Jersey, would also require labeling of unsolicited, commercial e-mail (Kleiner, 1997). A private citizen, Frank Elbel, has created a spam web site that contains information about these bills - <http://www.csn.net/felbel/jmemail.html> (Mannes, 1997). [18]

Currently, four states (Connecticut, Nevada, New York, and Rhode Island) have legislation pending to ban spam (Stapleton, 1997). In mid-June 1997, the FTC promised a crackdown on fraudulent and deceptive e-maiL and also said it would ask the new Internet E-Mail Marketing Council for its assistance (Mannix & Thomas, 1997). FTC Commissioner Christine Varney wants both spammers and spammees to communicate with each other and come back in mid-August, 1997 with recommendations (Kleiner, 1997). The Council has available at its web site, <http://www.iemmc.org>, a form one can fill out requesting removal of one's name from senders' lists (Mannes, 1997).

PRINCIPLE XII: Online Advertising Aimed at Children May Face Increasing Regulation

Protecting children from those who would take advantage of them is a time-honored goal. Perhaps especially ripe for regulation are web sites that target children. Potential harm of children is a topic designed to raise the hackles of parents, politicians, and watchdog groups, such as the Washington, D.C.-based Center for Media Education. In May 1996, the Center asked the FTC to investigate the activities of "Kidscom" web site, operated by Spectracom. The

---

[18] The numbers and titles of the bills are:

"The Netizens Protection Act of 1997" (H.R. 1748, introduced on May 22, 1997, by Rep. Smith).

"The Unsolicited Commercial Electronic Mail Choice Act of 1997," (S. 771, introduced on May 21, 1997, by Sen. Murkowski).

"The Electronic Mailbox Protection Act of 1997" (S. 875, introduced on June 11, 1997, by Sen. Torricelli).

Center charges that the real purpose of the site is to collect data from children for market research, while the site pretends to be an educational and entertainment site. Available at <http://www.kidscom.com>, it uses four languages and advertises itself as "A Communication Playground for Kids Ages 4 to 15." According to SpectraCom, children from 74 countries access the site. Its president, Jorian Clark, maintains that her company does not release information to anyone. Before a child can visit KidsCom, however, he or she must register, giving information such as age and geographical location. And to receive premiums such as CD-ROMs or baseball cards, a child must answer additional questions and have his or her parents and teachers visit the site. Perhaps raising the most concern is KidsCom's "kidfinder," which provides children who have registered with "kidfinder" the e-mail addresses of other registered children with similar interests. The father of Polly Klaas, a 12-year-old who was raped and murdered, expressed alarm that "kidfinder" could be yet another avenue for persons seeking to sexually exploit children. He is the founder of the Klass Foundation for Children (Butterbaugh, 1996).

On June 13, 1997, the FTC urged all online marketers to gain consent from parents before gaining information online from children (Gellene, 1997). FTC Commissioner Christine Varney said that rules were needed to restrict sale of information about children to third parties. Spokespersons from the Center for Media Education, testifying in front of the FTC, related survey results from 38 web sites for children. Although 90% of the sites requested personal information, only 20% advised children to get their parents' permission, and none required permission from parents. One site required children to answer 20 personal questions in order to receive a compact mirror, while another asked for the information in exchange for free candy. The Center for Media Education's director, Jeff Chester, testified that Kidscom remains "one of the more invasive sites on the Web," asking children about their favorite televisions programs, commercials, sports, music groups and even their future career plans (Pietrucha, 1997).

The FTC is currently considering rules to protect children, and a Presidential task force plans to release guidelines on gathering information from children, perhaps in July 1997 (Armstrong, 1997).

PRINCIPLE XIII: The Long Arm of the Law Generally Extends to Internet Advertisers

Jurisdictional questions test how long the long arm of the law really is. In order for a plaintiff to sue a defendant in a particular court, the plaintiff must show that the court has jurisdiction over the defendant. Courts talk in terms of "minimum contacts." A principle of due process of the law is that a defendant must have "minimum contacts" with a state in order to be sued in that state. The question is: How minimal can those contacts be and still satisfy the minimum-contacts requirement? The following cases from the Internet indicate that courts split on whether use of the Internet satisfies minimum contacts for suits in distant courts, but the tendency is to approve of the long arm of the law.

Could "The Blue Note" jazz club in New York City sue, in a New York federal court, "The Blue Note," which is a small club for live music in Columbia, Missouri? The court said "no" because merely having a World Wide Web site on the Internet that could be accessed in New York was insufficient contacts with stat New York state for the owners of the Missouri club to be sued there (Bensusan Restaurant Corp. v. King, 937 F. Supp. 295 (S.D.N.Y. 1996), aff'd, 126F.3d 25 (2d Cir. 1997)).[19]

Could a Connecticut corporation sue a Massachusetts corporation in Connecticut? The Massachusetts corporation, Instruction Set, Inc., advertises its computer technology and support over the Internet. The long arm of Connecticut could reach the defendant, the court ruled. The court reasoned that the Internet advertising, which "unlike television and radio advertising, . . . is available continuously to any Internet user," was enough for "minimum contacts." By advertising over the Internet, the defendant had "purposefully availed itself of the privilege of doing business within Connecticut." Therefore, it could also be sued in Connecticut (See Inset Systems, Inc., v. Instruction Set, Inc., 937 F. Supp. 161 (D. Conn. 1996)).

Could CompuServe sue a Texas man in Ohio, where CompuServe has its headquarters? The trial court in Ohio said the electronic links between the Texan and Compuserve were "too tenuous to support the exercise of personal jurisdiction." But the federal court of appeals overruled this decision. The Texan had never stepped foot in Ohio, but he did place "shareware" on the CompuServe system and entered into a "Shareware Registration Agreement" with Compuserve (CompuServe, Inc. v. Patterson, 89 F.3d 1257 (6th Cir. 1996)). CompuServe sought a "declaratory judgment" to declare that it had not violated the defendant's trademarks when Compuserve started marketing software that the defendant thought had markings and names too similar to those on the defendant's software.

Jurisdictional matters concerning the Internet are not clear cut. But jurisdictional questions generally can be difficult. Advertisers using cyberspace need to be aware that even if they have never visited a state in person, if they have made their presence known in that state via cyberspace, they may have to stand suit in that jurisdiction.

Criminal prosecution in a state far removed from one's home is also a possibility, as Californians Robert and Colleen Thomas could attest. They were

---

[19] Hearst Corp. v. Goldberger, 1997 U.S. Dist. LEXIS (S.D.N.Y. 1997) (A New York federal court ruled it lacked personal jurisdiction over a defendant whose Internet web site had been "visited" by New York residents; the defendant, whose business was no yet in operation, had sold no products or services to anyone in New York.)

convicted in Memphis, Tennessee, for distributing obscenity. They advertised their bulletin board service as "the Nastiest Place on Earth." The Sixth Circuit Court of Appeals said that by accepting money from a person in Memphis, the Thomas's could be tried in Memphis. In the court's words:

> . . . Defendants had in place methods to limit user access in jurisdictions where the risk of a finding of obscenity was greater than that in California. They knew they had a member in Memphis; the member's address and local phone number were provided on his application form. If Defendants did not want to subject themselves to liability in jurisdictions with less tolerant standards for determining obscenity, they could have refused to give passwords to members in those districts, thus precluding the risk of liability. (*United States v. Thomas*, 74 F.3d 701, 705 (6th Cir. 1996))

The court rejected the argument that there is an Internet community whose standards should be applied for determining obscenity.

CONCLUSION

Old law still applies, be it First Amendment law, damage control (libel, negligence, invasion of privacy), copyright and trademark matters, or jurisdictional questions. But the Internet, replete with cookies and spam and easy availability to many children, offers new wrinkles on these old areas of law. As Internet advertisers go boldly forward where advertisers of old could not go, they must remain cognizant of the old precepts that controlled their predecessors. "Thou shalt not deceive" is just as viable as it ever was. Junk ads are just as undesirable as they ever were; spam by any other name is just as annoying. However, the opportunities of online advertising are just beginning to be explored. The protective shadow of the First Amendment falls on Internet advertisers just as surely as it does on those advertising through more traditional media. The World Wide Web beckons. It is not as tangled a web as some would say - so long as one remembers to apply old legal principles to the new digital market.

REFERENCES

Armstrong, L. (1997, June 30). Pssst! Come into my Web . . . . *Business Week, n3533*, p. 67.
Ballard, M., & Riverz-Sanchez, M. (1996, December). Settlement: FCC's newest strategy to address indecency? *Communications & the Law,18*, 1.

Barnett, S. R. (1994, December 19). The big chill: Free speech in advertising, *Legal Times*, 21.

Black's Law Dictionary (6th ed). (1990). ("Trademark" definition, "Trade name distinguished," citing American Steel Foundaries v. Robertson, 269 U.S. 372).

Butterbaugh, S. (1996, June 1). May be unsafe...KidsCom service draws data cops' scrutiny; SpectraCom's KidsCom Website. *Cowles Business Media Inc. Direct, 8*(7), p. 1.

Cooper, B. (1996, September 8). They're watching you surf the Internet, and you give away valuable information about yourself. *The Cincinnati Enquirer*, I05.

Davidson, S. (1997, Winter). Blood money: When media expose others to risk of bodily harm. *Hastings Communications and Entertainment Law Journal, 19*, 225.

Dean, R. (1996, September 15). Millions of pieces of junk mail invade Internet, *Weekend Edition Sunday* (NPR), Transcript # 1193-12 (available on Lexis/Nexis computerized database service).

Donatiello, G. T. (1997, March 24). Internet domain names: What's all the confusion? *The Legal Intelligencer,* 3.

Erickson, J. (1996, June 30). Are those who go online to send junk mail out of line? Growth of unsolicited direct mail on Internet raises questions of privacy. *Star Tribune*, p. 3D.

Firms fight for names on World Wide Web (1996, July 8). *Indianapolis Business Journal. 17*(16), 40.

Gellene, D. (1997, June 14). FTC urges rules on getting info. from kids online. *Los Angeles Times*, p. 1.

Hassell, G., & Thompson, C. (1997, July 11). Let us bury Joe, not praise him, some say. *The Houston Chronicle*, p. 1.

Hilzenrath, D. S. (1996, November 5). Judge rules AOL can block direct-marking firm's ads. *The Washington Post*, p. C01.

Hopkins, J., Dorman, B., Katayama, F., Wilson, J. Q., & Tucker, B. (1997, July 3). Stock market soars; Lockheed Martin buys Northrop Grumman; Mississippi makes deal with tobacco company. *CNN Moneyline with Lou Dobbs*, (available on Lexis/Nexis computerized database service).

Judge: Firm has no right to send junk e-mail (1996, November 5). *The Columbus Dispatch*, p. 2D.

Kleiner, K. (1997, June 21). Can anyone slow the ascent of spam?" *New Scientist, 154*(2087), 7.

Lesser, J. (1997). Discussion with AOL's deputy director for law and public policy.

Levin, M. (1997, July 11). RJR agrees to pull Joe Camel from ads, *Los Angeles Times*, p. D1.

Loundy, D. J. (1997, June 12). Internet users aim to can unwanted spam. *Chicago Daily Law Bulletin*, p. 5.

Mannes, G. (1997, June 22). Flood of spam has net users sizzling: Pesky junk e-mail can invade your home computer. *Daily News* (New York), p. 36.

Mannix, M., & Thomas, S. (1997, June 23). Exposed Online. *U.S. News & World Report*, p. 59.

National Public Radio (1993, May 9). Telemarketing - Pesky pests or way of life? *All Things Considered*.

Neergaard, L. (1997, May 28). FTC seeks to shield kids from Joe Camel campaign. *Chicago Sun-Times*, p. 3.

Nowell, P. (1997, July 11). Joe Camel is put to sleep after years of controversy. *The Chattanooga Times*, p. B8.

Pietrucha, B. (1997, June 16). Regulations needed for children's Web sites. *Newsbytes*.

Stapleton, M.A. (1997, June 12) "Ban all junk computer mail, federal regulators urged. *Chicago Daily Law Bulletin*, p. 1.

Stern, A. (1996, September 9). Playing the game of names. *The Denver Post,* p. G-12

The media business: Advertising; Joe Camel, a giant in tobacco marketing, Is dead at 23 (1997, July 11). *The New York Times*, p. D1.

Wildstrom, S. H.(1996, November 11). They're watching you online. *Business Week, n3506*, p. 19.

APPENDIX

Protection for Online Service Providers Who Screen

47 USCS @ 230 (1998)

@ 230. Protection for private blocking and screening of offensive material

(a) Findings. The Congress finds the following:
  (1) The rapidly developing array of Internet and other interactive computer services available to individual Americans represent an extraordinary advance in the availability of educational and informational resources to our citizens.
  (2) These services offer users a great degree of control over the information that they receive, as well as the potential for even greater control in the future as technology develops.
  (3) The Internet and other interactive computer services offer a forum for a true diversity of political discourse, unique opportunities for cultural development, and myriad avenues for intellectual activity.
  (4) The Internet and other interactive computer services have flourished, to the benefit of all Americans, with a minimum of government regulation.
  (5) Increasingly Americans are relying on interactive media for a variety of political, educational, cultural, and entertainment services.

(b) Policy. It is the policy of the United States--
  (1) to promote the continued development of the Internet and other interactive computer services and other interactive media;
  (2) to preserve the vibrant and competitive free market that presently exists for the Internet and other interactive computer services, unfettered by Federal or State regulation;
  (3) to encourage the development of technologies which maximize user control over what information is received by individuals, families, and schools who use the Internet and other interactive computer services;
  (4) to remove disincentives for the development and utilization of blocking and filtering technologies that empower parents to restrict their children's access to objectionable or inappropriate online material; and

(5)   to ensure vigorous enforcement of Federal criminal laws to deter and punish trafficking in obscenity, stalking, and harassment by means of computer.

(c) Protection for "good samaritan" blocking and screening of offensive material.
(1)   Treatment of publisher or speaker. No provider or user of an interactive computer service shall be treated as the publisher or speaker of any informationprovided by another information content provider.
(2)   Civil liability. No provider or user of an interactive computer service shall be held liable on account of—
(A)   any action voluntarily taken in good faith to restrict access to or availability of material that the provider or user considers to be obscene, lewd, lascivious, filthy, excessively violent, harassing, or otherwise objectionable, whether or not such material is constitutionally protected; or
(B)   any action taken to enable or make available to information content providers or others the technical means to restrict access to material described in paragraph (1).

(d) Effect on other laws.
(1)   No effect on criminal law. Nothing in this section shall be construed to impair the enforcement of section 223 of this Act [47 USCS @ 2231, chapter 71 (relating to obscenity) or I 10 (relating to sexual exploitation of children) of title 18, United States Code [18 USCS @@ 1460 et seq. or @@ 2251 et seq.], or any other Federal criminal statute.
(2)   No effect on intellectual property law. Nothing in this section shall be construed to limit or expand any law pertaining to intellectual property.
(3)   State law. Nothing in this section shall be construed to prevent any State from enforcing any State law that is consistent with this section. No Cause of action may be brought and no liability may be imposed under any State or local law that is inconsistent with this section.
(4)   No effect on communications privacy law. Nothing in this section shall be construed to limit the application of the Electronic Communications Privacy Act of 1986 or any of the amendments made by such Act, or any similar State law.

(e) Definitions. As used in this section:
(1)   Internet. The ten-n "Internet" means the international computer network of both Federal and non-Federal interoperable packet switched data networks.
(2)   Interactive computer service. The term "interactive computer service" means any information service, system, or access software provider that provides or enables computer access by multiple users to a computer server, including specifically a service or system that provides access to the Internet and such systems operated or services offered by libraries or educational institutions.
(3)   Information content provider. The term "information content provider" means any person or entity that is responsible, in whole or in part, for the creation or development of information provided through the Internet or any other interactive computer service.

(4) Access software provider. The term "access software provider" means a provider of software (including client or server software), or enabling tools that do any one or more of the following:

(A) filter, screen, allow, or disallow content;

(B) pick, choose, analyze, or digest content; or

(C) transmit, receive, display, forward, cache, search, subset,

(D) organize, reorganize, or translate content.

Part 4

Applications

16

Old-Fashioned Salesmanship in a Newfangled Medium

Keith Reinhard, Chairman
DDB Needham Worldwide

Some scholarly camps have appropriately subscribed to "an evolutionary approach" to the infinite and almost incomprehensible new opportunities presented by new technologies. Such a thoughtful approach is needed at a time when so much of what we read in the trade and business press seems to suggest that we drop everything and log our lives - business and personal, onto the Internet. *Advertising Age*, for example, will sometimes devote almost half of its pages to the new technologies causing one of its editors to privately complain that the magazine is literally becoming "*Interactive Age*."

The purpose of this chapter is to offer a practitioner's perspective to the subject of advertising and the Internet. I do not try to quantify the extent to which advertisers are or are not succeeding with the new technologies. These are early days and we are going to need a lot of experimenting before we find the best ways to use the new media. Nor will I attempt to predict the extent to which advertisers will be using the Web by the year 2000 or the year 2050. I hope we will be taking a much more holistic approach to selling goods and services and when all the technologies finally converge, it will be both difficult and irrelevant to try to divide advertising expenditures by media type. For now, let us just say that the Internet adds an important instrument to our orchestra - it does not replace anything.

I am an advertising man and therefore a salesman. Although I believe within a very short period of time all the functions now performed by my Sharp Wizard, my 500 channel TV, my Nintendo, my AM-FM radio, my Walkman, Discman, my credit cards, ATM cards, and my computer will converge into one hand-held unit, I do not expect to understand the technology that will allow all this to happen.

Robert Sarnoff said, "Whatever the mind of man can conceive, modem technology can achieve." When I began my career as a copywriter, I might have been able to conceive of the Budweiser Clydesdales playing football, but I could not have achieved it. Today, we can - quite easily.

So, my objective here is to let some of the air out of the overblown hype about the new media technologies and bring the subject down to a manageable size. In fact, the World Wide Web provides the perfect opportunity to get back to the basics of selling and back to the unchanging aspects of human behavior. It can be noted that the people and the ideas one encounters on the Web are pretty much the same as the people and the ideas one encountered before the Web. Some content is good, some is awful, and most of it is somewhere in between. In the category of religious content, for example, the old fashioned tent meeting brought us Elmer Gantry, television brought us Jim Bakker, and the Web brings us the Church of Elvis.

If someone can provide religion on the Internet, selling goods and services ought to be relatively easy. We can examine the subject of old-fashioned salesmanship in the newfangled media.

Advertising is salesmanship and it always has been. Advertising was first salesmanship in print - newspaper, magazines, posters or through the mail. Then salesmanship was broadcast - radio and television. Now, salesmanship has entered the new electronic media. Yet, for reasons never clear to me, the term "salesmanship" has never been popular either in academic circles, nor, for that matter, in our own industry.

Yet, salesmanship is the sparkplug of the free market systems. I've always liked the way an old ad from Wheelabrator-Frye expressed this truth. I've excerpted from the copy:

> Until a product or service is sold, nothing happens.
>
> No wages are paid. No taxes are paid. A household can't function. Neither can a government.
>
> A person can't buy a can of soup; a fire engine can't move. The clock stops. So does America. So do you.

Selling is why the advertising industry exists. Bill Bernbach, the "B" in our company DDB Needham, revolutionized the advertising industry in the 1960's had this to say on the subject:

> The purpose of advertising is to sell. That is what the client is paying for and if that goal does not permeate every idea you get, every word you write, every picture you take, you are a phony and you ought to get out of the business.
> -Bill Bernbach

What the newfangled media allows us to do is to sell more efficiently and more effectively than ever by combining the special capabilities of the new technologies with the traditional strengths of the old. If the one-way advertising on conventional television can be likened to putting up a roadside sign along the highway, then advertising on a web site is more like opening a roadside stand. It is a place where a marketer, having created awareness and brand equities through conventional media, can now allow the customer to more closely examine the product and make the purchase.

Before we go any further, let us remind ourselves that interaction between buyer and seller is not a new idea. The activity of a door-to-door salesman was to knock on a door. The occupant either slammed the door or extended an invitation to the salesman to enter and demonstrate his wares. If every door was slammed in his face, he changed either his product, or his face.

For advertisers, the key point of difference between the electronic media of the past fifty years and the newfangled electronic media is that the consumer is once again in control. On the Internet, the consumer, not the seller, will decide which salesmen to spend time with, and which to shut out.

As a first step in applying old-fashioned selling principles in the newfangled media, let me offer the following premise: If our view of the history of selling through media begins with the television era, we will see the process of selling through interactive multimedia as one that requires radical change. But, if we take a longer view of marketing history and view it from the turn of the century, we might well conclude that the television era was in fact an unnatural act in the art of selling. Selling has always been, from the days of the first street vendors, an interactive process, and marketing activity has always been directly influenced by consumer desires and consumer behavior.

Rather than using the last fifty years as a point of reference, let's go back one hundred years to 1887 (see Fig. 16.1). In that year, Americans were provided with an unprecedented opportunity to "interact" with a merchant without being present at the store. The original Sears catalog is a good paradigm because, once the "technology" - that is, the catalog - was in the home, the customer, not the advertiser, decided when the communication would take place. And the customer, not the advertiser, decided which department would be shopped, how much time would be spent in each section, be it farm machinery, undergarments, even automobiles. The customer, not the advertiser, decided how much information to absorb, to review, or to avoid.

Assuming the marketer had done a decent job of consumer research, there would invariably be an item or two of interest to the shopper. In this event, an order form was completed and mailed, and in a few weeks' time, the product was delivered. An early, low-tech example of remote, interactive selling. It is this basic interactive process that the newfangled media will enhance and facilitate.

With conventional television, the consumer had to sit down when the program started and stay seated there. Viewers only received, they did not send. There was no interactivity at all. People were told what to watch and when to watch it. I suppose that's why it was called "Tell-a-vision, " but selling has always been a lot more than telling.

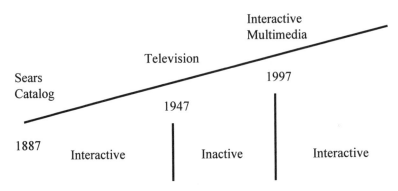

Fig. 16.1: History of selling through the media.

So, I propose that it was television which interrupted the natural interactivity of marketing by requiring that the customer sit silently inactive, captive to the medium and therefore to the seller. Now that we have returned to the natural, interactive track, we need to get back to the fundamentals of selling - some of which may have gotten lost on the one-way streets of conventional television.

What are those fundamentals again? My checklist goes something like this:

Fundamentals of Selling
- Know, honor, and love your customer
- Offer the right merchandise
- Present your product in an inviting way
- Spell out features and benefits clearly
- Make it easy to buy

The task we face as marketers is to apply these fundamentals in the fractionated and computerized marketplaces of the future.

As a one-to-one marketing tool, the Web is an excellent way to engender true two-way communication with customers. The ability to track user habits, trends, and preferences is unprecedented. With the Web, a marketer is able to know more than ever about his customer, and to be more accommodating and deferential to the customers needs, wants and wishes. By accessing the Federal Express site, for example, customers can track their shipments without resorting to the telephone.

A favorite site of mine that demonstrates the ability to know and honor the customer is <FireFly.com>. Because I have been to the site before, they already know my name. They ask if I am interested in music or movies today. I choose music, and because they know my favorites - their database tracks my previous visits, the focus is on jazz. They ask my opinion on several albums they've selected. In giving my opinion, I contribute more knowledge to their database and they can make additional suggestions using a process of affinity clustering to recommend more CDs I might be interested in knowing about or even buying. They come back with some new suggestions, one of which I think I will add to the CD collection.

Offering the right merchandise includes having the right amount of the right product available. In the analog world, a retail establishment has to rely on experience, research, gut instinct, fickle consumer trends, and luck to make sure his inventory meets consumer demand in the right quantity. A mistake can make for a disastrous selling season. The Web provides all the benefits of catalog merchandising with one major difference: Product offerings can be adjusted in real-time to fit consumer demand.

Another example of offering merchandise on the Web that is just right for each individual customer. It is Cover Girl's "Personal Makeup Recommendation Page." Makeup is a very personal choice so to offer the customer a product she'll try, Cover Girl needs to know something about the customer. The response of the computer to the customer's input increases the perception of interactivity and has a life offline - the same categories of "Warm," "Cool," and so forth are used at the makeup counter in the real world. Online the input leads to the assortment of products that is right for the customer.

There is no substitute for being able to see and touch a product in front of you, but of all media, the Web presents the ultimate (to date) combination of elements to enhance the second-hand shopping experience. Video, audio, photography, text 3D animation, virtual reality - all the key means of communicating the imagery of a product with one element most other media do not provide time. The customer is not limited by the linear nature of a broadcast media and although print may allow the time, it cannot compete with the depth of the media experience. Of course, all this means nothing if the product is not presented in a creative and engaging way.

Saab's web site illustrates the principle of spelling out your product features and benefits clearly. Although the site does a wonderful job of communicating the benefits and features of the product through a virtual tour with the aid of the latest in web tech, Saab recognizes that nothing can compare to experiencing these features first-hand. So, they offer the customer the opportunity to schedule a real world test drive. The customer puts in their zip code and fills out a form to set up an appointment to be picked up at their home for a Saab test drive.

Amazon is the "Earth's largest bookstore," but lives only online. It is a superbly organized, simple-to-use site, and if you are tempted to spend more time there than planned – it is because the content (reviews, snippets from best sellers, interviews with authors and reader forums) is so engaging, not because you have any problem getting to what you want. You can check out the Book of the Day, decide on your purchase, and in very little time place your order, have it shipped to arrive immediately, and even choose a gift wrap and add a personal note.

Selling through the newfangled media will not be without its special challenges - standards are needed as are ways to measure effectiveness. The ability to segment the universe of buyers into infinitely smaller groups will require us to be even sharper in terms of strategic thinking. If clutter is a problem with conventional media, the sheer number of options available to surfers can serve as a bothersome distraction to customers on the way to a destination site.

It is an exciting new world of selling to contemplate. Creativity is released from the prisons of the printed page and the television screen. Consumers shop in electronic malls from digital shelves stocked with virtual products. Creative people are not only charged with selling to consumers but to "Things that Think!" By this, I mean that in order to reach the consumer, you may have to get on the shopping list of a consumer's personal digital assistant (PDA), which recognizes the consumer's voice and hand movements, knows the consumer's personal brand and lifestyle preferences, and has intimate knowledge of all the consumer's demographic data. If you want to sell your product to the consumer, you first have to sell it to his PDA, an inanimate, but highly intelligent digital device.

It is exciting to contemplate an advertising industry made young again by a whole new breed of creative people who think, not in terms of putting words with pictures, but much more holistically to create ideas and ideas for the new medium. When I asked one of our website designers what he most liked about being in the advertising business at this time, he said without missing a beat "no old pros to contend with." The old pros, on the other hand, must embrace the new technologies. As Bill Bernbach said years ago, you have to live in the idiom to create in the idiom.

The mind boggles at the many ways creative people will be able to put the new technologies to work. Even though language translation software is still primitive and fully capable of producing laughable results: A similar example of faulty "Fuzzy logic" was the computer that translated the phrase, "The spirit is willing, but the flesh is weak" from English to Russian, then back into English. The phrase came out, "The vodka is good . . . but the meat is rotten." A favorite mistranslation legend is the one about the Chinese translating program that turned the aphorism "Out of sight, out of mind" into "blind and insane." There will certainly come a day when, even as I become fluent in universally understood non-verbal languages, I will be able to translate my global theme into Arabic or Japanese with the touch of a key.

Living in the idiom of the new technologies means that, as a creative person, I could create my own chat room where I could gather beer drinkers and let them react to my ideas as they are forming.

It is an exciting future to contemplate - one that presents unprecedented opportunity to (a) know, honor and love your customer, (b) offer the right merchandise, (c) present your product in an inviting way, (d) spell out features and benefits clearly, and (e) make it easy to buy.

Most exciting is that the future can be what we make of it. And on that note, I conclude this chapter with the advice I received from a client years ago. He was a scientist employed by Xerox in Palo Alto, California, where the computer mouse was born, along with laser printing. When asked about the future, he said, "The best way to predict the future is to invent it." With all the possibilities of the newfangled media, it is a great future that is ours to invent.

17

An Audience Survey From the First Gridiron Cybercast

Lynn R. Kahle
Robert Madrigal
Nancy P. Melone
Kerry Szymanski
University of Oregon

The University of Oregon cybercast the football game between the University of Oregon and the University of Illinois on September 16, 1995. Audience members could listen to the audio (radio) feed from the Oregon Sports Network, including all inserted advertisements, through their computers, from anywhere in the world. During the cybercast, they could click buttons on their computer screens to find out more information about the University of Oregon academic and athletic programs, to purchase novelty items, to learn more about the cybercast sponsors, and to participate in a survey.

Survey participants (120 of them, 10% of logons, 1% of attempted logons) were affluent young adult and middle-aged adult males, well educated. They liked novelty and sports. They did NOT hate advertising or advertisers. They owned software. They received 23% of their sports information from the Internet. They valued (more than others) self-fulfillment and sense of belonging. They devalued (less than others) warm relationships with others and security. As expected, they also strongly value sense of accomplishment. Individuals who tended to view internal values as being less important and who were highly attracted to the cybercast as a form of new technology reported receiving a significantly greater percentage of sports-related information over the Internet than did those who were highly motivated by internal values and novelty.

An Audience Survey From the First Gridiron Cybercast

In the past, users of the Internet have bellowed their negative sympathies toward advertisements and marketing in cyberspace; however, in recent months these

275

negative sentiments may have been changing to become more supportive of advertising over the Internet.

> Marketers are crowding onto the net as fast as they can, each trying to outdo the other with flashy graphics and deep databases. As recently as six months ago, however, marketers shied away from the Internet, fearing flames from angry computer users. But those fears have gone by the wayside as the WWW, a portion of the Internet containing multimedia pages that are linked together has gained popularity. (Donaton, 1995a)

Partly due to changing demographics and partly due to changing experiences, Internet users may be moving toward a more favorable view of advertising on the Internet. As cyberjunk gives way to carefully targeted information, interest will shift (Mehta & Sivadas, 1995).

If the Internet is the wave of the future, marketers may need to create new forms of passive advertisements that vary considerably from the active print and television ads. Internet users require information and entertainment. Consumers access a web site because they are interested in a topic or product. Therefore, advertisements should contain information and entertainment for the user. If advertising is done effectively, a company may gain recognition and loyalty from consumers; however, if advertisements are intrusive or distasteful, they may damage a company's image. The popular theory about Internet advertising was expressed articulately by Donaton (1994): "To succeed, on-line ads probably will not be ads at all. At the least, they will not be intrusive. Instead, these ads will be interactive information, education and entertainment services sponsored by marketers."

September 2, 1995 was historical. Over Labor Day weekend, Molson Breweries was the first to sponsor live video broadcast over the Internet. Molson promoted chances to win free tickets to the Metallica concert at Tuktoyaktuk, in the Northwest Territories, 200 miles north of the Arctic Circle. For those who could not attend the concert in person, they could participate via the cybercast. In addition to the cybercast, Molson has its own web site with over 70 pages of video clips, games, and even offers a computerized brewery tour.

Electronic Commerce and Customer Relations

Developments in electronic commerce are changing traditional business transactions. The Internet provides a new forum for companies to promote and sell their products and services. Sales over the Internet have been increasing - 2.5 million people have made purchases via the Internet (Williamson, 1995). "The interactive industry - including consumer online/Internet services, PC/ multimedia software, and video games - tallied 5.7 billion in spending last year according to a recent Investment Banker's Report. That figure is expected to reach 14.2 billion by 1999, a hefty 19.9% annual growth rate. By contrast, the entire communications industry is expected to grow only 6.8% annually through 1999, from 233.5 billion last year to 323.7 billion in 1999. . . . Leading most of that growth will be the online segment, which has grown dramatically over the past year with the rise of the World Wide Web" (Williamson, 1995).

The Internet provides a new format for companies to interact with their customers. This allows advertisers to segment the market by targeting their products to specific individual customers. Tracking via the Internet enables companies to measure the volume of hits a site receives on a particular day, in turn enabling companies to develop close contacts with their consumers. In this medium, advertisers can segment the market without losing a broad consumer base. Advertisers can provide services to fairly narrow markets worldwide. Although the accuracy is not perfect, the opportunities for tracking probably are much greater than with other mass media.

Examples of market segmentation can be seen across gender lines and among the collegiate marketplace. Males comprise 66% of Internet usage, motivating web sites to create new tactics to attract women. Lang's Women Web enables women to network and receive business advice. *Elle* magazine offers beauty advice. The Express Company has opened a web site that enables women to preview new fashions and receive coupons by registering for the mailing list. In turn, the list enables Express to more accurately target their customers (Hodges, 1995). Demographically appropriate ads can be interspersed through useful or entertaining information for most audiences.

The college market also shows a great degree of segmentation. Universities across the country are linked to the Internet, enabling students to gain easy access. Research and entertainment drive students to cruise the WWW. With that fact in mind, companies are gearing Internet marketing campaigns to target this large audience. Students show aversion to advertisements that interrupt or intrude their search; therefore, advertisers are changing their strategies to lure college students to their sites. The telephone company, Sprint, created a web site that is synonymous with modern day soap operas. Each time a student activates a site, he or she can find games, puzzles, surprises, and new information about the characters in the Sprint drama. The drama encourages students to come back to the site to follow the lives of their favorite characters. The Sprint site also enables students to talk directly with a Sprint representative about their calling plans and to receive discounts and promotional items. Booksellers, Barnes and Noble, recently created a site based upon their consumer survey. The research found that internet advertising is acceptable but that excessive amounts of it are not. This research reinforced the fact that advertisers have to create new methods of marketing on the Internet.

Support Base for Worldwide Electronic Commerce

At present, financial support for the Internet comes both from subscribers and advertisers; however, analogous to the television industry, the Internet may soon be predominantly sponsored through corporate advertising.   More and more companies are getting involved in Internet advertising.   Marketers are going online at a rate of 10% per month (Shermach, 1995). The logic of Internet sponsorship in many respects mirrors the logic of other types of sponsorships. In order to advertise on the Internet, a company may rent space on an existing web site or create its own site.

Commercial online connections such as America Online (AOL) and Prodigy are not making it inexpensive for advertisers to develop a presence the Internet.   AOL currently charges advertisers $300,000/year for their own web site, and Prodigy is asking for $100,000 per year (Donaton, 1995b); however, advertising on the Internet requires a relatively small investment for the potentially high rate of return.   It also enables companies to save on mailing costs, to update information constantly, and to form close relationships with consumers. Maintaining web sites after creation can also be expensive. Because the Internet goes across the global market, advertising over this medium allows marketers to disseminate information at the same domestic and international rate.

Advertising and Sports on the Internet

In the past, the advertising industry found a successful marketing mechanism through the sponsorship of sporting events. To date, advertisers have perhaps saturated the market. Sports' appeals to audiences with specific demographics, and they have often proven to be quite effective as media vehicles for conveying information. Advertisers may have an opportunity to use the Internet for certain types of sports information. Advertisers will be able to increase the speed of their message via transmission over the Internet, and they will be able to broaden their user base at a lower cost than television advertising. The Internet is a new sports communication device that will enable advertisers to sharpen their tools to provide a new means of advertising across cyberspace.

One of the largest Internet advertising purchases to date was made by Gatorade on ESPNet Sports Zone (Marx, 1995). Gatorade conducted a preliminary three-month test on ESPNet Sports Zone, spending under $100,000. Following increased profits, Gatorade signed a $300,000 advertising contract for a year with ESPNet. It is interesting that Gatorade does not do extensive advertising on television.

Another historical cybercast event took place on September 16, 1995, when the University of Oregon was the first to cybercast a live football game over the Internet. More than 6,000 people logged on to the sports cybercast, which used Real Audio software from Progressive Network. The cybercast was transmitted in real time, as the game was being played. Alumni and fans from around the world tuned into the event. Advantages of a cybercast include international transmission and multiple replays of an event.

The cybercast essentially sent out over the Internet the audio feed from the Oregon Sports Network radio coverage of the college football game (Oregon vs. Illinois), complete with all advertisements. The home page for the cybercast displayed logos for the sponsors - Sierra Online, Apple, Gatorade, and Bank of America, as well as the University of Oregon and the Warsaw Sports Marketing Center. Audience members could listen to the audio (radio) feed from the Oregon Sports Network, including all inserted advertisements, through their computers from anywhere in the world. During the cybercast, they could click buttons on their computer screens to find out more information about the University of Oregon academic and athletic programs, to purchase novelty items related to Oregon sports (e.g., "Duck lips") by mail from the Oregon Bookstore, to learn more about the cybercast sponsors and organizers (Sierra On-Line, Apple, Gatorade, Bank of America, and the Warsaw Sports Marketing Center), and to participate in a survey. They could complete the survey while listening to the cybercast. They could listen to the cybercast during real time as the game was being played, or they could retrieve the cybercast after the game to listen to the complete game or portions of it. The time-delay option was especially popular among European participants, for whom the real-time cybercast came earlier in the morning than prime football-consuming time.

The game itself provided good entertainment value in that it was tightly contested. Oregon finally won the game, coming from behind in the final few minutes by converting a recovered fumble into a touchdown. The reported quality of the audio transmission was comparable to radio.

This paper reports on the results of the survey, which provided an opportunity to discover who listened to this cybercast, and why. In addition to the descriptive questions regarding who listened and why, as well as their attitudes toward advertising, we had one additional research question: To what extent can the use of a new technology as an information source be predicted by the novelty of a new technology as a motivater for connecting to a cybercast and personal values?

METHOD

The participants were approximately 10% of the people who logged on to the cybercast at some time during or after the game. The survey and audio files were available for one week after the game. Survey participation was voluntary and self-paced. Participants could select response categories by pointing and clicking with their mice.

Instrument. The questionnaire addressed five areas of interest.   First, background data were collected (age, gender, marital status, number of children in the household, education, continent from which the respondent was listening, and income).   The second area of interest addressed why the respondent was connected to the cybercast.   Specifically, respondents were asked to indicate along a nine-point continuum ranging from "not at all important" to "very important" the extent to which their interest in listening was: (a) novelty of new technology, (b) interest in sports, (c) University of Oregon supporter, and (d) supporter of the opposing university.   Third, two questions wee asked related to respondents' attitudes toward corporate sponsors of cybercasted sports events. The first item asked respondents about their attitudes toward advertising during cybercasts, whereas the second asked about corporate sponsorship of these events (1 = very bad idea, 9 = very good idea).   Respondents were then asked to indicate the amount of sports information they received from the Internet as a percentage of all media sources (television, radio, newspapers, magazines, computers).   Finally, respondents were asked to complete the List of Values on a 9-point scale ranging from "important to me" to "extremely important to me."

RESULTS

Profile of Respondents.   The 120 respondents constituted 10% of cybercast log-ons and 1% of attempted log-ons.   An unspecified larger number of people failed to be identified as attempted log-ons due to the limitations of the distribution and tracking system.   Table 17.1 gives the age, marital status, and education distribution of survey participants.   Most respondents were 25 to 49-years-old, married, and college educated.   The sample was 91% male and had a mean of .79 dependent children living in their households.   The median annual household income was $62,000.   Of the respondents, 5% had graduated from the University of Illinois, and 33% had graduated from the University of Oregon. Europe produced 2% of the respondents, and Asia produced another 2% of the respondents.   More nonrespondents, who nevertheless listened to the cybercast, came from Asia - including several hundred from Japan, a number from Singapore, and a smattering from other countries such as Germany, Bosnia, Russia, and South Africa.

Reasons for Listening.   Table 17.2 reports the means for the reasons for listening.   The novelty of the new technology was one important motive for listening; however, interest in sports received a similar rating.

TABLE 17.1
Age, Marital Status, and Education of Respondents

Demographic	Range	Percentage
Age	Under 18	8%
	18-24	15%
	25-34	39%
	35-49	41%
	50-64	13%
	65	1%
Marital Status	Single	40%
	Married	55%
	Divorced	5%
Education	Some High School	7%
	High School Graduate	5%
	Some College	27%
	Trade School	2%
	College Graduate (4 year degree)	28%
	Some Postgraduate	23%
	Postgraduate Degree	10%

Attitudes Toward Advertising. In response to the item, "Which of the following best describes your attitude toward commercial sponsorship of athletic events that are cybercast on the Internet? Please answer on a scale from 1 to 9, where 1 = *Very good idea*, and 9 = *Very bad idea*," the mean was 4.9, very close to neutral. In response to the item, "Which of the following best describes your attitude toward advertisements on the Internet during cybercasts? Please answer on a scale from 1 to 9, where 1 = *Very good idea*, and 9 = *Very bad idea*," the means was 4.39. The mean was 2.94 in response to the item, "How would you describe your attitude toward companies that sponsor athletic events? Please answer on a scale from 1 to 9, where 1 = *Very positive*, and 9 = *Very negative*."

Source of Sports Information. We asked respondents, "Considering all types of media (television, radio, newspapers, magazines, computers, etc.), what percentage of your sports information during the past month did you get over the Internet?" The mean response was a surprisingly high 23%.

TABLE 17.2
Reasons for Listening to the Cybercast

Reason	Mean
Novelty of New Technology	6.87
Interest in Sports	6.35
University of Oregon Supporter	5.38
University of Illinois Supporter	2.18

Scale: Reasons in terms of importance (1 = *Not at all important*, 9 = *Very important*).

Respondent Interests. Table 17.3 describes respondent interests. Respondents obviously liked football, but they have nearly the same level of interest in baseball and basketball. They own and are likely to purchase sports software, but they are even more enthusiastic about educational software. Marketers can certainly view cybercast audiences as potential consumers of at least some classes of products.

Values. We asked respondents to reply to the List of Values (LOV) items (Kahle, 1983). They valued (more than others) self-fulfillment and sense of belonging. They devalued (less than others) warm relationships with others and security. As expected, they also strongly valued sense of accomplishment.

Diffusion of Innovation. Of primary interest in the current study was the extent to which cybercasted events might be viewed in terms of diffusion of innovation. Specifically, we were interested in predicting whether the percentage of sports information received interactively from the Internet might be predicted on the basis of personal values and novelty of a new technology as a basis for connecting to the cybercast. In order to increase the power of analyses, we pooled the data from a surveys of subsequent cybercasts that asked some different questions but asked the identical questions for topics discussed in this section. The sample size for these analyses is 198. As commonly performed (Homer & Kahle, 1988; Madrigal & Kahle, 1994), the LOV items included in this study were factor analyzed to enhance parsimony. The principle components, varimax extraction yielded a one-factor solution. Four of the six items typically comprising the internal motivation factor loaded predominantly (all factor loadings greater than .87) in the factor analysis: self-fulfillment, warm relationships with others, a sense of accomplishment, and fun and enjoyment.

Internally-oriented individuals tend to be more self-motivated and believe that they are able to influence events and control outcomes in their lives (Kahle 1983). Given their predominance in the analysis, the four items were summed to form an internal motivation dimension.

A tercile split was then performed on the internal motivation dimension and novelty of a new technology as a motivater for listening. A 2 (internal motivation dimension) X 2 (novelty in new technology) analysis of variance (ANOVA) was then performed in which only those individuals scoring in the upper and lower terciles on each variable were included. The results of this analysis are shown in Table 17.4. The analysis yielded a significant two-way interaction, $F(1, 107) = 3.09$, $p < .05$. As shown in Fig. 17.1, individuals who tended to view internal values as being less important and who were highly attracted to the cybercast as a form of new technology reported receiving a significantly greater percentage of sports-related information over the Internet than did those who were highly motivated by internal values and novelty, $M = 36.51$, $M = 15.5$, respectively, $t(62) = 3.06$, $p < .01$. In contrast, no differences in internal motivation were found among those classified as having less interest in listening as a result of the novelty of the medium.

TABLE 17.3
Interests of Respondents

Interest	Type	Mean/Percentage
Interest in Sports Activity	Extreme-type games	4.27
	Football	6.77
	Baseball	6.33
	Basketball	6.33
	Hockey	4.73
Interest in Purchasing Software	Sports	5.55
	Education	6.11
	Action	5.31
Ownership of Software	Sports	53%
	Education	79%
	Action	68%

Scales: Interest (1 = *Not at all interested*, and 9 = *Extremely interested*).

TABLE 17.4
Interaction of Internal Values and Novelty on
Percent of Sports Information from the Internet

	Low Novelty	*High Novelty*
Low Internal	23.0%	36.5%
High Internal	24.2%	15.5%

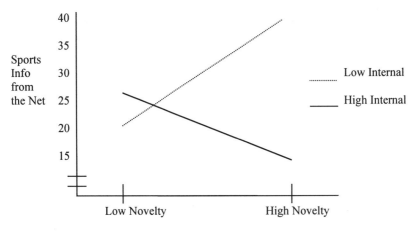

Fig. 17.1. Values X Novelty: Sports Info from the Net

DISCUSSION

The respondents were affluent, young and middle-aged males, mostly interested in the technology, which describes a predictable profile given that football often attracts a male-dominant audience and computers require some specialized, new knowledge and some money. The value profile fits what might be expected from an audience with these demographics. Accomplishment and fulfillment are upscale values. The pattern with warm relationships and sense of belonging might suggest that computer cybercast listeners are more lonely than others (Kahle, 1996). As Internet usage becomes more widespread, we expect the demographics and values of cybercast consumers will become more mainstream.

We were surprised by the high level of sports information obtained over the Internet. Either a dramatic trend is occurring in how people follow sports or we had a very computer-oriented group of respondents. Or both. Where immediacy of information is valued, as is the case with sports fans and game results, the Internet may be a particularly attractive medium. Listeners can find out results very quickly.

The data suggest that survey participants were neither excited about nor hostile toward commercial sponsorship of cybercast athletic events on the Internet. Likewise, survey participants were at best mildly positive toward advertisements on the Internet during cybercasts. Interestingly, respondents had a positive attitude toward companies that sponsor athletic events.

When the upcoming cybercast was publicized in newspapers, television, radio, and newsletters, we received no complaints. When the cybercast was publicized over the Internet, four people responded with suggestions that such communication is inappropriate. No one complained during or after the cybercast about the advertising included in the audio feed. When faced with the actual execution of the cybercast, most participants perceived something quite similar to radio and did not find it particularly offensive. Potential commercial sponsors should find this information encouraging.

One interesting interactive feature of the cybercast is the ability to listen to replays. All of the 5% of listeners who claimed to be graduates of the University of Illinois logged on prior to the fumble that changed the outcome of the game. Many University of Oregon graduates listened to the game-winning play repeatedly in the week following the game, but Illinois graduates apparently did not want to relive the unpleasant result by listening to the fumble again. Cialdini and his associates discussed BIRGing and CORFing - Basking In Reflected Glory and Cutting Off Reflected Failure. People clearly showed a bias toward wanting "no bad news," consistent with what the theory behind BIRGing and CORFing would predict.

Individuals who tended to view internal values as being less important and who were highly attracted to the cybercast as a form of new technology reported receiving a significantly greater percentage of sports-related information over the Internet than did those who were highly motivated by internal values and novelty. Presumably people who have a greater internal motivation also have more of an achievement motivation for exploring the Internet, whereas people without the internal values may emphasize curiosity more.

Clearly sports on the Internet has a bright future. The NBA is making sure that basketball will have a presence in cyberspace (Bernker, 1995). The NFL wants to see Internet retailing of its goods flourish (Pesky, 1995). Sports from baseball to canoe polo have a large presence on the Internet, and companies from the smallest all the way to IBM and Walt Disney are using sports to attract attention to their activities.

CONCLUSION

We concluded from our experience that cybercasting sports has a potentially bright future. Subsequent events corroborate this conclusion in that some very high fees have been paid (not to us) to coordinate more recent sport cybercasts. Our subsequent cybercasts have likewise generated considerable interest, ranging from appreciative letters to reports of alumni tailgate parties around computers in Singapore.

REFERENCES

Bernker, M. (1995). NBA gets on web with Starwave's ESPN Sportszone. *Broadcasting & Cable, 125(44),* 69.

Cialdini, R.B., Borden, R.J., Thorne, A., Walker, M.R., Freeman, S., & Sloan, L.R. (1976, September). Basking in reflected glory: Three (football) field studies. *Journal of Personality and Social Psychology, 34,* 366-375)

Donaton, S. (1995, January 23). AOL seeks big bucks for ads. *Advertising Age, 66,* 15.

Hodges, J. (1995, November 6). What women want online. *Advertising Age,* 30.

Homer, P. M. & Kahle, L.R. (1988, April). A structural equation test of the value-attitude-behavior hierarchy. *Journal of Personality and Social Psychology, 54,* 638-646.

Kahle, L.R. Ed. (1983). *Social Values and social Change: Adaptation to Life in America.* New york: Praeger.

Kahle, L.R. (1996). Social Values and Consumer Behavior: Research from the List of Values. In C. Seligman, J.M. Olson, & M. P. Zanna (eds.) *The Psychology of Values: The Ontario Sympoisium, Vol. 8.* Mahwah, NJ: Lawrence Erlbaum Associates, 135-151.

Madrigal, R. & Kahle, L.R. (1994, Winter). Predicting vacation activity preferences on the basis of value-system segmentation. *Journal of Travel Research, 32,* 22-28.

Mehta, R., & Sivadas, E. (1995). Direct marketing on the Internet: An empirical assessment of consumer attitudes. *Journal of Direct Marketing, 9,* 21-32.

Pesky, G. (1995). Pro leagues join the Internet: Serve up electronic retailing. *Sporting Goods Business, 28(6),* 22.

Shermach,K. (1995, October 23). *Advertising Age,* 40.

Williamson, D. (1995, August 6). Digital media future looks rosy. *Advertising Age,* 13.

18

Conversations With Practitioners

Edited by David W. Schumann
University of Tennessee

Five speakers representing four companies were invited to offer their insights at the Advertising and Consumer Psychology Conference held in Bloomfield Hills, Michigan, during the summer of 1996. Each had direct responsibility for the development of commercial web pages. Michael Samet, President of Edmund's Publication Corporation, offered an overview of his popular web page addition. Carole Walters and Teresa Denova, representing Cincinnati's Northlich, Stolley, LaWarre Advertising Agency, provided an interesting perspective on targeting and direct web page research with children. Bruce Gorlich from DMB&B Corporate Media offered four criteria by which to consider commercial advertising on the Internet. Finally, David King, President of DDB Needham Interactive Communications, shared both historical and present day perspectives on interactivity, positioning the Internet as an evolving, exciting, yet unknown future medium.

Fifty Million Data Points - Consumer Behavior on the Web

Michael G. Samet, President
Edmund's Publication Corporation

A psychologist as a used car salesman? I know nothing about cars, not the slightest thing at all about cars. It is all about methodology. We facilitate the sales of used cars on the World Wide Web. We rate safety, reliability, performance, comfort, pleasure to drive, and value. Edmund's employs a multiattribute ratings system that rates every one of 5,000 used cars. To weight these attributes, we initially placed a form on the Internet and asked people what was the most important feature of a used car? Inside of two days, we had over 7,000 responses to that question. The most important thing to buyers was reliability, 3 to 1 over safety. The second most important thing was value.

I believe the Edmund's web page draws more people to it than does the major automobile manufacturers' web pages. Why? Information and advice. People want a third party, not an advertiser. People want to compare and contrast. When it comes to succeeding in advertising or selling on the Internet, you have to see yourself as a presenter of information, advising the consumer, helping the consumer make a decision.

What are the important features of a web page that is designed to sell? The first is "success stories. Edmund's gets thousands of e-mails a day. Many of them relate success stories, how the page saved them money. One woman wrote, "I am a single woman and your cite gave me the information I needed before I talked dollars with the dealer." If you watch a great infomercial, it is all about success stories.

You have to update constantly. The web site updates every two weeks with new cars and trucks. You also have to offer numerous links into the database. You have to provide the latest information on how to buy a new car, how to negotiate. You have to be perceived as being on the consumer's side. The automobile manufacturers do not like Edmund's because the site teaches people how to negotiate the best deal on a car. People who come to the site want three pieces of information: "What should I buy?", "How should I pay for it?", and "Where do I get it?".

When you arrive at the Edmund's web page you are greeted with a set of options to include: New Car Prices & Reviews; New Vans, Pickups, & SUV Prices & Reviews; Used Car and Truck Prices & Reviews. Visitors to the site can go immediately to a town hall, a chat room to talk with people about cars. One can click-on the Incentives & Rebates and receive information about current dealer holdbacks, incentives, and rebates. There a section on road tests with a list of the latest cars tested. There's information from the latest news releases and car shows. If you are interested in selling your car, clicking-on "used cars" allows you to find your make of car and its current value. Data is provided on both trade-in and market value by year and make. In addition, the value of additional features is presented on a table so one can determine the exact value of the present car they own.

If you're interested in buying a new car, you can get the latest Edmund's test information and can click to Auto-by-Tel to purchase a car. One can also secure financing over the web site. It's a one-stop shopping center for used cars.

Women on the Internet is a big issue. More women need to use the Internet. Women buy 50% of the cars in the United States; they also make 80% of the decisions. On our site, you will find 77% to be male.

Loopy: Keeping You In the Loop

Carole Walters and Teresa Denova
Northlich Stolley LaWarre Advertising Agency, Cincinnati

Let us begin by giving you a little background. This is less a research study and more a history of a living, breathing web site. Northlich Stolley LaWarre is an advertising agency in Cincinnati that just recently broke $100 million in billings. Two years ago, when all the press starting getting hot and heavy about the Internet and World Wide Web, we started getting lots of questions from our clients. "Should we be there?" "What role should it play in our marketing communication?" We did not have the answers to these questions. We had absolutely no hands-on knowledge of this new medium. And, because there were no current measures that we were familiar with, we could not even say, "Let me look it up in my Nielsen Book." There was nothing we could go back to provide them any kind of a point of view.

We decided to put together a new technology task force within the agency composed of three people who had some working knowledge of the Internet and online services. We started this as very much an exploratory process. After six months, we evolved to heavy discussions concerning what we really needed to do to create the credibility to have a point-of-view about the Internet for our clients. We discussed the options of putting up an agency web site. We really did not like that idea because agency web sites were, at that time, not much more than agency brochures on the Internet. We did not feel that we could learn anything from that. We talked about investment spending with the client, going to one of our clients and stating "We will build a Web site for you on our dollar." We felt a little uncomfortable with this idea because it was like admitting to them that we did not know much about this medium.

We eventually got to the point where we linked up with another area in which we were cutting our teeth: understanding marketing to children. We eventually decided to build a web site with the objective of gaining insights from kids. This was perceived as risky business because there was only one other group that had attempted such an effort, America Dialog, who are now linked up with Yankelovich and are called Cyber Dialogue. They have an exclusive arrangement with America Online (AOL) to access AOL subscribers to do research via computers. Basically, what they do is access AOL subscribers and invite them to do on-line focus groups. This is a very different technique from what we're doing.

As was suggested, our web site links up with another initiative we had going on in the agency, developing an expertise in children. We do all of Procter & Gamble's in-school programs; we develop curriculum-based programs for products like Crest toothpaste, Always, Noxima, and Clearasil. We wanted to see whether or not we could learn something from the Internet in order to bring some insights to this kids' initiative we had going.

We attempted to put together a web site to see if we could get kids to interact with a site and give us information about themselves. We wanted to ask certain types of questions about them: age, sex, where they live. We ask them for their e-mail addresses but it is not required that they give it to us. We get responses like "I don't know it", or "It's my Mom's and I can't tell you." Presently, we are into Phase 2. Phase 1 was basically to see whether or not we could get kids to the site. We launched the site eight months ago and the only advertising to get kids to the site was via search vehicles on the Internet. We have nothing out in print form or running on television. This must all be paid for by the agency, so we are working with a very small budget. Phase 1 lasted about three month; however, we learned within the first 6 weeks that we could get kids to the site, and that we could get them to take a survey.

We now going to take you through a discussion of the site and explain the different sorts of evolutions that we have gone through, even in this short period of time. Please keep in mind that the main reason we developed this site is so that we, as an agency, could see what it takes to maintain a living, breathing organism on the World Wide Web. Thus, we purposely built this site and targeted to a group that needs to be stimulated on a very regular basis. We built a site that needs a lot of management as evidenced by the number of changes we have made over the course of three months.

We started as complete novices; we were clueless. We had never been on the Internet. We did not know anything about it. We did not know anything about children. So, we walked in totally blank for the first couple of months, sort of flailing because it was not obvious what we needed to do. We decided to go back to the resources we did have at the University of Cincinnati, taking a Ph.D. seminar in media. After reading and discussing a number of interesting articles primarily from M.I.T., we came to the conclusion that we did not know what the term *interactive* meant. Our simple definition had been "what happens on the web," but Internet is a bit broader. Thus, there is no real clear operational definition of Internet interactivity. We evolved to a viewpoint that it is two-way communication, that we are encouraging the kids to talk to each other, and to us. One gets the feeling kids love to talk because they feel that no one is ever listening.

I think one of the most interesting things we do on this site is give the kids an outlet to talk, and they voice an appreciation for our effort in their comments back to us. The second aspect is that each child can experience the web site in their own way, controlling how they go through it. This also seems to be part of a definition of interactivity. We have provided more and more activities that have allowed the kids to do their own thing.

The very first screen children see is "Welcome to Loopy. Please sign our guestbook." At present, there are five activities going on in Loopy: "In the

Loop" is a message area. "Stuff" is just a miscellaneous area of activities. "Survey" allows kids to participate in a survey. "Favorite Sites" is a jumping off point to other for other web sites. "Puzzle" is a source of interactive word games. One of our concerns is whether kids ever get beyond the opening banner. We suspect that many people surf right to here and never look at the rest of the page. We invite them to do so by the statement "We want to get to know you." Once they sign in, the next screen has a message to both kids and parents describing what Northlich Stolley LaWarre is and the purpose of the web page. The objective of Loopy as defined as "to gain consumer insights from children ages 12 to 19, to enable us to create products that they can use as well as improve how we communicate to them." Parents are encouraged to interact through an interactive help desk, and to be involved in the activities with their children. It is interesting to note that, to date, we have not had a single message from a parent.

Children are invited to sign the guest book, which asks for name, age, gender, grade in school, occupation if employed, address (city and state), e-mail address (we get email addresses from about 50% of those who sign the guestbook), how they found Loopy (typically while surfing employing Yahoo under "entertainment" or "surveys"), and to provide any comments or ideas at this point. After completion, a request to return to the homepage follows.

Children can select from these five areas. The survey is focused on how children spend money and influence family purchase decisions, and it is restricted to children between the ages of 9 to 19. It is dynamic in that new surveys can be initiated at any time. Currently, we are on our third survey. As an example, the present survey begins by asking some name, city and state address, gender, e-mail address, whether they plan to work during the summer (almost everyone says they are employed, even if it is babysitting or lawn mowing, etc.), and an open-ended question on what they plan to do with the money they earn (most were saving for college or a car). The next page requests information concerning family decision making. A number of products are listed and respondents are asked whether the choice is "my choice," "shared choice," or "parent's choice." They are asked whether they have their own credit card and/or checking account. Next, they are asked about the frequency of certain shopping activities (e.g., going to a mall, going grocery shopping, going to a restaurant, renting a video, going to a movie, going to a convenience store, going to a drug store). Finally, there is a space for comments. We actually had our first classroom response where an entire class from Big Piney, Wyoming filled out the survey. Most of them were saving their money to go to the Cheyenne Rodeo, so there is a big difference across the country in terms of children's priorities. Overall, the survey has been dominated by girls, about 75%.

The activities on the site are user friendly and highly interactive. "In The Loop" provides a set of discussion groups. Children are prompted to keep their conversation "family-friendly." Each discussion group lists previous messages, e-mail addresses, and specific subject. The message board is designed to give something back to the kids for participating in the survey. However, we have found that the message board also provides a great deal of information. For example, we are exposed to language and the most recent expressions. Kids provide information on the latest trends on a number of topics (movies, clothes, etc.). This allows us to become more effective in our own communication with the kids because we can truly "talk their language." Examples of discussion groups include the following:

- E-mail Pen Pals
- Homepages and favorite web pages (Announce your homepage...or your favorite WWW site
- Movie stars (If you could have a dream date with a movie star, who would it be?)
- Movies (Give your opinion on the latest movie, videos, etc.)
- Chat (open discussion)
- Talk back
- Comics (Talk about your favorite comics)
- Are uniforms in public schools a good idea? (Looking for opinions...)
- Music! (List your top 10 groups)
- Create a topic

"Favorite Sites" and "Towering Achievements on Internet" include listings of other interesting sites for children. Each is underlined and hotlinked directly to the site. Each site is reviewed on a regular basis for good taste and appropriateness for the audience. Finally, under the "Puzzle" section, Loopy offers a number of interactive educational word games. Each game asks the child to feed the game with words, adjusting to the child's age and ability.

A new feature we are working on is the transmission of greeting cards. This might include Valentine cards, graduation announcements, birthday cards, and so on. This is not unique to web sites, but we are trying to create a means for viewing the card and changing it before it is sent. The Loopy character (a sniffing dog) is the main character featured on the cards. The name Loopy came out of a brainstorming session and the graphics people came back with really complex ideas. We rejected this in terms of the KISS rule (Keep It Simple Stupid). We were concerned with the time for downloading, recognizing that a shorter period of time for downloading is desirable.

There are a number of future opportunities for us. We now have about 500 e-mail addresses, which will allow us to go back to our participants and ask them about participating in online focus groups, for example. We will be marketing Loopy to teachers in the classroom, and be adding more educational programs. Another exciting initiative targets involvement with "Kid Link," a global communication, noncommercial network for children that already exists on the Internet. To date, they have 42,000 kids registered in Kid Link society, and many of them are active in Kid Link projects. We are presently involved in getting underwriting sponsorships for Kid Link. Our payback is that Loopy be allowed to conduct a project on Kid Link. Hopefully, we will get some of those Kid Link kids trafficking into Loopy and the prospect of having 40,000 to 50,000 kids globally aware of the site is very exciting.

Interactive Media: An Agency Perspective

Bruce Goerlich
DMB&B Corporate Media

My topic concerns why we are participating in interactive strategic discussions with our clients, about when and where we think interactives are important. Interactive and other media are of primary importance because we are really in the business of relative comparisons. What is the value of this medium versus another for a particular client? So, we attempt to talk about interactive in the context of other media, the choices that our clients have. Then, some of our evaluational equations that we use to determine how valuable a particular web-site or interactive media might be for this particular client are discussed.

Who are we? We are the fifth largest AT network in North America, with about $2 billion in annual billings. We have 2,600 employees in seven cities. Some of our clients include Burger King, General Motors, NBC, Procter & Gamble, and Southwestern Bell. We just won, and I spent the last three months doing it all, Coca-Cola USA's media planning in the United States for all their branches. That is over $350 million in business.

Well, why an interactive medium? Why bother? Now, I use the term *interactive media* because when we really started looking into this in-depth in 1993 and 1994, the Internet was part and parcel of many different forms of electronic interactive delivery systems. There is an entirely separate discussion about the problems with the Internet, from an infrastructure point of view - from a communications point of view - but I still think we should not just limit the question of interactive media with the Internet. That is where we are today. Maybe six months from now, cable modems will work and we will be into cable interactivity, but any use of any media should reflect our client's strategic needs. Interactive media are no different in that way, whatever form they take.

Basically, when we think that in terms of interactive media there are really four key areas that you need to start thinking about: leadership, relationship marketing, conversations, and target.

We have a whole body of work on the importance of leadership, the value of leadership, and where leadership comes from. It is really clear that leadership brands are not simply so because they are big but because consumers are able to distinguish and tell you what is a leadership brand. Leadership brands are more trusted and they have greater marketplace leverage. So, if there is a problem and a brand is perceived as a leader, the consumers are more likely to give it the benefit of the doubt. And it is clear from our work that leadership brands need to be seen in leadership media; if you are a leader, you need something bold and dramatic. If you are saying that you are leaders, that you are trusted, you need to be in places where people expect leaders to be. As a result, if you are a leadership brand, you need to start thinking about cutting into media because you need to be seen as a leader.

If a brand is doing relationship marketing, interactive may be the future. At this moment however, it is the promise, it is not necessarily the actuality. The idea with relationship marketing is that you are communicating back and forth and, if you and a client are involved in this, any form of relationship marketing, you need to start looking at the interactive media as a viable vehicle to use.

In the interactive literature, there is a whole category about community and conversations relating to the Internet. Although you might be thinking, "I do not need to be in interactive with my client," you do a search and you find 20 mentions of your client out there on the internet. So, there may be a conversation happening out there and you are not part of it. If there is a conversation out there - you need to join that conversation. For example, before Coca-Cola had their web site up, there were 200-plus web sites that mentioned Coca-Cola, and by the time they first tried to put up a web page, most of the existing pages were a lot better than Coke's. So, in other words, if someone is talking about you in a mental institution or whatever, if there is a site up there and you are being mentioned, you are the one joining that conversation.

Finally, targeting is very important for those of us in the media. We need to have numbers, and the numbers are certainly there on the Internet. There are no income ratings currently, but the directional indicators suggest a relatively young consumer uses the Internet, the 25 to 44 age range. For a large number of advertisers this group is a natural target audience, so if you have a consumer target that is in that general neck of the woods, from a targeting perspective, the Internet makes some sense.

Now, it is interesting when you take those four things and say well now how does this work, what is interactive media competing with? Maybe its greatest competitor, in terms of other media, is really direct marketing. This sort of nontraditional positioning is both a blessing and curse. The blessing is it eases the pressure because, if I do not have to take a traditional cost per thousand mentality to targeting, you can say to the client, "This is an investment, you are doing this for leadership, you are doing this for conversation, and you are trying to get direct response numbers up." The curse is not being able to attribute media spending to increases in the bottom line. And if cable TV's experience is of any value, it is going to take some time for revenues to grow. Take a look at Thompson, the Purple Bar, and then the percent of national products and revenue. You can see that, for cable, the revenues have lagged far behind their penetration. Now, why is that? That is because the ratings, too, are still quite small; the networks still dominate television. Although 22 or so cable networks have 30-share, the networks have managed to maintain a strong perception of delivery. For example, when Late Night With David Letterman came in, it brought a lot more money into the late night arena, and basically there was a perception that network television, compared to cable, gave advertising more value. Some of it is audience size, some of it is less commercial clutter, and so forth.

I am bringing this up to sort of give you a sense of the challenges that interactive media faces, because interactive as an advertising vehicle is not in isolation, it is competing with these other vehicles for a share of our client's dollars. So, what are some of the things that interactive media needs to do? Revenue growth has developed an independent rating system but the cost per thousand approach is not going to go away. You saw the same thing happen when cable came up, a lot of people whining about how unfair the cost per thousand basis was. Business is not going to change because this new medium has arrived. The cost per thousand is going to be with us and that requires an agreed-upon currency. We are working very hard on that currency - I mean, a rating system. A rating system is a common myth that we agree to that this thing is worth this amount that is revenue rating. We are not there yet at all, but we are certainly working on it.

Venturing into interactive is also going to require going after some lucrative targeting of users. There is a sense that the medium itself has to really position itself for certain kinds of targets, especially expanding the female user base. We have done some initial project work, and it really seemed that when you start talking about concepts that women are interested in, shopping Pea Pods for example, there is more interest. Thus, there has to be some sort of a new positioning of the medium to go after targets that will provide advertising value. There is a lot of promise in interactive media relationship marketing but there is not that much delivery yet. The question of providing database management to work on that relationship, to work on that kind of conversation stuff would be, I think, of value.

So the point we're at today is primarily a selective nonprofit buy. But even in that environment we still need to evaluate how to select one interactive medium over another and then measuring how well this one site worked over another. Our planners ask: How interesting is this web site to our target? Would this be a hot site? By that, I mean some of this is when you are evaluating magazines, for example, you go through and you might find that the *National Enquirer* has got a great cost per thousand for people who are going to buy the Catera (automobile), but there is no editorial compatibility. What is the compatibility? What are they providing in the way of hot links (the site where they provide a hot link to our site)? Will this be something our clients and targets are interested in? Will this be something that editorially fits well with us and perhaps provide some link to our site if we have one? These are subjective questions.

What about positioning opportunities, e.g., top of the first page banner, and so on.. There is some work done that says if you are not there at the banner on the first page, then you may not be seen at all, so we will try to get the prime position as we are trying to ensure leadership. Now, it is interesting how many of you can use that media, but there is a company now that is selling something that strips out those banners. Anyway, being in the first position for the banner is probably pretty important in terms of a price-value relationship. What is the level of clutter and competition? Are there a lot of other folks on that page? Are your competitors there? Are you going to get lost? These are some of the things that you need to ask yourselves.

Now, let us get more into the nitty-gritty of how we have to start evaluating the material on a daily basis. A web site provides two distinct values: exposure and interaction. One possible approach that we are working on is: the exposure value plus the interaction value equals the total value. This the kind of thing were doing now, trying to numerically develop the amount of exposure, the amount of direct interaction, and the value of each to the bottom line. Some disadvantages to this approach include the need for accurate client performance data. To supply this information, we need third party currency. We need site dates, independently developed demographic profiles to make this more valuable for us. It does not reflect the influence of the audio-video, and I think as bandwidth increases, this will certainly be more important to consider. It does not reflect the position on the page and we talked about the different exposure opportunities. But in summary, even with this model, clients really evaluate the needs of interactive in terms of strategic value: the strategic value of an interactive medium for you. It is not really a cost per thousand by the day. It tends to be more of an investment buy, more of a direct-market buy. We are working on developing tools to make it a better value across interactive alternatives. So, that is kind of where we are today, taking this from a day-to-day business perspective.

Relevance, Originality, and Impact: A New Marketing Communications Model

David King
DDB Needham Interactive Communications

Bandwidth. The more I see and the more I hear, the more things just kind of keep popping up in front of me. Take cognac for example. Do you know where cognac came from? It is as though the monks had an extra century or two on their hands. Cognac is made the same way it was made back in the - whenever - 16th century, and the distillation process has not much changed since that time. The Scandinavian, Dutch, and English traders discovered that the humble white wine of the cognac region traveled better and took one eighth of the space of their ships when converted into brandy. So, the next time you are sitting in front of the fireplace with a snifter full of brandy and admiring its bouquet and its clarity, you can sit there and state "now that's a compression technology."

As the chairman of our company is very fond of pointing out, the first interactive marketing tool was the Sears and Roebuck Catalog. When you think about it, what was the first interactive piece of hardware? The telephone. How long has that been around? This year is the 25th anniversary of the Automated Teller Machine (ATM), so interactivity as a marketing tool and interactivity as a means of communicating has been around for a long time, it is just getting more sophisticated.

There was an article in the *New Yorker* about two months ago about a parish priest, or he was a little higher than that, whatever is higher than that; but he was an activist priest in Paris, and he kept going on TV and shooting his mouth off and making demands. The more senior clergy members asked him to continue to help the downtrodden but not to do TV interviews. He would not stop, so they assigned him to a new diocese. It was a very old diocese, one of the original dioceses, and it was in the corner of the Algerian desert - like the south corner of the Algerian desert, so there is a church there and no people. So, they assigned him to this diocese, like a "So, we're going to show you" behavior. What his parishioners did was go out and set up a web page so that this diocese is now available to the entire world. At the end of the article, the authors were discussing the World Wide Web and how it is a distributed wide-area communications network, it is borderless, and it does not recognize any civil borders. It is totally cross-platformed and is able to leap language barriers and it basically spurs the idea of an authoritative hierarchal information fluff. So, if you want to know what the original World Wide Web was, it was the early Christian church, because it kept all of those categories, or all those parameters.

So, none of this is really new, just the technology has changed a little bit. I would like to go through how I, and we as an agency, look at the whole issue of interactivity, the Web, and the Internet from a creative marketing perspective as opposed to from a technical perspective. For better or for worse, the World Wide Web is now a commercial medium, and that is not something that sits well with a lot of people. But I am afraid the dye is cast, the deed is done, and I do not think there is any going back. That means that perspectives will change, the way we communicate will change; and that the web will continue to open up to new ways of communicating; and there will be change, and change can be good. So, where are we in all of this?

The computer is now the fastest-growing home appliance. Ellison and the folks from Oracle, and some of his buddies were announcing this week at the E3 conference, that they are pushing hard on the new network computer, a little $500 device that will take the computer from being out of range for the masses. Computer sales have gone up and the reports are now that their starting to level off; there is a price point that is hard to get below, as far as computer sales is concerned. Until this appliance comes along that allows greater penetration into the household, the Web will not be a mature medium. But still, computers are outselling televisions two to one, because television – we have all got three or four of them now – so, what more do we need? Every 18 months, the processor capacity doubles and the price is cut in half, and we see that in the way that the computer chip is now a part of everything that we do, and demand is increasing for information. I think the days of passive viewing are on their way out the door, not tomorrow, but soon and forever. Then entertainment is a way to "engagement," and you know that if you have ever watched your kids play Nintendo. Engagement is that like a drug-induced coma or more like just hypnotism. Engagement drives interactivity, and coupled with the ability to self select, the ability to determine what it is you want to be communicating with, the Internet is the new medium of exchange for ideas.

So, what is the Internet? From a practical physical standpoint, a pragmatic standpoint, it is a worldwide server network of networks, and I am sure you all know how the Internet works. No one owns it and it manages itself, and that's certainly important in the sense that it is not under the control and it probably never can be under the control of any one entity. From a practical standpoint, it is a pipeline for education - that's basically where it started. Expression, entertainment, the size and growth rate defy conventional measurement in the sense that as a medium and the way that it is being used at least from a commercial standpoint, it is exploding exponentially. From a less pragmatic standpoint, looking at it from a marketing perspective and from a creative perspective, it is a unique medium for one-on-one interaction. That is a pretty basic statement. However, it goes beyond any other context of activity because of its immediacy. It is constant, dynamic, and immediate.

We have clients that come in and say, "I've got to be on the Internet tomorrow, if not tomorrow, then the next day." Then it happens, then the first phone call is, "What'll I do? What'll I do now?" It's up and where we start with all our clients now is this: You are about to put on the air a 24-hour television station that reaches the entire world that is all blank all the time. If you are selling office products and you are Office Depot, it is the Office Depot channel. It is all Office Depot, all the time. So, you not only have the problems that traditional media have of getting people to come back, tune in, and stay tuned in. What do you do to make that compelling - it never goes off and it can be reached by anyone, and you go beyond that and what can you do to make it a part of a person's personal culture?

That is the key. You can do games, you can do trivia, you can do this or that, you can do a lot of things, but what do you do to make it a part of a person's personal culture? It is both a vehicle and a destination, an entity and a mind-set. It is like you go and turn on the TV, sit down, then you change the channel, and turn it off. It is a box that has pictures or sound on it and keeps you occupied for a while. When you sit down at a computer and you start surfing the Web, you are doing something more than just observing what is going on. You become a part of the process. That is the difference in this medium and others.   More important than the fact that the growth rate is phenomenal is the fact that the scope and depth of the resources is infinite. Where can it stop? I guess when we are out of silicon - and when is that going to happen? When we are out of people, and how many web sites can you have? What are the ranges of interest? I think it is when we are out of plugs, personally.

There is no end in sight. Why is it important? As a linkage of defense researchers and active divisions, it has evolved to a self-sustaining information medium. In other words, the government and academia built it, so it can never be killed, and it will never go away. As we talked about before, the fact that it has this constant, dynamic environment that is always changing, there are always different places to go with always different things to do. The fact of the matter is there's always a reward if you look for it. The interactivity is genuine because you are on line. You have the ability to get an immediate response as opposed to having to wait. The ability to communicate imagery is growing more and more important. And, that takes us to the last one, the fact that in my mind, this is interactive TV. The web passes 25 million homes. The web doesn't take 2.5 billion dollars in the infrastructure to build to pass – that is an awfully long run for a very short slide - to make that kind of investment to reach that small number of people. It is already there. As you see the convergence of the appliance as I call it, as you see the appliance happen, with interactive TV, it is there.

How does the Internet differ from conventional media? Obviously, you've got an active user versus a passive user and self-selection. In conventional media the commercial message can be the content which is one of the key parts to growth and the eventual dominance of the web's media. In conventional media, the commercial message interrupts the program content when you're reading a magazine or watching television. The idea of display advertising and its impact is or continuing interest. For example, one Fortune 100 company recently did their best to put a bullet in interactivity recently when they announced they were not going to pay for ineffective advertising. When is an impression not an impression? When you're on the Internet. All of a sudden, this company decided that - well, if you do not click-on it and go and see the rest of it, then that is not an impression, and we are not going to pay for it - which is kind of like saying, if somebody does not inquire about a product from after seeing my ad in *Life* magazine, I am not going to pay you for it. So, I think that the way that the commercial message becomes interpreted on the web is still something that we all have a long way to go in figuring out how it is going to work. Obviously, you've got less constrained message parameters in the way you can structure your message, a more empowering medium obviously, and one where the user has ultimate control.

19

Thoughts Regarding the Present and Future of Web Advertising

David W. Schumann
University of Tennessee
Esther Thorson
University of Missouri

Advertising and the World Wide Web has attempted to present and discuss a number of issues focusing on promoting on the Web: interactivity, consumer factors, advertising strategy on the Internet, public policy, and special interest groups. All are addressed in the present. Yet, consider the following scenario:

Dan's son Michael, 7-years-old, had been after him for weeks to buy a basketball standard and backboard for their driveway. Michael told his Dad how much fun he had playing basketball at his friend's house and "Couldn't we get one?" "Please, Dad." Liking to think of himself as athletic, having played a little "b-ball" himself as a kid, Dan knew it was time. That night after Michael went to sleep, Dan sat down in his living room and turned to the 42-inch screen embedded in the wall.

"Computer." Dan said.

The screen flashed on and a voice responded.

"Yes?"

Dan thought to himself, "why don't I try that new database from *Consumer Reports* I just starting subscribing to?"

"Computer, access *Consumer Reports* Database and show me the latest product comparisons on basketball standards and backboards. I want to see the 5 best brands with a picture of each."

In less than an instant, the *Consumer Reports* Database title page flashed on screen and was gone. It was replaced by a list of the 5 best basketball backboard and standards with a picture of each out to the side. They all looked good but had slightly different shapes to the backboard. Two of the backboards were actually transparent. All appeared to have springs that allowed the hoop to spring back and could be adjusted to any height.

"Computer, I want to see the ratings by major features."

A new screen appears with a matrix comparing each product on several features: durability, strength, price, and so on..

"Computer, backup."

The previous screen comes on and Dan looks at the picture of the one with the best ratings. He thinks to himself, "looks good."

"Computer, link me to the web page for MJ Sports."

A title page for MJ Sports flashes across the screen and a voice welcomes Dan to the corporate web page, complete with its founder slamming home the basketball in his traditional flight pattern to the basket. The action concludes and a logo screen appears.

"Computer, I want to place an order for the MJ200x model."

The computer responds with a new company voice, "We appreciate your interest in our products. We will need the following information to complete the purchase. Please note that the information you provide is guaranteed secure." The required information prompts come on the screen: name, address, phone, credit card information.

"Computer, provide the necessary information."
The computer provides the information for Dan automatically and shows the correct information on the screen.

The company voice comes back on, "Please verify information is correct."

Dan states, "The information is correct."

"Please confirm the purchase of the MJ200x model you have just ordered."

"I confirm the order."

The following message on the screen appears, "Thank you for selecting MJ Sports. Your order will be shipped tomorrow and you can expect it the day after by UPS. Have a good evening."

Dan follows with "Computer off, television on. Select PBS." Dan settles in to watch his favorite public television show.

Is this scenario 10 or perhaps 20 years in the future? Someday soon, will we be ordering the majority of our products this way? Perhaps someday is closer than we think. A good portion of the technology employed in this story is available now. *Consumer Reports* already has a subscription database accessible on the Web (see *Consumer Reports'* web page). Flat-mounted, wall-screen technology is available now but extremely expensive. Most major corporations have web sites and many provide direct purchasing as well as order tracking capabilities. Finally, voice-activated, natural language is quickly becoming a reality for general use (Gross et al., 1998).

Twenty-four percent of Web users now shop online. They make airline reservations, buy and sell stocks and mutual funds, and purchase many of the products and services known to humankind. Half the nation's auto dealers, approximately 22,000 in number, use the Internet to sell cars (Hughes, 1998). Auto-by-tel Corporation, an online car purchase service, has 2,700 franchises and actively turns away dealers and limits franchises in market areas. Twenty percent of car buyers actually use the Internet before making a purchase. Although retail shopping is still the preferred way to shop by the majority of the world's population, Internet shopping is clearly making significant inroads. The story above also demonstrated a technology that included the merging of vehicles. With the advent of new creative products like interactive online television, voice activation, visual telephones, and mini-electronics, it seems only logical that the television, computer, radio, and telephone are all racing toward some common and uniform consumer space, accessible through one common tool. Perhaps an even more intriguing thought is the strong likelihood that some time in the near future we will all have Dick Tracy two-way watches and the capability to access television, radio, the Web, and each other on our wrists.

ADVERTISING AND THE WEB

The advertising industry has definitely found the Web and is there to stay. One needs to look no further than Internet advertising revenues to begin to see the dynamic growth of this new promotional medium. For the second quarter of 1996, $51.9 million dollars was spent on Internet advertising. One year later, second quarter advertising revenues topped $214 million (Hyland, 1998). What does this new medium offer to advertising? It appears it brings an exciting new level of direct interactivity with customers. Today, both traditional and novel promotional approaches can be found. A list of advertising techniques employed on today's web pages includes both established as well as some new innovative tools:

- Banner advertising – Banners can be purchased throughout the Web and provide direct links to homepages. They account for 54% of online advertising revenues.
- Sponsorship – Promotes certain forms of online content such as contests and give-aways.
- Sponsorship is somewhat analogous to event marketing.
- Content web sites – Business web sites promoting the company and its products/services.
- Classified advertising – Web site providing targeted promotion of products for sale. An example can be found in Chapter 18 (Edmunds Publications).
- Directory listings – Listing of companies can be found on certain homepages as well as search engines.
- Inline Ads – Online advertorials positioned within a web site.
- Interstitials – Flashes of branding information or imagery. These often appear between pages of a site.
- Pop-up windows – Separate windows that appear on top of site content while a page is loading.
- Split-screen ads – A web site screen is split between advertising and content.

Given the creative possibilities within an interactive environment, it is certain that new advertising techniques will surface on the net within a relatively short period of time. Already, promotional sites vary their content and offer consumers product/service information, product/service trial (e.g., magazine subscriptions, software), direct purchasing, and many creative forms of entertainment. The Web is the great equalizer in advertising. Both large and small companies can all promote on the Web. Combined with e-mail, the Web provides a low-cost means of accessing the global marketplace and communicating directly with existing and potential customers.

ADVANTAGES AND DISADVANTAGES
FOR ADVERTISERS

The great advantage of the Web to advertisers is that it provides a means of identifying customers, differentiating them, interacting with them, and then customizing purchasing and post purchase service. These actions increase the potential for satisfied and loyal customers. Web interactivity allows customers greater access to companies through customer discussion groups, e-mail, direct ordering, and links to more information.

The Web has disadvantages for advertisers as well. Unlike the straightforward means of interacting with a company portrayed in the opening story in this chapter, consumers today must go to considerable effort, typing, searching, and interweaving through the Internet. These activities may take significant time. For their customers' efforts, advertisers must keep their web pages current. Consistent updating of a web site will prevent audience wearout. A great deal of advertising research suggests that wearout due to repeated exposure to the same ad can lead to negative attitudes and responses toward the advertised product.

Web advertising needs to be viewed as a tool of an Integrated Marketing Communication (IMC) strategy. A strong IMC campaign strategy focuses on the value sought by customers, ongoing database management, targeting and customization of media according to viewer preferences, and the maintenance of a consistent message strategy across promotional venues. The need for consistency suggests a coordinated endeavor between different media formats including what is placed on the Web. A focus on media purchase and promotion on the Web will also need to rethink target segmentation strategy. Traditional media segmentation strategies may not hold up in a technology driven communications environment. New technology-based segmentation strategies may be necessary. A recent study by Forrester Research Inc. surveying 131,000 respondents discovered 10 technology-related segments (Judge, 1998). Six of the segments appeared to be optimistic about technology, while four did not. Segments were further divided on the basis of primary use, career, family, and entertainment and also took into consideration discretionary income that could be spent towards technology. "Fast-Forwards" (biggest spenders overall, early adopters, are focused on their careers); "New Age Nurturers" (big spenders on technology for the home); "Mouse Potatoes" (high spenders on the latest entertainment); "Techno-Strivers" (use technology to gain career edge, e.g., cell phones, pagers, online services); "Digital Hopefuls" (limited family budget but high interest in technology); "Gadget-Grabbers" (limited budget and favor online entertainment); are labeled as technology "optimists"; "Hand-shakers" (older consumers who leave technology to younger subordinates); "Traditionalists" (willing, but not sure upgrades are worth it); "Media Junkies" (seek entertainment through traditional forms of media); and, "Sidelined

Citizens" (no interest in technology), are viewed as pessimists when it comes to technology.

In the future, it will be important for Web advertisers to make the customer feel good by providing a personalized environment in which to interact with the company. The technology to facilitate this goal exists today and many new firms are experimenting with it. A personalized environment can be accomplished with personal preference profiles taken of visitors, and "match making engines" that will allow delivery of customized communication and information.

Another advantage of the Web for advertisers is the ability to conduct market research online. Consumers can be exposed to stimuli involving sight and sound, within 2- or 3-dimensional space. Data can be collected rather easily through surveys that employ both open-ended responses as well as quantitative scaling. For example, one research topic that can be facilitated by the Web is in the area of product design. Visual interactivity with the product will provide means for customers to experience the product through pictures and have accompanying information. Consumers can then make recommendations on how the product can be designed better to meet their needs (Stevenson, 1998).

Advertisers today live by traditional effectiveness measures that may pose a problem with new technologies. Comparing the "cost per thousand" between television and the Web is like comparing apples and oranges. As advertising media, they have very different objectives. Television is primarily a passive medium, where audience exposure to the product is key and is measured through the number of people viewing a program. Web viewing, on the other hand, is more proactive due to the high level of interactivity, where the audience for a certain product is based upon a perceived need for the product. To date, cost per thousand naturally favors television but such comparisons do not take into consideration the varied media ability to impact actual purchasing. The measure of impact of web advertising should include exposure measures such as information received by a server (hits) and "click throughs," but should also include number of inquiries, requests, and purchases.

ADVANTAGES AND DISADVANTAGES FOR CONSUMERS

Clearly, the greatest advantage to consumers is the ability to have access to, and control of, information. This global marketplace called the Web allows consumers to access information about products and services from around the world. Although the largest search engine (HOTBOT) has only been able to capture 35% of all web pages to this point can, this still represents a rather large number of businesses (current estimates are more than 320 million web sites exist). The consumer can select which information to process. In this sense, the consumer is in control. However, as the future unfolds, web sites with more personal preference-based information, may naturally restrict the amount and nature of the information provided. This personal preference information process makes assumptions about its audience: what they need and what they value. These assumptions will naturally lead to more subjective information being offered via the Web, and this will lead to elimination of some information. Indeed customization, viewed as an advantage to consumers, may in actuality lead to greater restriction of information and less control.

Finally, another advantage of the Web to the consumer is the ability to interact directly with business, to actually talk to the seller. This interactivity can facilitate information flow, purchase incentives, as well as direct purchasing. However this direct communication brings up one of the most significant disadvantage to the consumer: security of personal information. A recent *Business Week*/Harris Poll revealed 57% of poll respondents who use the web site list policies that guarantee the security of their personal data as affecting their decision to make an online purchases (Judge, 1998). Counteracting the typical desire for less government intervention, fifty-three percent want government to pass laws immediately for how personal information can be collected and used on the Internet. A *Business Week* check on the top 100 Web sites found that only 43% displayed privacy policies. To further the difficulties, due to the largess of the Web, regulating against deceptive advertising is far more difficult and complex.

CONCLUSION

Although the Web poses advantages and disadvantages for both the advertisers as well as the consumer, it is clearly moving us toward new strategies for relating to each other, and promoting and exchanging goods and services. The Web's ability to target, customize, and provide massive volumes of information on the spot, is unparalleled as an advertising medium. The Web is expected to increase 1,000% within the next few years. It will do more to decrease the perceptual size of the world than any single activity since long distance telephone. It is a global encyclopedia of our past and current knowledge, and it offers us a dynamic vehicle to communicate with each other as we move toward an uncertain future.

REFERENCES

Gross, N., Judge, P. C., Port, O., & Wildstorm, S. (1998, February 23). Let's Talk! (Special Report). *Business Week*, 61-64, 66-68, 72.
Hughes, J. (1998, March 2), Auto dealers see future in Internet, *Marketing News*, p. 12.

Hyland, T. (1998), Web Advertising, a year of growth, *Internet Advertising Bureau Online Advertising Guide*, p. 20a-22a, 24a, 66.

Judge, P. C. (1998, January 26). Are tech buyers different? Marketers say new consumer categories are needed, *Business Week*, p.64-66.

Stevenson, J. (1998, March 30), Interactive research can enhance new design, *Marketing News*, p. 12.

Author Index

Subject Index

HF6146.I58 A38 1999

Advertising and the
World Wide Web /
1999.